DELTA TEACHER DEVELOPMENT SERIES

Series editors Mike Burghall and Lindsay Clandfield

Teaching children how to learn

Gail Ellis and Nayr Ibrahim

DELTA
PUBLISHING

Published by
DELTA PUBLISHING
Quince Cottage
Hoe Lane
Peaslake
Surrey GU5 9SW
England

www.deltapublishing.co.uk

© Delta Publishing 2015

ISBN 978-1-905085-86-6

Edited by Mike Burghall
Designed by Christine Cox

Cover photo © Donald Sawvel/Shutterstock.com
Back cover photos © S. Lenormand

The Snowman illustration on pages 131 and 160:
© Snowman Enterprises Ltd
www.thesnowman.com

Printed in Greece by Bakis SA

Dedication

To children everywhere learning new languages.

Acknowledgements

We would like to thank:

Nick Boisseau for giving us the opportunity to write this book, for believing in us, and for his endless patience.

Mike Burghall, our editor, for his continuing support, his vision in bringing shape to the manuscript, and for his good humour.

Christine Cox for her excellent design of the book.

Sarah Philpot for her initial collaboration and, in particular, her contribution to the development of Principle 1.

Michael O'Brien for an illuminating moment during his session on action research on the British Council's Managing Teaching Excellence course in Johannesburg, February 2013, which sparked the idea to add a 'share' stage to the 'plan do review' routine to encourage home involvement.

Dr Barbara Sinclair for reviewing Part A and selected activities from Part C, and for her pertinent comments.

Eileen Connolly for piloting the *Learning English feels like …* activity, and the children for producing such creative responses and drawings.

Our colleagues, our learners and their parents, from whom we have learnt so much.

Doreen Trival and Fatima Wakrim for always being there.

Our families for their support and understanding during the writing process!

From the authors

My learning to learn journey began in the early 1980s at Ealing College of Higher Education in West London. Barbara Sinclair and I were responsible for running intensive, four-week summer courses for European Youth Leaders and Young Workers on behalf of the Council of Europe.

At this time, the Council of Europe was promoting autonomy in language learning, and a principle aim of the courses was to equip the students with the skills and strategies to carry on learning English. The courses also highlighted the need for teacher support materials.

My passion for helping students learn how to learn was ignited – and *Learning to Learn English*, published in 1989, was a result of this work.

The 80s also coincided with the global expansion of introducing languages into the primary curriculum, and my journey entered the world of primary education. I discovered that children are competent, insightful and spontaneous commentators on their own learning experiences, which links well with the development of learning to learn.

In 1998, I opened the first teaching centre for the British Council in France specialising in teaching children and teenagers. I made learning to learn an integral part of our approach: methodology, course information, lesson planning, induction and teacher training.

Nayr Ibrahim, one of the first teachers to join the centre, embraced this approach. Together, we began developing classroom and teacher development materials.

This book represents the evolution of our work, which we hope will reach future generations of children and teachers.

Gail Ellis

My contribution to this book is a result of 18 years of working with children in Portugal, Cairo, Hong Kong and now in Paris, as a teacher, teacher trainer, writer and manager.

When I joined what was then designated as the Young Learners Centre at the British Council in Paris in 1998, I was embarking on a wonderful journey that deepened my understanding of how children learn, which taught me that children are active learners in their own right.

By engaging the child, not only in the language learning process but also in the learning to learn process, I discovered that teaching and learning are reciprocal and that children, too, were agents in their own learning.

If initially I was listening to children instinctively, it was when I met Gail Ellis that I discovered a theoretical basis for metacognitive awareness and learning to learn, which would impact on my teaching, my action research and my teacher training.

My collaboration in *Teaching children how to learn* has consolidated a number of beliefs in my own teaching practice – ie systematic introduction of reflection opportunities throughout the lesson, assessment for learning as a whole-school approach – and informed my PhD methodology, which is based on eliciting the children's voices on their living and learning in multilingual spaces.

We hope this book will also be a journey in *your* discovery of learning as a reflective process, of the children as active participants in meaning making, and of the teacher as creator of optimum learning and teaching conditions in the primary English classroom.

Nayr Ibrahim

Contents

Contents

See pages 35 and 171 for information on all the downloadable materials available on the website.

Teaching children how to learn

- An essential condition for developing learning to learn is a classroom climate which scaffolds learning through interaction and reflection.

- You, as the teacher, are valuing the children as active participants in their own learning and encouraging dialogue about their experiences and understanding.

- This will enable the children to become aware of and respect individual differences, and recognise what and how they have learned and what they need to focus on next.

Teaching children how to learn

Learning to learn has always been an important aim of curricula throughout the world, but has often remained at the more theoretical level in official documents, due to a lack of practical guidelines for teachers on how to implement it.

Teaching children how to learn addresses learning to learn at a practical level, and will help you meet the diverse learning needs of children by equipping them from an early age with the critical learning skills required to meet the many social, economic and technological changes of the new century, and to foster lifelong learning and creativity.

Part A discusses the **theory and rationale** behind learning to learn, in order to establish a common working language and definitions:

- First, we set the context of primary English language teaching.
- Then we discuss the teacher's role, and the effective teaching strategies you can use to help your pupils learn how to learn.
- We look at our primary language learners and the range of socio-cultural and socio-linguistic factors affecting their learning.
- We consider the benefits of learning to learn – for the teacher and the children (and we recommend informing their parents of these) – and review the optimum learning conditions you need to create, to achieve the best results.

We also look at the **pedagogical principles** which underpin the activities in Part B of *Teaching children how to learn*:

- We look at the types of activities we use, and their intended main outcomes.
- We situate the learning of English within the wider context of the children's development, their general school activities and home experience.
- We show how the application of the 'plan do review' learning cycle to activities provides a framework to support and encourage effective teaching and learning.
- We refer to this support as 'scaffolding' – and model the different stages of each learning activity.

As your competence and confidence grows, this scaffolding can be reduced – until you feel empowered to function autonomously and generalise, by applying the 'plan do review' learning cycle freely to activities and lessons of your own choice.

Part A gives you an overview of the approach used in Part B, so you can relate this to your current practice – and prioritise, prepare and plan for the activities you decide to use.

An understanding of the theory and rationale of learning to learn as part of your planning is essential for the successful implementation of the activities. Before you begin, a knowledge of yourself and your teaching context will better prepare you for Part A …

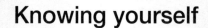

Knowing yourself

Before you begin using *Teaching children how to learn*, answer these questions and, if possible, discuss with a colleague:

1 How do you view children, and what is your perspective of childhood?*

2 How do you view your relationship with children?*

3 What has been your own experience of learning to learn: for example, at school, at university, on training courses ...?

4 How did you learn?

5 What learning strategies/approaches have you tried? Which were successful?

6 How would you define learning to learn in your classroom?

7 Do you encourage your pupils to reflect on their learning and to become more independent?

8 What challenges do you face?

* Questions 1 and 2 are adapted from:
Pinter, A and Zandian, S ''I don't ever want to leave this room': benefits of researching 'with' children' *ELTJ* 68 (1) (p72) 2014

Knowing your class

Classrooms in the 21st century are evolving rapidly, as a result of globalisation and a variety of contextual factors. For example, global mobility and migration mean that many children now speak more than one language at home, at school and in the community. Consequently, the terms L1/L2 are no longer necessarily valid. For these reasons, we use the following terms throughout the book:

• **Mother tongue** refers to the first language or languages the children learn in the home from their parents when they are young – usually it is the language the child is most familiar with, uses most or knows best, and the one they identify with.

• **Shared classroom language** refers to the language that all the children in a particular classroom share with the teacher and each other, and use on a daily basis.

• **Target language** refers to the language the children are in the process of learning in a classroom context, especially a foreign or a second language – in this case, the language is English.

For further information on the factors affecting children's English language learning, see page 21 and the first activity in Part B, which shows you how to complete a profile to deepen your knowledge of your class.

Knowing your resources

Find out what resources and technological aids are available in your school to help you in your teaching.

Many children are exposed to a range of technologies from a very early age in the home; and many school curriculum documents refer to the importance of learners gaining experience of digital technology as an integrated part of the curriculum.

However, there is unequal access to technology throughout the world: *'In many schools, computers remain a luxury and internet access is limited.'* (Garton, Copland and Burns)

Furthermore, learning to learn is best developed in a classroom context that considers learning as an affective, emotional, personal and social process which requires human face-to-face interaction.

For these reasons, we let *you* decide how and when to best integrate learning technologies into your classrooms – depending on your own context and the resources you have at your disposal.

Garton, S, Copland, F and Burns, A *Investigating Global Practices in Teaching English to Young Learners* British Council 2011
http://www.teachingenglish.org.uk/biblio/investigating-global-practices-teaching-english-young-learners

1 Primary English language teaching

Over the past decades, there has been an ongoing global repositioning of English as a basic skill [1], an increase in English as a world language and a belief that 'earlier means better'.

Consequently, English is introduced to ever more and ever younger children. In many countries, English is now compulsory in primary education. Richard Johnstone [2] describes this as *'possibly the world's biggest policy development in education'*.

However, the British Council 'Survey of Policy and Practice in Primary English Language Teaching Worldwide' [3] reveals a great deal of variation in policy and in models of English language instruction from one country to another, and even within countries: meaning that children receive language learning experiences of differing types and quality.

Teachers are, therefore, finding themselves with classes of children with diverse learning needs, as well as with varying levels of English.

In order to accommodate these variations, there is a growing recognition and acknowledgement amongst primary English language teachers of the importance and benefits of developing 'learning to learn' with children as a key goal in a 21st-century curriculum.

The first thing, then, would seem to be to answer three fundamental questions – in order to identify, define and explain three essential terms.

What is learning to learn?

Learning to learn is an umbrella term for a wide variety of activities designed to develop metacognitive awareness and learning strategies.

Learning to learn is primarily concerned with the *processes* of learning, and aims to focus the child's attention on what they are doing – and why – in order to develop their awareness of the learning process and better understand *how* they learn, in addition to *what* they learn:

- We can assume that *'the more informed (and aware) learners are about language and language learning the more effective they will be at managing their own learning'* (Ellis and Sinclair [4]).
- Yet there is a gap between teaching and learning that children have to negotiate, in order to construct new ideas or concepts based upon existing knowledge.
- Learning is an active process and something learners have to do – the teacher cannot learn for the child. However, children *can* learn the skills of learning *with the intervention* of a teacher.

Learning to learn is based on a philosophy of constructivism, originating in the work of Piaget [5] and Bruner [6], and more recent theories of social interactionism based on Vygotsky [7/8] – as well as theories of motivation, ability and intelligence (see Claxton [9], Csikszentmihalyi [10], Dweck [11] and Gardner [12]).

In the field of language learning, the work of Dam [13], Ellis and Sinclair [14], Little [15], Holec [16], O'Malley and Chamot [17] and Wenden and Rubin [18] focuses on ways of teaching learners explicitly the techniques of learning a language, and an awareness of how and when to use strategies to help them become self-directed.

Learning to learn values diversity, and takes the following into account:

- Each child is unique, develops and learns in different ways and at different rates, and has individual preferences regarding learning activities and materials.
- Each child may use a variety of learning strategies at different times, depending on a range of variables such as:
  - the nature of the social context and learning conditions in terms of setting;
  - the learning task and topic;
  - the role of the teacher;
  - mood and motivation.

Understanding this will help teachers manage diversity and differentiation within a class.

Learning to learn underpins all learning in all areas of the curriculum and life:

- Its link with learner autonomy is one of the most important aspects of a child's overall educational development.
- It is something children start to learn from a very early age, as being autonomous means doing things for yourself: *'Thus learner autonomy requires the learner's full involvement in planning, monitoring and evaluating his or her learning'* (Little [19]).

Learning to learn requires the development of the explicit skills of reflection and analysis, and entails learning how to learn intentionally:

- In the primary English language classroom, this requires you – the teacher – to gradually lead the children to a conscious development of their own learning strategies and awareness of how they learn, so they can become more effective and independent language learners.
- Early language learning also aims to prepare the children for the more formal and exam-orientated courses that they will encounter in secondary school.

Learning to learn provides children with the basic learning tools for all this, as well as learning skills for life.

What is metacognitive awareness?

'Metacognition' is a term first coined in the 1970s, and there has been much debate over a suitable definition. Ann Brown – quoted in Nisbet and Shucksmith [20] – defines it as 'knowing about knowing'. This includes the knowledge and self-awareness a learner has of their own learning process, and can lead to effective learning.

Much research has shown (see Nisbet and Shucksmith [21] and Whitebread et al [22]) that even very young children possess a considerable degree of metacognitive knowledge and ability which they are rarely given credit for, and that this can be developed:

○ They are, furthermore, capable of understanding information about classroom procedures and benefit from being given this information.

○ They can be helped – given the opportunity, and asked the right questions – to express themselves in a purposeful and meaningful way about their learning experiences.

You, their teacher – as a catalyst in this process – have a crucial role to play.

Metacognitive awareness is an umbrella term which incorporates the following strands:

○ Self-awareness:
  knowing about oneself as a language learner.
○ Language awareness:
  knowing about language.
○ Cognitive awareness:
  knowing about the processes of language learning.
○ Social awareness:
  knowing about collaborative learning techniques.
○ Intercultural awareness:
  knowing about cultural similarities and differences.

Self-awareness helps children to better understand themselves as language learners, to become aware of their learning differences and preferences, to understand what affects their motivation, and to formulate realistic expectations and set and meet personal goals.

Language awareness stimulates children's interest and curiosity about language *'to challenge pupils to ask questions about language'* (Hawkins [23]) in order to develop understanding of and knowledge about language in general – including the target language, the mother tongue and, if appropriate and depending on the context, other languages.

This would involve understanding and using *metalanguage* (the terminology used to describe language – noun, verb, adjective, sentence, simple present, structure, etc – and the language used in language teaching – pairwork, matching, sequencing, organising, etc) in the mother tongue or in the target language for the following:

○ Stating the aims of a lesson.
○ Explaining the purpose of different classroom activities.

○ Identifying and negotiating the success criteria – what the children need to do, in order to succeed in the activity.
○ Signposting the different stages of a lesson.
○ Giving classroom instructions.
○ Describing and analysing language.
○ Making comparisons, to find similarities and differences between the mother tongue and the target language.
○ Discovering rules.
○ Developing positive attitudes towards the target language and language learning.

Cognitive awareness helps children understand why and how they are learning a language at school and that, in addition to linguistic outcomes, it also offers important personal, cognitive, cultural, affective and social gains. This involves:

○ explaining to the children how they are going to learn the target language in class, the type of materials they are going to use and the activities they are going to do;
○ getting them to think about how they learn, which strategies they use to help them to remember, to concentrate, to pay attention;
○ how and when to review, how to monitor their learning and to decide what they need to do next;
○ building their confidence and giving them the language which will empower them to take control of their learning – when, for example, they don't understand – to enable them to become more responsible and independent in the learning process, as well as creating positive attitudes to language learning.

Social awareness can be related to Vygotsky's theory of social construction of learning [24] – that higher cognitive functions are internalised from social interaction.

This will involve children in communication and collaborative activities to establish a class learning community which, in some contexts, may involve a new understanding of:

○ how to behave in class – towards the teacher and towards each other;
○ how to establish a working consensus, which will contribute towards building class, peer, teacher and individual respect;
○ how to learn to interact and cooperate in activities, and to develop positive attitudes to sharing and working together in the classroom.

Intercultural awareness involves the development of an understanding and openness towards others, to draw *'attention to the fact that the differences in relation to the pupils' own habits and day-to-day lives are to be seen in a positive light. This awareness adds to the sum of pupils' knowledge of humanity and of the world'* (Brewster et al [25]):

○ It would involve children in activities to enable them to discover similarities and differences between themselves and other people.
○ It aims to develop empathy and tolerance, as well as positive attitudes to the target language culture and people, and draw the children away from a monocultural perspective and into a broader view of the world.

These strands overlap to some extent and, in class, involve the global development of the child by building positive attitudes, self-awareness and self-confidence. Children need to develop a range of learning strategies and social skills – as well as linguistic and intercultural understanding – in order to foster positive attitudes, values and beliefs which contribute to their motivation to learn, to their realisation of their own capacity to improve, and to provide a solid and positive foundation for the future.

Underpinning these five strands of metacognitive awareness is the development of the children's creativity and imagination. This is established by developing the characteristics of creative people, through learning environments and activities which:
- foster questioning, patience and openness to fresh ideas;
- have high levels of trust;
- provide opportunities to enjoy experimenting and taking risks;
- provide opportunities to make choices and be independent;
- help the children see connections and make links in their learning;
- allow the children to learn from mistakes and failures, and build self-esteem and confidence.

What are learning strategies?

Learning strategies can be defined as techniques and efforts which a learner may use to acquire knowledge. It is generally agreed that it is useful to recognise the existence of two major groups of learning strategies.

Metacognitive strategies are more generalised – and are used to regulate learning:

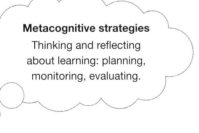

Metacognitive strategies
Thinking and reflecting about learning: planning, monitoring, evaluating.

Cognitive strategies are more task-specific, and involve actually manipulating the subject to be learnt – in this case, doing things with language:

Cognitive strategies
Task-specific and involving children doing things with the language and their learning materials, and relating to skills areas.

O'Malley et al [26] have shown through research that, by combining metacognitive and cognitive strategy training, learners are able to reflect on what they are doing – and why – and become aware of how they learn. They applied this scheme to language learning, and added a *further* category which they called 'socioaffective'.

Socioaffective strategies are more affective and social – and used by learners to involve themselves in social and group activities in order to interact with another person and expose themselves to language input:

Socioaffective strategies
Collaborating.
Co-operating.
Pairwork/groupwork.
Project work.

This three-part typology is useful, in that it is relatively simple to apply and to extend, especially in the primary English classroom. A typology of the learning strategies developed in *Teaching children how to learn* – there are others – is set out, organised alphabetically under each group, on page 12.

A *further* group of strategies is used by learners when there is a conscious awareness of a problem in communication, such as not knowing a vocabulary item.

Communication strategies are used to maintain communication, negotiate meaning and assist learning. They give the children practice in managing their own learning, build their self-confidence and allow for self-direction – as described by Dickinson and Carver [27]:

Communication strategies
Maintaining communication.
Negotiating meaning.

The major point here is that learning strategies can be *taught*, and self-awareness can be *developed*:
- You – as the teacher – play an essential role in this process, by providing the children with opportunities for reflecting on and experimenting with the process of language learning, as an integral part of the *language learning experience*.
- As their teacher, you can also remind them, when appropriate, that many strategies for learning English can also be applied to other subject areas – so that they learn to transfer these strategies, and develop an overall awareness of their learning *across the curriculum*.

Typology of learning strategies

Metacognitive strategies

- Activating prior knowledge
- Becoming aware of collocations
- Becoming aware of English in the out-of-school context
- Developing awareness of word stress
- Developing grammatical awareness
- Developing knowledge of metalanguage
- Expressing personal preferences about language learning and learning strategies
- Finding out about resources for learning inside and outside the classroom
- Identifying what to revise and work on next, based on self-assessment
- Keeping a language learning diary or English Language Portfolio
- Monitoring progress
- Planning and preparing for a language activity
- Prioritising learning based on self-assessment
- Reflecting on language learning
- Reviewing learning
- Selecting and negotiating success criteria
- Self-assessing
- Setting a clear focus for reading/listening
- Setting short term aims
- Sharing ideas about language learning

Cognitive strategies

- Analysing
- Categorising
- Classifying
- Collecting examples of English words used in the environment
- Comparing
- Concentrating
- Copying work into an English Language Portfolio
- Defining
- Discriminating between sounds
- Drafting
- Experimenting with language and learning strategies
- Following instructions
- Generating sentences/instructions/paragraphs/poems/recipes from a model
- Identifying
- Listening and repeating
- Listening for enjoyment
- Listening for general information
- Listening for specific information
- Making a mind map
- Making associations
- Matching
- Memorising
- Observing
- Organising vocabulary into meaningful groups
- Paying attention
- Personalising learning
- Predicting from context to guess what happens next
- Problem-solving
- Reading aloud to practise pronunciation
- Reading for specific information
- Reciting to practise pronunciation
- Recognising facial expressions as aids to meaning
- Recording information
- Risk-taking to try out some English
- Sequencing
- Sorting
- Using a chart or a graph
- Using a concept web
- Using a dictionary
- Using a KWL grid (see pages 29 and 41)
- Using actions, expressions and gestures to aid memory
- Using actions to reinforce meaning and aid memory
- Using colour-coding to aid visual memory
- Using rhyme as an aid to meaning
- Using rhyme to aid memory
- Using visual markers to identify word stress
- Visualising

Socioaffective strategies

- Collaborating
- Co-operating
- Discussing with each other
- Helping each other
- Listening to each other
- Negotiating success criteria
- Roleplaying
- Sharing language learning materials and ideas about learning with classmates and family members
- Singing English songs and chants together
- Working in pairs/groups

This typology includes the learning strategies developed in *Teaching children how to learn*. Other typologies exist – see, for example, the work of J Michael O'Malley and Anna Uhl Chamot; Annamaria Pinter; and Peter Skehan.

2 Primary English language teachers

You may be a general primary school teacher who teaches all the subjects in the curriculum, including English, or you may be a specialist teacher of English, and English may or may not be your mother tongue. Whatever your situation:

- A teacher of another language to children needs to have the knowledge, skills and sensitivities of a teacher of *children* and a teacher of *language* – and *'to be able to balance and combine the two successfully'* (Brewster et al [28]).
- Teaching children how to learn should ideally be incorporated into all subjects, so the children can learn to transfer learning skills from one task to another across subject areas, as we have pointed out.

Voicing the teachers' views

Many teachers have strong views and concerns about incorporating learning to learn into their English classes:

○ **We didn't learn like this!**
Many teachers have not been taught or trained in a way that encouraged them to reflect actively on how they were learning. They may, therefore, feel dubious and anxious about implementing an approach they themselves have not experienced.

○ **Children are too young for this aspect of learning.**
Many teachers do not believe that children are capable of expressing their opinions or views about how they learn, or of understanding explanations about what they are going to do and why. However, as stated above:
  ○ Research and classroom practice have shown that even quite young children possess a considerable degree of self-awareness.
  ○ Given the opportunity and asked the right questions, they can talk about their learning in a purposeful and meaningful way that they are rarely given credit for.

Furthermore, this can be developed. Even very young children can be brought to *reflect* on their learning in a conscious way, although they are less able to *analyse* – as this is linked to their cognitive ability.

○ **We don't have the time.**
Teachers are busy people, often struggling to complete the syllabus. They may feel pressurised into feeling they cannot deal with anything else in an already crowded curriculum.

○ **Our materials don't show us how to do it.**
There is a general lack of practical guidelines for incorporating learning to learn into lessons:

  ○ Some materials now include activities which ask children to review what they have learnt, but these often focus on the product or the linguistic content of a learning unit and not on the processes involved.
  ○ Accompanying teacher's books rarely offer guidance on the type of questions teachers can ask to get children to think about their learning.

Many teachers, pressurised in addition by constraints of time, often omit these activities altogether, thus denying the children early opportunities to reflect actively on their learning.

○ **You have to use the mother tongue.**
In the initial stages, the language used for developing learning to learn is often the child's mother tongue or shared classroom language, as they do not yet have the level to talk about this aspect of their learning in the target language.

Teachers may feel guilty about using the mother tongue, or see it as time lost for English learning, or the use of the mother tongue may actually be banned in the 'English' class.

○ **It takes a long time.**
Developing learning to learn is a lengthy and gradual process, and is closely linked to everyday procedures and routines for classroom management, time management and lesson planning.

Teachers need to develop techniques for integrating learning to learn into their lessons in a systematic and explicit way.

○ **We don't have enough evidence that learning to learn improves linguistic performance.**
Teachers, school heads, inspectors and parents want evidence that investment in learning to learn can be justified. They usually want to see this in the form of improved linguistic results.

Evaluating learning to learn is difficult and, consequently, we lack sufficient empirical evidence of its effectiveness. However, see the activities on pages 142 and 144 on evaluating learning to learn and the comments on pages 96 and 143.

○ **We are doing it anyway!**
Teachers may feel that because much of the work they are doing in the primary English language classroom is task-based, they are already contributing to the development of self-awareness.

However, such awareness does not necessarily generalise to other learning tasks and nurture autonomous learning – unless there is an element of conscious reflection and self-monitoring.

Teaching children how to learn offers solutions and techniques for overcoming these concerns through activities structured around the 'plan do review' cycle – showing how learning to learn can be integrated on a regular, systematic and explicit basis.

Expanding the teachers' role

'Instruction is a provisional state that has as its object to make the learner or problem-solver self-sufficient … Otherwise the result of instruction is to create a form of mastery that is contingent upon the perpetual presence of the teacher.' Bruner [29]

As Jerome Bruner states, teachers play a key role in teaching children how to learn in order to help them become self-sufficient. The process is long and gradual, to be integrated systematically into the language learning aims of each activity and lesson – but not overriding them, as the main goal remains language learning:

- You therefore take on an 'expanded role' (Wenden [30]).
- Your added 'pedagogical challenge' (Wenden [31]) is to find ways of developing the learners' efforts to learn by giving attention to the *process* of learning, rather than focusing exclusively on *content*.

This all needs to be carried out explicitly, so that the children are made consciously aware of what they are doing, and why.

Your role can be divided into four main areas (adapted from Read [32]).

Affective role

- To recognise and value that each child is unique and has their own learning differences and preferences.
- To create an atmosphere of mutual trust and respect.
- To set up a collaborative and cooperative learning environment.
- To value diversity.
- To motivate the children to think and talk about how they learn.
- To use the mother tongue or shared classroom language, as necessary, for reflection activities.

Procedural role

- To integrate learning to learn into lesson plans, and ensure there is sufficient time for reviewing and self-assessment.
- To combine the development of metacognitive and cognitive strategies systematically and explicitly, through the application of the 'plan do review' learning cycle (see Principle 6 on page 26).
- To provide opportunities for self-direction and choice.

Behavioural role

- To explicitly demonstrate and model learning strategies.
- To explain strategy use – eg naming the strategy and saying why to use it.
- To inform the children about language learning.
- To encourage the children to transfer learning strategies to other tasks.
- To be a positive role model, by demonstrating the attitudes and values that language teaching should encourage and promote.
- To encourage the children to take on more responsibility for their own learning.
- To teach the children to 'account for' their own learning, so they can tell their parents what and how they have learnt.
- To encourage parental involvement.

Interactive role

- To encourage discussion about learning strategies.
- To scaffold and encourage active reflection, by using effective questioning techniques to develop greater understanding and self-awareness.
- To give feedback on learning and performance.
- To use methods that encourage the children's voices, so they talk about their opinions and preferences about language learning, and to listen to their perspectives and act upon these.
- To develop the interpersonal and communication skills to liaise effectively with parents.

Introducing Wilbur the Worm

Throughout *Teaching children how to learn*, Wilbur the Worm – a friendly mascot figure – can be used in various ways as a teaching aid to support both you and your learners, and to assist you in creating the optimum conditions for teaching and learning. (For more on these 'optimum conditions', see pages 30–31 and Part C.)

Wilbur originates from the 'Can of Worms' concept which was released at the 2006 IATEFL conference in Harrogate, UK, to help *'unravel some of the 'interlinked strands' of learner autonomy'* (Everhard et al [33]).

Wilbur is personified – that is, given human traits – to help the children relate to him and to stimulate their imagination. Like you, the teacher, he plays several roles:

- He plays a *behavioural* role, and can be used as an 'intermediary' to present learning strategies and information about language learning, which can take the focus off the teacher and show the children that they play an important part in their own learning.
- He plays a *procedural* role, through the use of Wilbur's 'Learning suggestions' speech bubbles (see page 15), to remind the children to use various strategies and encourage them in their learning.
- He also plays an *affective* and *interactive* role, by fostering collaboration and interaction in the classroom.

Once the learners have been introduced to the English Language Portfolio (see Principle 2 on page 25), Wilbur should be presented *before* you use the rest of the activities in Part B, so the children get to know him and understand his role. Two activities introduce Wilbur:

- *Wilbur the Worm: the facts* (page 40) introduces the children to the world of the earthworm, in preparation for …
- *Wilbur the Worm: the puppet* (page 42), where they learn how to make their own puppet.

The children can use their Wilbur puppet with any activity related to reviewing or reminding classmates about learning tips, etc. They can also chant the Wilbur chant, as part of beginning or ending lesson routines: see page 42.

Introducing Wilbur's toolkit

Teaching children how to learn is to be used *alongside* your core teaching materials and resources – flashcards, realia, posters, etc. However, to facilitate the preparation of your lesson plans, as well as the children's enjoyment, downloadable material for Part B can be found in Wilbur's toolkit on the website.

These materials are also reproduced in reduced format in Wilbur's toolkit in the book, and can be copied onto the board.

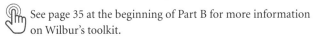 See page 35 at the beginning of Part B for more information on Wilbur's toolkit.

Wilbur's learning suggestions

In the Teachers' toolkit, you will find a downloadable 'Wilbur's learning suggestions' speech bubble template. This can be used to display learning suggestions around your classroom. For example:

- To prompt the children to use English as much as possible.
- To remind them of learning tips.
- To encourage/motivate them in their English language learning.

You can write learning suggestions in the speech bubbles to suit your learners' needs. We provide some suggested phrases opposite:

- You can write a phrase in the speech bubble yourself. Write the phrase in the children's shared classroom language if appropriate.
- You can get the children to copy the phrases themselves.
- Alternatively, the children can write phrases of their own choice, as this will give them ownership and make the phrases more meaningful and memorable.

You can refer the children to the learning suggestions in the speech bubbles when necessary. Gradually, they will refer to them and recall them independently – without your intervention.

 See pages 149 and 171 in Part C for more information on the Teachers' toolkit.

Wilbur's storybook recommendations

Worms are also popular characters in children's literature, and Wilbur plays the role of a 'bookworm' – by recommending storybooks that can be used alongside the activities in Part B:

- These storybooks can be used to consolidate and extend the language or themes presented through each activity.
- They therefore provide opportunities for more language learning.

The key to successful storytelling is having the right storybook for the linguistic and cognitive ability of the children. Children may have limited target language, but they have the ideas, concepts and aspirations that are relevant to their age:

- To guide you in your selection, there is a short synopsis in the Teachers' toolkit on the website of each storybook he recommends.
- For further guidance on the criteria for selecting storybooks, and a story-based approach, see Ellis and Brewster [34] and the activities *Selecting storybooks* and *Storytelling skills* in Part C.

| Learning suggestions |

To maintain communication in English

- *How do you say 'xxxx' in English?*
- *Can you repeat, please?*
- *Can you explain, please?*
- *What does 'xxxx' mean?*

To suggest learning tips

- *Listen carefully!*
- *Organise your work in your portfolio.*
- *Group the words by topic.*
- *Use a dictionary.*
- *Review your work.*
- *Don't forget to put the date on your work.*
- *Remember the success criteria.*
- *Listen carefully to each other.*
- *If you don't know, ask.*
- *Ask yourself 'Why'?*
- *Use your imagination.*
- *Do your best.*
- *Try harder.*
- *Take risks in your English language learning.*
- *Concentrate!*
- *Talk about your learning.*
- *Focus!*
- *Ask questions.*
- *Think about what you already know.*
- *Learn from your classmates.*
- *Be flexible.*
- *Try out different strategies.*
- *Learn from your mistakes.*
- *Persevere! Keep going!*
- *Be determined!*
- *Help your classmates.*
- *Organise your work and your time.*
- *Share your ideas.*
- *Work with your classmates.*
- *Monitor your progress.*
- *Revise your work.*

Asking for help

- *I need some help, please.*
- *Can you help me, please?*
- *Is this correct?*

Praising

- *Well done!*
- *Good effort!*
- *Good work!*
- *I like your work because ...*

Reviewing and self-assessing

'Good learners are flexible. They watch how they are going and change things as they go along.' Claxton [35]

Reviewing and self-assessment are about encouraging children to reflect on and make judgements about their and others' learning:

- This helps the children develop a better understanding of what and how they are learning – so they become more confident in themselves and understand that their learning can be improved.
- It teaches them to monitor their progress, maintain motivation and identify their strong and weak points – so they know what their next steps need to be.

Developing an understanding of themselves as language *learners* enables children to become more versatile and resourceful in the face of new challenges. And it benefits *teachers*, as you gain insights into their learning – which informs your planning and deciding which children require additional support:

- Unfortunately, this metacognitive dimension of learning is not always incorporated into the primary English classroom.
- Research shows (Buzan [36]) that over 80% of a lesson can be forgotten – if reviewing doesn't take place *immediately* or *shortly* after a learning period. Just doing an activity is not enough!

Some English language materials do attempt to encourage a degree of reflection by including an end-of-unit self-assessment. However:

- This often involves the children in little more than mechanical acts of ticking boxes, drawing or sticking a smiley face if they like a unit – or an unsmiley face if they don't – with no consideration of the reasons why.
- In this case, the emphasis is simply on *'learning something rather than on learning to learn'* (Wenden [37]).

Children can be confused by these activities and may not understand their purpose:

- They may feel there should be a 'right' answer and they should receive a mark for such work.
- They should be informed, therefore, of the *purpose* of self-assessment – so they understand there are no 'right' or 'wrong' answers. Self-assessment is a personal activity, which helps each child become aware of and monitor their own progress.

When to use the mother tongue or shared language

This vital metacognitive dimension may also be missing, due to the young age of the children and their limited knowledge of the target language. However, children are capable of – and enjoy – reflecting on their learning. Classroom practice shows there is no loss of the learning to learn benefits when the mother tongue or shared classroom language is used to discuss learning and for reviewing:

- It can improve children's self-expression.
- It is efficient, and valorises and empowers the children's voices.
- It also has an affective function for many young children.

When to review

Reviewing can take place at different stages of a lesson or activity:

- At the beginning – to review previous learning, and help the children make connections to what they did in the previous lesson or activity and what they know or can do.
- During learning – between stages of the lesson, to help the children stay focused, see how what they have done relates to the next stage of the lesson and make improvements as they go along. It also allows them to voice any difficulties during the progression of the activity.
- After learning – to help the children become aware of what they can do well, how they learnt and the areas they need to improve.

How to review

To ensure the children's reflection is focused, they need to be informed of the learning aims of a lesson or activity and of the success criteria:

- You will play a guiding role, modelling both the process and the language for reflection, in order to develop the children's ability to talk systematically and explicitly about their learning.
- You will need to plan and manage reflection time carefully – so the children perceive it as 'special time' when what they say really matters.

Initially, reviewing can be conducted as a whole-class plenary review. You can demonstrate and model the questions and prompt the children's reflection, as you are inviting them to think about an aspect of their learning that is abstract and, for many, will probably be new.

In the early stages – in response to a question like *What did you learn today?* – the children will reply very literally:

- They will want to talk about *all* the activities they have done, without analysing *each* activity.
- You need to be skilful in keeping them focused. (See the activity on page 122, the transcripts on page 123 and the transcript notes on page 155.)
- They will, this way, develop their listening skills – as they listen to each other, learn from others, and become aware of and value individual differences and preferences.

At later stages – as the children become more familiar with reviewing and self-assessment – group discussion, led by individual children, or peer assessment can be introduced from time to time:

- The initial teacher-guided review will have modelled the questions that the children can ask each other.
- This allows the children to check against the success criteria, discuss and compare the quality of their own work and of others, and develop empathy and social skills.

What follows are some further techniques you can use:

- to support active reflection, inviting the children to think about and discuss their learning;
- to get the children to organise, and keep a systematic record of, their learning;
- to involve their family in their learning – not just the school.

Encouraging active reflection

The main purpose of encouraging active reflection is to deepen and advance children's understanding of new concepts and learning. Getting the children to reflect on their learning can be motivating – if you ask questions that challenge them to think. The right questions provide a connection between teaching and learning.

Here are some guidelines on how to ask effective questions that encourage active reflection.

- **Effective questioning:** Ask questions that are clear and directly related to a concrete learning experience. Unless the questions are well-formulated, in language that is accessible to the children, they will not understand and will not be able to reply in a way that helps them, or you their teacher, become aware of their learning processes. A good question, then:
  - must be probing and an invitation to think, so that it makes the children justify their responses;
  - must focus their attention and encourage observation, invite inquiry and stimulate, because it is open-ended;
  - should be productive and seek a response, and generate *more* questions (see Fisher [38]).

In reply to questions like *What helped you learn?* and *What did you enjoy most/least?* children are likely to give minimal responses. For example: *'The song.'* This tells you or the child little, so you need to probe further – *Why?* – in order to lead the children to a greater understanding of themselves as learners. See pages 123 and 155.

- **Give 'thinking' or 'wait' time:** Give the children time to think before answering a question. Increase 'wait' time to three seconds to encourage longer answers, more of the children to answer, and better-quality responses.

- **Use 'think-pair-share' time:** This gives the children time to think by themselves, discuss with a classmate, and then share by discussing with a group or the whole class.

- **Use 'talk partners':** These develop thinking, speaking, listening, collaborative and cooperative skills, and ensure all the children are involved in the lesson. This gives those who might not be as confident in a whole-class situation time to think, discuss and 'rehearse' – before speaking to the whole class.

- **Encourage the children to ask questions:** To the teacher, to another learner.

- **Use processing strategies:** Give the children two minutes to think of or write three things they remember about 'xxxx'.

- **Explaining an activity:** Get the children to explain how to do an activity or play a game to other children. Reflecting on the procedures, rules and stages of an activity or game will focus their attention on the processes involved and is extremely motivating. It also provides language practice, either spoken or written.

Encouraging organised learning

Successful learners organise their time and materials in ways which suit them personally, and fully exploit the language learning resources available to them inside and outside the classroom.

- It is therefore important for them to learn how to organise their learning materials efficiently and effectively.
- Although your school will no doubt have its own systems in place, a key pedagogical principle of the activities in *Teaching children how to learn* is the creation and systematic use of an English Language Portfolio.
- A portfolio enables the children to record and reflect on their language learning and intercultural experiences.

As part of this class methodology, learning becomes *'more child-centred and collaborative – the children and you become partners in learning. Because this empowers the children, they develop feelings of trust and respect for you as their teacher'* (Ioannou-Georgiou and Pavlou [39]). (See Principle 2 on page 25, and the corresponding activity in Part C.)

Encouraging parental involvement

'Learning and sharing English experiences in a family can be bonding.' Dunn [40]

The most important people that teachers see besides their pupils are the children's parents, and teachers of young children come into contact with parents more often than teachers of other age groups:

- You need to be prepared to take on this additional aspect of parent care as part of your day-to-day role, by making yourself available to talk to parents about what their child is doing, and why, and to update them on their progress.
- You need the appropriate attitudes, interpersonal skills and strategies for working with parents, and on how best to involve them in their child's learning.

Everyone benefits when parents and teachers work together:

- Most parents are prepared to invest personal time and effort in their child's English language learning.
- They see the provision of English in schools as a basic life skill and career enhancer for the child's future in a globalised world.

However, unlike other subjects – such as Maths, Science, Geography, etc – where parents share a common language and possess some content knowledge, helping their child with the target language can be more difficult if they do not speak *any* or speak *only a little* of it:

- These parents feel insecure, inadequate and unable to support their child's learning. They need to understand that they can still provide an enormous amount of support and encouragement. See the concept of 'translanguaging' on page 34.

Other parents may have unrealistic expectations, in terms of results, about how much and how fast their child can learn, because they evaluate progress solely in terms of linguistic outcomes. Part of the teacher's role, then, is to help parents formulate realistic expectations.

Parents need to understand that learning a foreign language:
- contributes to a child's holistic development;
- offers important personal, cognitive, cultural, social and affective gains.

Although parents may be very good at praising and encouraging their children, they are often unsure as to how they can help their children in *practical* terms. However, they can soon be helped to understand that they can use a lot of their everyday household paraphernalia and clutter to support their child's English language learning – by the following:
- Looking for words in English on food packaging, clothes, etc.
- Creating an English corner.
- Reading storybooks.
- Singing songs or saying rhymes in English together.
- Using natural situations at home – such as meal time, bed time, etc – to integrate some English.

Schools, therefore, need to establish effective communication channels with parents to facilitate parental involvement. The Language Triangle opposite highlights the three-way relationship between child, parent – and you. See also the activity on page 125.

Encouraging parental understanding

An important aspect of communication with parents is to help them *understand* the approach used to teach their children English – which includes helping them learn how to learn. This may differ from the way the parents themselves learned a language, and from the way the children are taught other subjects:
- Parents often have strong views on how languages are learned, and how they should be taught.
- They may perceive modern methodologies as 'less formal', 'not serious enough', 'less disciplined', and their value may be questioned.

To dispel such misconceptions, parents need to understand:
- the aims of English language learning, and how these are to be achieved;
- the language learning process;
- the methodological approaches and materials used.

It is important that parents have positive attitudes towards their child's English language learning:
- They are much more likely to react positively to this approach if they are informed about, and understand, the rationale behind it.
- They will thus be in a better position to support their child's language learning, and maximise their learning time.

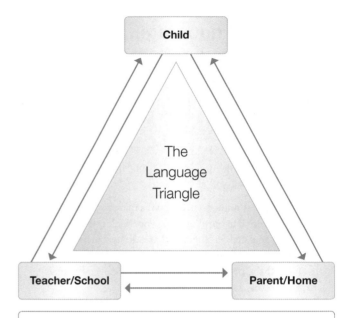

The Language Triangle ...
- reinforces family–school connections, through the establishment of clear and effective communication channels between the school/teacher, the child and the parent/home;
- maximises parental involvement and mutual understanding and relationships, by developing a partnership between teachers, parents and their children.

Your school will know the best way to communicate effectively with parents, such as through newsletters, parents' meetings, or letters:
- On page 19, you can find information you can adapt or translate, to inform parents about English language learning and learning to learn.
- There is also a 'child-friendly' version on page 20.

Children benefit in many ways when their parents are interested in, and involved in, their education – and understand the benefits:
- of early language learning;
- of the methodology used.

Parents need a clear understanding of the benefits of an early start in English, otherwise they may question its value. This questioning is often based on the premise that older children:
- will have developed more efficient learning strategies;
- will make more rapid progress in less time;
- will catch up with children who started earlier.

It is important to look *beyond* narrowly-defined, linguistic 'returns' – to look to the broader, longer-term benefits.

For further guidelines on how parents can support their children's language learning and teachers can communicate with the parents, see Brewster et al [41] and Linse et al [42].

Information for parents

Here are some suggested answers to two questions parents frequently voice.

Why should my child start learning another language at a young age?

- The early years of childhood is the period when children can most naturally apply the mechanisms through which they acquire their mother tongue to the learning of another language.
- It gives them more exposure to, and time for, learning English: 12 years of schooling, rather than the five-to-seven years at secondary school.
- Language learning programmes, if the children start early and then continue, can benefit from increased efficiency in learning as the child matures.
- Children are less self-conscious, and are more flexible and open to differences at this age.
- They have fewer negative attitudes and are willing learners.

What are the benefits for my child of an early start?

- Some elements of language are more easily acquired at earlier ages – such as pronunciation, and the development of the ability to discriminate between the different sounds of a language.
- There are motivational, socio-affective and cultural benefits of early language learning, such as developing empathy and understanding of others – in addition to linguistic benefits.
- There are cognitive benefits – such as the development of better memory, listening skills, visual-spatial skills and creativity.
- Children develop their self-confidence.

Language teaching methodology

Children 'learn by doing', and by active involvement in the learning process.

They learn best:

- when the approach is structured and accessible, in which they realise English has a real purpose for communication, and when they are involved in activities which relate to their personal experiences and environment;
- when they participate in activities which are interesting and enjoyable, as motivation is a key factor in order to develop positive attitudes towards language learning and to build their confidence;
- when there is a variety of resources from the English-speaking world – such as poems, songs, rhymes and storybooks which introduce them to the culture and literature of the English-speaking world;
- when they are immersed in an English language learning environment – which enables them to acquire English naturally, through a variety of activities which are both enjoyable and challenging;
- when they are encouraged to use English actively – to develop listening and speaking through activities which build grammar, vocabulary, communication skills and pronunciation. Reading and writing activities will develop basic literacy in English.

Learning to learn

During your child's English classes, the teacher will spend some time helping your child learn 'how to learn'.

- Learning to learn focuses the children's attention on *how* they learn, in addition to *what* they learn:
  - It helps them become aware of the process of language learning.
- Learning to learn is not new, but we will be using a systematic framework that allows an explicit approach to integrating learning to learn into your child's English lessons:
  - It will help both your child and their teacher perceive their progress.
- Your child will be informed of what they are going to learn, and why, at the beginning of each activity:
  - We will discuss how to complete the activity successfully.
- Your child will be encouraged to reflect actively on *what* they are learning, *how* they are learning, and to assess *how well* they are doing:
  - They will also be encouraged to reflect on the work of other children in their class, to build and deepen their understanding of quality learning.
- Your child's teacher may sometimes use the mother tongue or shared classroom language for learning to learn activities, as it is more efficient and valorises and empowers the children:
  - There will be no loss of the learning to learn benefits.
- Your child's teacher will ask lots of questions in the classroom, to stimulate your child's thinking:
  - The teacher will encourage your child to participate actively in their English classes: to 'take a risk' and try out English.

How will learning to learn benefit your child?
- They will increase their self-esteem, confidence and motivation.
- They will become more resilient and independent as learners. ▶ ▶ ▶

- They will develop awareness of the learning strategies that suit them best, and learn how to assess their performance.
- They will become more resourceful and organised.
- They will develop the ability to talk about English language learning, account for their learning and tell you about their classes.
- They will change their relationship with their teacher, so they become 'partners in learning'.
- They will become more actively and personally involved in their English language learning.
- They will become aware of general learning strategies that they can transfer to other subjects in the school curriculum.
- They will be more prepared for the more formal learning at secondary school.

How will learning to learn benefit the teacher?
- Becoming more concerned with *learning* than *performance*.
- Becoming more reflective about their own practice.
- Giving more control to your child.
- Listening and responding to your child's opinions and preferences about English language learning.
- It will improve your child's relationship with their teacher.

How can you help?

- Talk to your child about what they are learning – show interest!
- Look at your child's English Language Portfolio regularly, do the 'share' activities together and write your comments.
- Encourage your child to 'take a risk' and try out using English, even if they are uncertain.
- Encourage your child to ask questions and be curious about English and English language learning.
- Value all the attempts your child makes to speak English – making mistakes is part of the normal learning process.
- Praise and reward your child's efforts and encourage them to keep improving.
- Involve other family members, and look for English in the environment together.
- Ensure your child's computer safety at home. Consult the following guidelines: *http://learnenglishkids.britishcouncil.org/ en/parents/articles/internet-and-computer-safety*
- Give your consent, when it is requested, for activities which involve interviewing, filming or photographing.

Let your child teach you!

Information for children

Learning to learn

- During your English classes, we will do lots of language learning activities to help you learn English and practise listening and speaking in English.
- We will spend some time thinking and discussing *how* you learn, as well as *what* you learn. This will help you understand that everyone learns in a different way, and that you can learn with and from each other.
- Your teacher will ask you lots of questions, to get you to think about and discuss your learning with your classmates.
- You will be asked to assess how well you did your activities, to help you see your progress and identify what steps to take next.
- You will use an English Language Portfolio to organise your work. Your teacher will help you make the portfolio.
- You will take your portfolio home regularly – to share with your family, involve them in an English activity and ask them to write their comments.

Don't forget to bring your portfolio back to school with you for your next English lesson!

How will learning to learn help you?

- It will increase your self-esteem, confidence and motivation.
- It will help you become more resilient and independent in your learning.
- It will help you understand better how you prefer to learn.
- It will help you assess how well you are doing and see your progress.
- It will help you become more resourceful and organised.
- It will help you become more actively and personally involved in your English language learning.
- It will help you talk about your language learning, and help you tell your parents *what* and *how* you have learnt.
- It will help you become a better language learner, and it will prepare you for English language learning at secondary school.

You and your teacher will become partners in learning!

3 Primary English language learners

In many educational systems, children begin primary school at around age six and make the transition to secondary school around the age of 10 or 11, although it can be earlier – and later – in some contexts (ISCED [43]). In some countries, children at six will already be reading and writing; in others, they are just beginning.

Within this age range, individual differences in children are especially marked. There are vast social, emotional and cognitive differences, as well as physical and psychological differences.

Primary children are not yet in control of their lives, and still have a great deal to learn. Generally, they:

- have a lot of energy, and need to be physically active;
- have a wide range of emotional needs;
- are emotionally excitable;
- are developing conceptually, and are still at an early stage of their schooling;
- are still developing numeracy and literacy in their mother tongue;
- learn more slowly and forget things quickly;
- tend to be self-oriented and preoccupied with their own world and interests;
- can get bored easily;
- can concentrate for a surprisingly long time, if they are interested in what they are doing;
- can be easily distracted, but also very enthusiastic;
- are excellent mimics.

Moreover, in our 21st-century global arena, technological developments and an increasing number of social, cultural and contextual factors (see below) are affecting children's English language learning and influencing their achievements. Consequently, many teachers are finding themselves with diverse classes of children with varying learning needs and levels of English.

These factors need to be taken into account when assessing the language learning needs of children in school environments where relatively limited amounts of time are available for English language learning, and class sizes are large.

They will provide the 'drivers' for your making informed decisions – regarding which activities to select or adapt from this book, for example, and when creating your own activities.

School

- Status given to English in the school and curriculum.
- Quality of teacher input and teaching.
- Continuity of learning across school classes.
- Appropriacy of teaching approach and assessment.
- Approach to teaching mother tongue, and age literacy is introduced.
- Resources and technology.
- Home–school connections.
- Class size.
- Quality of school leadership.

Individual

- Age.
- Attitudes.
- Motivation.
- Self-confidence and self-concept.
- Gender.
- Cognitive ability.
- Mother tongue writing system (Roman, Arabic, Cyrillic, etc).
- Previous exposure to English in pre-school or private programmes.
- Other languages spoken.

Factors influencing children's achievements

Policy

- The age English is introduced into the curriculum.
- Lesson frequency and intensity.
- Pre- and in-service teacher education.
- Type of teacher, and level of fluency in English.
- Language aims.
- Curriculum development.
- National teacher support, and online materials provision.

Society, home and environment

- Socio-economic status.
- Role and status of English in the learners' society.
- Home background, parental attitudes and family support.
- Parents' level of education.
- Parents' use of English.
- Exposure to English in local environment.
- Local linguistic landscape.
- Access to English outside the classroom through media, technology, etc.

Managing learners' motivation

Generally, children bring with them many well-developed cognitive capacities which help them to learn another language:

○ By the age of six, when many children begin learning English, they have already acquired their mother tongue and possibly another language or languages:
  ○ They are, however, still developing cognitively, physically, socially and emotionally.
  ○ This will impact on their motivation to learn English, as the strong intrinsic motivation to learn their mother tongue may not necessarily be so strong for another language.

It may also seem quite alien for some children to speak another language when they already have their own language for communicating:

○ At the age of six, eight or ten, a child does not have specific foreign language needs.
○ However, some may be under pressure, usually from their parents or the school system, to pass English language examinations.

They may also have unrealistic expectations:
  ○ They believe that they will be able to learn English quickly.
  ○ They may become frustrated when they realise it will take time before they speak, read and write in English as they do in their mother tongue.

Dweck[44] describes two mindsets or beliefs about learning ability and how learners respond to challenge. These are the 'fixed' mindset and the 'growth' mindset:

○ Children with a *fixed* mindset think they have either 'got it' or not, and believe that their ability, not effort, should help them overcome a problem. When they experience frustration or failure, they see it as something lacking in themselves and link this to their own lack of ability.
○ In contrast, the *growth* mindset is about being resilient in the face of frustration or failure, and believing that effort can lead to success:
  ○ These children believe in themselves as learners with the capacity to improve, and are robust, resourceful and reflective.
  ○ This shapes their attitude, motivation and commitment to learning, and has a significant impact on success.

So motivation and affective factors are likely to impact on whether children are willing to engage with the new language.

However, if the children are involved in the *management* of their own learning – and are able to mould it according to their developing interests – there are better chances that they will utilise and sustain their intrinsic motivation.

With more and more children learning English at ever younger ages, the challenge for the teacher is to manage classes of mixed levels of language skills and diverse needs, and to maintain or restore motivation through transition from pre-primary to primary to secondary school.

You can help:
○ by explaining to the children the *reasons* for starting to learn a foreign language at an early age;
○ by helping them understand the *value* of learning another language – and why the language they are learning is important.

In this way, *'we can empower children to participate more fully'* (Curtain and Dahlberg[45]).

Managing learners' memory

For learning to take place, information needs to transfer from working memory to long-term memory. Once information and knowledge is stored in long-term memory, it is learned and available for recall:

○ Working memory does not store knowledge, and it disposes of information relatively quickly.
○ When the brain disposes of information from working memory, it results in catastrophic loss and it cannot be recalled.

Working memory capacity increases with age during childhood, but differences in working memory capacity between children of the same age can be very large. Consequently, a particular activity may be within the capacity of one child but exceed that of another. In this way, the learning behaviour around instructions or words 'going in one ear and out of the other' is to do with working memory:

○ Success for many children requires approaches that ensure learning transfer, and reduce the loss from working memory.
○ 'Stickability' is a term that has been coined for learning transfer into long-term memory (Crabtree[46]).

Much of what happens in working memory happens in the classroom. So what techniques can you the teacher use, to help learning 'stick' in the long-term memory?

○ Stating the aims of an activity or the lesson and presenting these in a variety of ways, including visually.
○ Discussing and negotiating success criteria.
○ Presenting new language and information in different ways.
○ Breaking down tasks and instructions into smaller components.
○ Repeating information as required.
○ Encouraging children to request information as required.
○ Ensuring activities and materials are meaningful.
○ Using memory aids or reminders, eg Wilbur the puppet, Wilbur's learning suggestions, visuals, etc, around the classroom.
○ Engaging the children in higher-order thinking – to make sense of whatever the input or activity was, and for learning to be meaningful and to last. This involves asking the children a series of probing questions, such as those included in the 'review' stage of each activity.

Managing multiple intelligences

People process information in different ways and each person has their preferred way, which can be linked to different types of intelligence as initially defined by Howard Gardner in 1983 in his work on multiple intelligences [47].

The eight intelligences defined by Gardner are:

- **Linguistic or verbal intelligence:**
  A child with good vocabulary, who enjoys reading and listening to stories, and likes word puzzles.

- **Visual/spatial intelligence:**
  A child who enjoys drawing, learns from using pictures, maps, charts, diagrams.

- **Logical-mathematical intelligence:**
  A child who is good at planning and problem-solving; likes sorting, classifying, sequencing, ranking activities.

- **Physical intelligence:**
  A child who learns through manipulating and moving objects, and physical activities.

- **Musical intelligence:**
  A child who learns well through the use of chants, rhymes and songs.

- **Interpersonal intelligence:**
  A child who learns well by interacting with others in pair- or groupwork activities such as interviews, games, surveys, etc.

- **Intrapersonal intelligence:**
  A child who likes to reflect and can evaluate their own performance; likes working alone; likes creative writing.

- **Naturalist intelligence:**
  A child who is good at recognising patterns, who notices similarities and differences between things, and is good at classifying and organising things into groups; likes the outdoors and is curious about the world.

Traditional schooling has put an emphasis on verbal-linguistic and logical-mathematical intelligence, which may disadvantage children with strengths in the other areas.

A knowledge of multiple intelligences can help teachers ensure they provide variety in the activities and materials they use. In this way:
- They cater for a range of intelligences.
- They allow each child to maximise their potential.

The table opposite shows the kinds of activities which can develop each of the eight intelligences.

Linguistic or verbal intelligence	Visual/spatial
• Concept mapping • Giving instructions • Word games • Storytelling • Show and tell • Roleplay • Crosswords/anagrams • Tongue twisters • Gap fills	• Pictures/flashcards/ photographs/illustrations • Concept maps • Graphs • Charts and diagrams • Films • Symbols • Drawing • Construction • Maps • Shape puzzles
Logical-mathematical	**Physical**
• Problem-solving • Sequencing • Critical thinking • Predicting • Classifying/categorising • Analysing • Number puzzles • Ordering	• TPR (Total Physical Response) • Crafts • Roleplay • Drama • Physical games • Mime • Action rhymes • Dance
Musical	**Interpersonal**
• Songs • Chants • Action rhymes	• Groupwork • Pairwork • Dialogue/roleplay • Interviews and surveys • Peer teaching • Peer assessment
Intrapersonal	**Naturalist**
• Individual study • Self-assessment • Diaries/personal journals • Reflection • Personal goal-setting • Project work • Creative writing	• English in the environment • Observing nature • Patterns in nature • Protecting the environment • Classifying • Nature projects

We have discussed the theory and rationale behind learning to learn. We can now move on to present the pedagogical principles which underpin the activities in *Teaching children how to learn* – and how to create optimum learning and teaching conditions.

4 Pedagogical principles

Principle 1
Mode of input and type of response

The first pedagogical principle is based on the two main modes of input that teachers use to present and contextualise language in order to convey meaning and make this comprehensible:

○ *Verbal* input includes any form of *spoken* English, such as the teacher's speech: questions, instructions, stress, intonation, descriptions; songs, rhymes, stories and dialogues can also be presented via CDs, DVDs, etc.

○ *Non-verbal* input includes any form of *unspoken* English – such as written instructions, descriptions, short paragraphs, tapescripts, movement, mime, gestures, facial expressions, still or moving images, or objects.

In this way, meaning is conveyed through a combination of multimodal resources, and allows for a range of options in reaching children in the different ways they learn so they can engage actively in the processing and construction of meaning. For example:

○ Flashcards (*non-verbal* input) are used in the *Leisure time* activity (see page 64) to elicit vocabulary for games.

○ At the same time, the teacher scaffolds the activity *verbally* by asking questions, eliciting, confirming, explaining, etc.

But it is the *main* mode of input – in *Leisure time*, this is non-verbal – which provides the starting point for designing activities which involve the children in learning opportunities to find, share and express meaning and to use language in meaningful contexts, such as in the two tables below.

Activity *response* also takes various modes – from physical, spoken, written, creative, analytical or personal, or a combination of these – in order to offer different ways of demonstrating understanding and accommodating learner differences.

Verbal input: Listen and respond

Physical/TPR	Spoken	Written	Creative	Analytical	Personal response
Listen and ... • point/put up your hand. • follow instructions/ directions. • select. • arrange/match.	Listen and ... • repeat. • answer. • complete roleplays, dialogues, rhymes, chants, jokes. • predict.	Listen and ... • tick. • sequence. • match. • complete.	Listen and ... • draw/ colour. • make something. • mime/act out. • sing/recite.	Listen and ... • identify (right/wrong). • predict. • spot the odd one out. • identify part of speech/sound. • sort/categorise/ classify/rank. • find information.	Listen and ... • say what you think / express a personal opinion. • identify a message, mood, feeling, emotion. • prioritise. • collaborate.

Non-verbal input: Read and respond

Physical/TPR	Spoken	Written	Creative	Analytical	Personal
Read and ... • point. • follow instructions/ directions. • move/select/ arrange. • locate/find/ match.	Read and ... • answer. • complete sentence stems. • predict. Read aloud (drill, tongue twister, rhyme, chant).	Read and ... • tick. • sequence. • match. • complete – gap fill/ sentence. • write from a model.	Read and ... • draw/colour. • make something. • mime/act out/roleplay dialogues. Read aloud / recite.	Read and ... • identify (right/wrong). • predict. • spot the odd one out. • identify part of speech. • sort/classify/rank. • find information.	Read and ... • say what you think / express a personal opinion. • identify a message. • identify mood/ feeling/emotion. • prioritise. • collaborate.

Principle 2
English Language Portfolio

Principle 2 establishes the use of an English Language Portfolio as an integral part of the methodology of *Teaching children how to learn*, and of each activity.

The activity on page 38 explains how to introduce and make the portfolio with your class.

The portfolio is based on models of the European Language Portfolio developed by the Language Policy Unit of the Council of Europe [48]. Its main aims are stated as follows:

- *to help learners give shape and coherence to their experience of learning and using languages other than their first language;*
- *to motivate learners by acknowledging their efforts to extend and diversify their language skills at all levels;*
- *to provide a record of the linguistic and cultural skills they have acquired (to be consulted, for example, when they are moving to a higher learning level or seeking employment at home or abroad).*

Portfolios enhance children's motivation as they allow them to personalise their work, which they build up during their English language learning ('ownership' is a motivating influence):

- They help the children reflect on their own learning and achievements by asking them to make choices, review, compare and organise their work.
- They lead to greater independence, learner responsibility and parental involvement.

Portfolios provide evidence of the children's progress, help them monitor this and become aware of what they need to do next:

- They store the Activity worksheets they complete when carrying out the activities in *Teaching children how to learn*.
- They also store their self-assessments, which we have included on the My Activity Record pages for each activity.

Portfolios allow the children to express their individuality. In the initial stages:

- You help them choose work they would like to include.
- You discuss criteria together for guiding their selection of work and organising the portfolio.

They can add other samples of work from their English lessons:

- A record of storybooks they have listened to or read.
- Rhymes and songs they have learnt.
- Recipes, postcards and vocabulary banks.

Principle 3
Assessment for learning

Principle 3 draws on assessment for learning (Black and William [49]), which is closely linked to the aims of learning to learn and helping children take responsibility for managing their own learning.

It is a holistic approach to assessing the children's progress, which engages them more deeply in the learning process:

- It is based on the principle that children progress best when learning aims are made explicit and shared with them, when success criteria are identified and negotiated with them, so they know where they are in their learning journey and are given the tools to assess what they need to do to reach their learning aims.
- It is supported by a philosophy of interactive dialogue: immediate teacher-led oral and written feedback, child-led peer assessment and self-assessment, effective questioning and reviewing of learning.

Each activity in *Teaching children how to learn* states the learning aim(s), and lists the success criteria in age-appropriate language:

- Success criteria are the parts of the learning activity that are essential in achieving the learning aim(s).
- They also provide criteria which both you and the children can use later in review activities, to evaluate how well they have done.

Principle 4
The children's voices

The fourth principle includes a children's rights perspective, based on the UN Convention on the Rights of the Child (1989) in which Article 12 defines a child's right to be heard: '*You have the right to give your opinion and for adults to listen and take it seriously.*'

- A child-friendly version of the UN Convention is also available [50].

Hence, a movement began towards listening actively to children talking about their lived experiences and to accepting them as social actors in their own right (Clark and Moss [51]).

In the English language classroom, this means:

- *Children* are given opportunities to voice their opinions and preferences about language learning.
- *Teachers* listen and act on these opinions and preferences.

Each activity involves the children in discussing their learning with their teacher and classmates, so they become active subjects in the learning process – and not empty vessels to be filled with knowledge.

The activity *Our language learning rights* on page 74 was inspired by the work of Francisco Gomes de Matos:

- He paved the way for what he called a 'human rights embedded' methodology.
- He published 'Children's Language Learning Rights' (a checklist for teachers) in 1995 [52].
- He himself was inspired by the work of Paulo Freire [53] and Gertrude Moskowitz [54].

For a more humorous approach to the rights of the language learner, see *The Rights of the Language Learner* [55]:

- You can also get *your* learners to illustrate *their own* convention on English language learning rights. See the activity on page 74.

Principle 5
Informed activities

The fifth principle is that each activity in *Teaching children how to learn* is 'informed'.

In the language classroom, children receive a lot of implicit practice in experimenting with different cognitive strategies – for example, activities that get them:

- to sort or classify;
- to compare;
- to match;
- to select;
- to predict;
- to guess;
- to sequence.

But most classroom situations and materials rarely inform children explicitly about *why* they are using certain strategies, or get them to reflect on *how* they are learning. In other words, the metacognitive dimension is missing – and so the children are not helped to understand the significance of what they are doing.

Sharing information explicitly about the learning activity means activities are 'informed' rather than 'blind' – as explained by Wenden [56]:

- An 'informed' activity is one where the learners are aware of its aims and purpose.
- A 'blind' activity leaves the children in the dark about its purpose and relevance.

As O'Malley et al explain: '*Students without metacogntive approaches are essentially learners without direction and ability to review their progress, accomplishments and future learning directions.*' [57]

The idea, then, is that the children are involved in a cycle of reflection and experimentation on their learning, in order to combine both metacognitive and cognitive strategy training – as you will see in our next principle.

Principle 6
Routines

Principle 6 is based on the value of learning routines:

- Routines are an important aspect of any primary classroom, as young children generally '*learn more easily when they know what to expect in a lesson and what the teacher expects of them*' (Dunn [58]).
- Routines enable children to develop a sense of timing, as stages in a lesson or an activity happen at regular intervals and in predictable ways.
- Routines ensure that phrases in English are repeated and recycled regularly, through interaction in well-known situations – thus they increase exposure and '*provide opportunities for meaningful language development*' (Cameron [59]).
- Routines also provide similar security for you, their teacher, and facilitate classroom management.

The Plan, Do, Review routine

The 'plan do review' learning cycle (see Hohmann et al [60]) is applied to all the activities in *Teaching children how to learn*, as it provides a routine which the children quickly get to know.

These three stages correspond to the typical structure of a lesson, and ensure that each activity has a clear beginning, middle and end:

Applied to the skills areas – for example, listening to a story – these stages are commonly referred to as *pre-*, *while-* and *post-*listening.

These three stages also provide a framework in which you can, systematically and explicitly, help the children learn how to learn and become aware of their own learning preferences and differences – through *reflection*, *experimentation* and *further reflection* – thereby combining metacognitive and cognitive strategy training, and representing the ongoing cyclical nature of learning as follows:

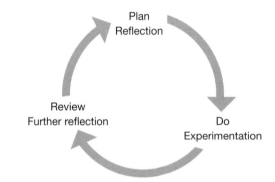

This routine helps the children feel secure, enables them to concentrate on an activity and gain the confidence to move on to the next stage, gradually making preparations themselves.

Plan

In this stage, the children are informed of the learning aims of an activity and encouraged to reflect on what they already know and how best to plan for the activity:

- They identify and negotiate the success criteria with you.
- You will, initially, need to provide success criteria, explicitly modelling how these are generated.
- Gradually, the children can become involved in negotiating and generating their own.

This planning stage involves the children in reflection, and develops metacognitive strategies and prepares them linguistically for the next stage of the activity: *Do*.

Do

The 'do' stage provides step-by-step guidelines for each activity. This stage involves the children in experimenting and doing things with the language and their language materials, thereby developing cognitive strategies.

Do more

The 'plan do review' learning cycle now incorporates a further stage: *Do more*.

This stage is optional and will depend on a number of factors, such as time available, the children's interests, etc:

- It provides opportunities to further extend and consolidate learning that has taken place in the 'do' stage.
- It gives the children opportunities to work independently, and personalise their work.

Review

The review stage involves the children in further reflection on their learning by responding to five reflection questions:

- *What did you do?*
- *What did you learn?*
- *How did you learn it?*
- *How well did you do?*
- *What do you need to do next?*

The first three questions above engage the children in a variety of familiar activities, which include:

matching	choosing the correct sentence
sequencing	gap fill
prioritising	*Simon says …*
ranking	miming
categorising	creating a cartoon strip
identifying	using a talking stick
completing a sentence	talk partners
choosing the odd one out	think-pair-share

These first three questions encourage the children to reflect on:

- What they did. What they learnt. How they learnt.

How well did you do?

The fourth question invites the children to assess how well they did, by reflecting on both the *content* and the *process* of learning:

- The self-assessment activities use familiar techniques – such as smiley faces, thumbs-up and traffic lights – in order to make self-assessment accessible and enjoyable:
  - Additional techniques are used – so that each self-assessment activity is linked to the language or topic of the activity, to provide further consolidation and to maintain the children's interest and motivation.
  - After each self-assessment activity, the children are asked to justify their assessment and discuss with the teacher and with the class.

This builds their self-esteem and confidence in talking about and accounting for their learning, and leads them to a greater understanding of themselves as learners – that different children learn different things, and have their own preferences about content and learning.

The self-assessment/*How well did you do?* activities are varied and visually appealing – so that the children will look forward to them, and enjoy taking on responsibility for assessing how well they did.

These activities are included in the My Activity Record pages and are downloadable from Wilbur's toolkit:

- The children share their My Activity Record pages with their families, and involve them in their English language learning.
- They organise and store the pages in their English Language Portfolios, to keep an ongoing visual record of their learning and progress.

What do you need to do next?

This last question refers the children back to the success criteria, and encourages them to identify areas they need to revise or understand better.

The five reflection questions we include stimulate the children to think and process information about the content of an activity, discuss their learning strategies and assess their performance in order to identify next steps.

The questions further develop metacognition.

We suggest ways for you to conduct these activities, as part of your classroom procedures, but you, as their teacher, can choose the interaction mode that best suits your class. For example:

- Plenary/whole class.
- Groups or pairs.
- Individual/personal reflection.

Once the children have become familiar with the questions, and gained some experience of how to reflect on and assess their own learning, they will gradually start asking themselves the questions independently.

Principle 7
Home involvement

Our seventh pedagogical principle focuses on encouraging home involvement. The ELLiE research (Enever [61]) highlighted the following:

- The impact the out-of-school context can have on children's learning.
- The importance of enhancing both children's and parents' awareness of the possibilities of contact with English outside the school.

The activities in *Teaching children how to learn* have been designed as follows:

- The children take the *in-the-school* experience into the home.
- They bring the *out-of-school* experience back into the classroom.

This is achieved by incorporating a final 'share' stage:

The 'share' stage enhances the children's self-esteem, encourages them to take pride in their work and take responsibility for sharing their achievements and progress with their family.

The English Language Portfolio provides 'an important vehicle' (see Linse et al [62]) for communication between the school and the home, and maximises English language learning time:

- This school–home involvement will strengthen the children's feelings of ownership and responsibility for the portfolio. Each 'share' activity is included in the My Activity Record page:
  - Parents and other family members are invited to write their suggestions and comments in English or in the home language.
  - If no English is spoken at home, the child can tell their family about the activity in the home language – and use the opportunity to teach them some English!
- Regular school–home involvement will make English language learning a dynamic living process, the children will develop pride in their work, learn to account for their English language learning and take on responsibility for informing their parents about this.

Consent should be sought from parents for any activities involving interviewing, filming or photographing (see page 34). This will also provide further opportunities for contact with parents.

Principle 8
Values

Principle 8 promotes a philosophy based on valuing self, others and the environment.

Values are the principles that guide behaviour:

- The teachers are encouraged to model values, and to give time for reflective practices.
- The children will be empowered to become effective learners and global citizens, by improving their capacity to learn and to succeed in life, connecting with other people and other cultures.

The values which are promoted through the activities in this book, and contribute to children's personal development, are:

- **Accountability**
  Taking individual and class responsibility for the environment, for the class community and for English language learning and reporting to parents.

- **Caring**
  Caring and respecting others and the environment. Listening to and valuing the ideas and opinions of others. Learning from and sharing with others.

- **Flexibility**
  Finding creative solutions, and adapting to a range of new situations. Being resourceful.

- **Resilience**
  Dealing with difficulties and setbacks, enjoying challenge and high achievement.

- **Tolerance**
  Seeing similarities and differences in a positive light, and valuing diversity.

Principle 9
Cross-curricular links

The ninth principle is that each activity can also be linked to, and used to develop, other subject areas in the primary curriculum, or to raise awareness of seasonal and cultural events:

- This makes learning more interesting and meaningful, and provides a broader view of learning English and of the world.
- It moves away from a traditional sequential and 'English as a subject' approach to a *holistic* approach to learning and general education.

Integrating content into activities from other areas of the curriculum provides challenge and the opportunity for children:

- to develop cognitive strategies, such as classifying, measuring, contrasting, hypothesising, etc;
- to use different kinds of graphic organisers and charts.

The water cycle on page 86, for example, allows the children to develop and use language to describe and sequence a process, and to label a diagram.

If you are the children's main class teacher, you will be in the ideal situation for integrating English with other subjects, as you will know exactly what your class has been working on:

- This integration can reinforce certain key content areas and concepts that cross subject boundaries, and underpins more general learning across the curriculum.
- It can also maximise the limited time often given to English language learning, by offering opportunities to revise or review relevant language as the opportunity arises – for example, by taking a little time to revise numbers in the Maths class.

If you are a specialist teacher of English who visits the school, you should liaise with the children's class teacher to find out what the children have been studying and how the teacher could collaborate with you.

Principle 10
A main outcome

Our final principle is that each activity has a main outcome.

Informing children at the beginning of an activity where their work is leading will make learning more meaningful, purposeful and motivating, and will provide them with an incentive:

- A main outcome provides the opportunity to bridge the gap between language *study* and language *use*, and also links classroom learning with the world outside.
- Main outcomes encourage the children to personalise language, pursue their interests and use language in an independent way.
- They also show that learning English means interest, creativity and enjoyment.

The main outcomes are varied, and take many forms, such as:

- making a poster;
- writing a senses poem;
- conducting a listening experiment;
- making a snowflake;
- doing a quiz.

The main outcomes are produced through whole-class or individual activities. When appropriate, the children organise their main outcomes in their portfolios – and share with their family.

Applying the pedagogical principles

The key features of the activities in *Teaching children how to learn* are the following:

There is an emphasis on the oral/aural mode throughout:

- It forms the main mode through which language is encountered and practised in the early stages of language learning.
- It is needed, to build a strong base for both spoken and written language.
  - More of the activities, therefore, involve the children in developing the skill of *listening and speaking*.
  - Activities focusing on the *written* mode are generally more suitable for older, literate children.

There is a mixture of both experiential and analytic activities, focusing on the following:

- Form, in which attention to certain aspects of language is the central part of the activity:
  - *My school day* focuses on using time linkers as discourse markers.
  - *A royal feast* focuses on discriminating phonemcs.
- Language awareness:
  - *English around me* encourages the children to become aware of English used in the environment.
  - *Leisure time* develops awareness of collocations.
- A topic, from which the language derives naturally:
  - The topic of environmental protection provides the springboard for the activity *How green am I?*
  - The topic of bullying generates the activity *Don't be a bully!*
- A particular learning strategy, such as how to use a KWL grid (a technique to activate the children's prior knowledge, encourage personal involvement with the topic, confirm information they already know, and focus their attention on what they want to find out) or a concept web:
  - *Wilbur the Worm: the facts* shows how to use a KWL grid.
  - *A friend is someone who …* shows how to use a concept web.
- A cultural aspect:
  - *Fireworks safety*
  - *H is for Halloween*

Age/level suitability

Age and level indications are provided. However, given the number of variables and factors affecting children's language learning, as we saw on page 21:

- Many activities can span the primary age range – by varying the amount of scaffolding, according to the cognitive ability and language level of the children.
- Although CEFR level descriptors – as benchmarks for primary foreign language learning – are not considered to be entirely appropriate (Enever [63]), the activities are nevertheless mapped to these, in order to give approximate indications of level.

The activities remain within the A1 and A2 CEFR levels (see page 36), which are the attainment levels to be reached at the end of primary school as defined by many ministries of education (Enever [64]).

Time

The time required for each activity is flexible to suit different teaching contexts:

- You can decide when best to use each activity alongside your core English language teaching materials, depending on the following:
  - Age
  - Language level
  - Cognitive ability
  - Stage of literacy
- Alternatively, they can be used as stand-alone, separate activities.

All the activities aim to build vocabulary and create confidence and motivation, whilst raising awareness of the learning process.

Summarising the pedagogical principles

To summarise, then, each activity:

- follows the 'plan do review' routine, to combine metacognitive and cognitive strategy training;
- allows for a variety of responses;
- is contextualised with a real purpose, and offers challenge;
- is informed, so the children are aware of its purpose and why a particular strategy can be helpful;
- involves the children in planning;
- involves the children in identifying and negotiating success criteria;
- has a main outcome;
- is linked to the English Language Portfolio;
- can be personalised according to the children's interests;
- provides opportunities for learner independence, responsibility and choice;
- provides opportunities to develop interaction and fluency;
- encourages creative use of language;
- involves the children in reflection and discussion on their learning and achievements;
- develops a broader view of learning English and of the world, via cross-curricular links and the promotion of positive values;
- teaches the children to account for their learning and report to their parents;
- fosters home involvement.

Creating optimum learning and teaching conditions

'Children learn best when they are given appropriate responsibility, allowed to make errors, decisions and choices, and respected as autonomous learners.' Tina Bruce [65]

As we have seen throughout Part A, the goal of effective pedagogy is to improve children's achievement and help them develop as autonomous learners and lead to their future success as lifelong learners in an ever-changing world.

This involves giving opportunities to make decisions and choices about their own learning, in order to develop a sense of responsibility.

We have already seen how the teacher plays a key role in this process.

By understanding how the activities in Part B are structured, and by following the pedagogical principles which underpin them – their conception, design and rationale – you can begin to create these 'optimum conditions' to support each child in the process of reaching their full potential and becoming enthusiastic and motivated about learning language and learning how to learn.

'Let us take our children seriously! Everything else follows from this. Only the best is good enough for a child.' Zoltán Kodály [66]

These optimum conditions are promoted through four core elements of effective pedagogy:

- by creating a positive classroom climate;
- by enabling children to experience success in early language learning;
- by planning interesting and stimulating learning experiences;
- by encouraging parental support and involvement.

These are illustrated on page 31 – as a visual representation and reminder of your multifaceted role as a primary English language teacher, and of the range of teaching strategies at your disposal.

Good quality teaching will involve a combination of these teaching strategies working together at different times. The very best teachers are those who demonstrate all of these features, and motivate the children and make a difference to their academic, social and behavioural outcomes.

As you experiment with the activities in Part B, you can refer to this visual representation regularly – to check to what extent you are able to create the best possible conditions for learning and teaching:

- *Are there any teaching strategies you are not able to use? Why?*
- *Are there any you need to improve?*

There will be further opportunities (see the *Self-assessment* activity in Part C) for you to review and reflect on the pedagogical principles underpinning the activities, as well as other teaching strategies.

Planning interesting and stimulating learning experiences

- Planning challenging lessons.
- Using familiar routines.
- Providing authentic input to create an acquisition-rich learning environment.
- Making links to other areas in the primary curriculum.
- Giving opportunities for the children to relate things to their personal experience.
- Developing intercultural understanding.
- Giving meaningful exposure to the language.
- Using age-appropriate and varied activities and materials.

Creating a positive classroom climate

- Understanding that mistakes are learning opportunities.
- Creating a climate of mutual confidence and respect in the teacher–class relationship.
- Creating an inclusive classroom, and respecting diversity.
- Recognising and praising effort, and giving constructive feedback.
- Being a positive role model, and promoting positive values.
- Establishing a learning environment where the children feel confident to take risks with the language.
- Enabling the children to voice their opinions and preferences about language learning.
- Listening to and acting on the children's perspectives.
- Building a class learning community.
- Giving the children responsibility and opportunities to work independently and make choices about activities and materials.
- Using positive behaviour and classroom management strategies.
- Providing opportunities for the children to work cooperatively.
- Making effective use of the classroom space.
- Using effective questioning to create an enquiring classroom and quality dialogue.

Creating optimum learning and teaching conditions

Enabling children to experience success in early language learning

- Planning and integrating learning to learn explicitly and systematically into lessons.
- Discussing and reviewing learning.
- Encouraging the children to use the target language as much as possible, but also with the right to use the mother tongue or shared classroom language to help them learn.
- Using child-directed speech.
- Scaffolding learning.
- Discussing and negotiating success criteria.
- Giving opportunities to use language in context.
- Encouraging organised learning.
- Ensuring the children know what is expected of them, and how they are to be evaluated.
- Ensuring the children understand the purpose of what they have to do, and its relevance.
- Giving the children opportunities to work at their own pace and personalise their learning.

Encouraging parental support and family involvement

- Creating effective communication channels between the school and home.
- Enabling the children to share learning with their parents.
- Encouraging positive parental attitudes to foreign language learning.
- Fostering cooperation between teacher and parents.
- Planning activities which take the in-the-school experience into the home.
- Planning activities which take the in-the-home experience into the school.
- Supporting parents to help their child with their English language learning.

Bibliography

1 Graddol, D 'English Next' British Council 2006 *http://www.teachingenglish.org.uk/article/english-next*

2 Johnstone, R 'An early start: What are the key conditions for generalized success?' In Evener, J, Moon, J and Raman, U (Eds) *Young Learner English Language Policy and Implementation: International Perspectives* (p33) Garnet Education 2009

3 Rixon, S 'British Council survey of policy and practice in primary English language teaching worldwide' British Council 2013 *http://www.teachingenglish.org.uk/article/british-council-survey-policy-practice-primary-english-language-teaching-worldwide*

4 Ellis, G and Sinclair, B *Learning to Learn English. Teacher's Book* (p2) CUP 1989

5 Piaget, J *The Language and Thought of the Child* Routledge 1963 3rd reprint edn. 2001

6 Bruner, J *Towards a Theory of Instruction* (pp49–53) Cambridge MA: Harvard University Press 1966

7 Vygotsky, L *Thought and Language* MIT Press 1962

8 Vygotsky, L *Mind in Society* MIT Press 1978

9 Claxton, G *Building Learning Power: Helping Young People Become Better Learners* TLO Ltd 2002

10 Csikszentmihalyi, M *Flow: The Psychology of Optimum Experience* HarperCollins 1990

11 Dweck, C *Mindset: The New Psychology of Success* Ballantine Books 2007

12 Gardner, H *Frames of Mind: The Theory of Multiple Intelligences* Fontana 1983

13 Dam, L *Learner Autonomy 3: From Theory to Classroom Practice* Authentik 1995

14 Ellis, G and Sinclair, B *Learning to Learn English. Teacher's Book* CUP 1989

15 Little, D *Learner Autonomy 1: Definitions, Issues and Problems* Authentik 1991

16 Holec, H *Autonomy and Foreign Language Learning* Pergamon 1981

17 O'Malley, J M and Chamot, A U *Learning Strategies in Secondary Language Acquisition* CUP 1990

18 Wenden, A and Rubin, J 'Incorporating Learner Training in the Classroom' In *Learner Strategies in Language Learning* Prentice Hall 1987

19 Little, D 'Democracy, discourse and learner autonomy in the foreign language classroom' *Utbildning & Demokrati* 13 (3) (pp105–126) 2004

20 Nisbet, J and Shucksmith, J *Learning Strategies* (p33) Routledge 1986

21 Nisbet, J and Shucksmith, J *Learning Strategies* Routledge 1986

22 Whitebread, D et al 'Metacognition in Young Children: Evidence from a Naturalistic Study of 3–5 Year Olds' Paper presented at the 5th Warwick International Early Years Conference, March 2005, and the 11th Biennial European Association for Research on Learning and Instruction (EARLI) Conference, Cyprus, August 2005 *https://www.educ.cam.ac.uk/research/projects/cindle/news.html*

23 Hawkins, E *Awareness of Language: An Introduction* CUP 1984

24 Vygotsky, L *Mind in Society* MIT Press 1978

25 Brewster, J, Ellis, G and Girard, D *The Primary English Teacher's Guide* (p146) Pearson Education 2002

26 O'Malley, J M, Chamot, A U, Stewner-Manzanares, G, Kupper, L and Russo, R P 'Learning strategies used by beginning and intermediate students' *Language Learning* 35 (1) (p24) 1985

27 Dickinson, L and Carver, D 'Learning how to learn: steps towards self-direction in foreign language learning in schools' *English Language Teaching Journal* 35 (1) 1980

28 Brewster, J, Ellis, G and Girard, D *The Primary English Teacher's Guide* (p269) Pearson Education 2002

29 Bruner, J *Towards a Theory of Instruction* (p53) Cambridge MA: Harvard University Press 1966

30 Wenden, A 'Facilitating Learning Competence: Perspectives on an Expanded Role for Second Language Teachers' *The Canadian Modern Language Review* 41 (6) (pp981–990) 1985

31 Wenden, A 'Learner Development in Language Learning' *Applied Linguistics* 23 (1) (p41) OUP 2002

32 Read, C *500 Activities for the Primary Classroom* (p286) Macmillan 2007

33 Everhard, C J, Mynard, J and Smith, R *Autonomy in language learning: Opening a can of worms* IATEFL 2011

34 Ellis, G and Brewster, J *Tell it Again! The Storytelling Handbook for Primary English Language Teachers* British Council 2014 *http://www.teachingenglish.org.uk/article/tell-it-again-storytelling-handbook-primary-english-language-teachers*

35 Claxton, G *Building Learning Power: Helping Young People Become Better Learners* TLO Ltd 2002

36 Buzan, T *Use Your Head* Aerial Books/BBC 1982

37 Wenden, A and Rubin, J 'Incorporating Learner Training in the Classroom' in *Learner Strategies in Language Learning* (p160) Prentice Hall 1987

38 Fisher, R *Teaching Children to Learn* Nelson Thornes 2005

39 Ioannou-Georgiou, S and Pavlou, P *Assessing Young Learners* (p23) OUP 2003

40 Dunn, O *Introducing English to Young Children: Reading and Writing* (p75) Collins 2014

41 Brewster, J, Ellis, G and Girard, D *The Primary English Teacher's Guide* Pearson Education 2002

42 Linse, C, Van Vlack, S and Bladas, O 'Parents and young learners in English language teaching: global practices and issues in school–home contacts' British Council 2014 *http://www.teachingenglish.org.uk/article/parents-young-learners-english-language-teaching-global-practices-issues-school%E2%80%93home*

43 International Standard Classification of Education (ISCED) 2011 Available at *http://www.uis.unesco.org/Education/Documents/isced-2011-en.pdf*

44 Dweck, C *Mindset: The New Psychology of Success* Ballantine Books 2007

45 Curtain, H and Dahlberg, C A *Languages and Children. Making the Match: New Languages for Young Learners, Grades K–8* 4th edn. (p239) Pearson 2010

46 Crabtree, D 'In one ear out of the other: how knowing about memory might help us in the classroom' British Council 2013 *http://www.teachingenglish.org.uk/article/one-ear-out-other-how-knowing-about-memory-might-help-us-classroom*

47 Gardner, H *Frames of Mind: The Theory of Multiple Intelligences* Fontana 1983

48 Council of Europe. European Language Portfolio (Accessed 8 October 2014) *http://www.coe.int/t/dg4/education/elp/ELP-REG/Default_EN.asp?_sm_au_=iHVH7TQtPjVP2176*

49 Black, P and William, D *Inside the Black Box: Raising standards through classroom assessment* School of Education, King's College London 1998

50 UN Convention on the Rights of the Child in Child Friendly Language 1989 *http://www.unicef.org/rightsite/files/uncrcchildfriendlylanguage.pdf*

51 Clark, A and Moss, P *Listening to Young Children: The Mosaic Approach* 2nd edn. London: NCB 2011

52 Gomes de Matos, F 'Children's Language Learning Rights' *FIPLV – Fédération Internationale des Professeurs de Langues Vivantes – World News* 33 1995

53 Freire, P *Pedagogy of the Oppressed* Penguin 1972

54 Moskowitz, G *Caring and Sharing in the Foreign Language Class* Longman ELT 1978

55 *Rights of the Language Learner* Illustrated by Steve Weatherill b small publishing 2013 *http://www.bsmall.co.uk/sca/The%20Rights%20of%20the%20Language%20Learner.pdf*

56 Wenden, A and Rubin, J 'Incorporating Learner Training in the Classroom' in *Learner Strategies in Language Learning* (p159) Prentice Hall 1987

57 O'Malley, J M, Chamot, A U, Stewner-Manzanares, G, Kupper, L and Russo, R P 'Learning strategies used by beginning and intermediate students' *Language Learning* 35 (1) (p24) 1985

58 Dunn, O *Introducing English to Young Children: Spoken Language* (p90) Collins 2013

59 Cameron, L *Teaching Languages to Young Learners* (p11) CUP 2001

60 Hohmann, M, Epstein, A S and Weikart, D *Educating Young Children: Active Learning Practices for Preschool and Child Care Programs* 3rd edn. High/Scope Educational Research Foundation 2008

61 Enever, J 'ELLiE Early Language Learning in Europe' British Council 2011 *http://www.teachingenglish.org.uk/article/early-language-learning-europe*

62 Linse, C, Van Vlack, S and Bladas, O 'Parents and young learners in English language teaching: global practices and issues in school–home contacts' British Council 2014 *http://www.teachingenglish.org.uk/article/parents-young-learners-english-language-teaching-global-practices-issues-school%E2%80%93home*

63 Enever, J 'ELLiE Early Language Learning in Europe' British Council 2011 *http://www.teachingenglish.org.uk/article/early-language-learning-europe*

64 Enever, J 'ELLiE Early Language Learning in Europe' British Council 2011 *http://www.teachingenglish.org.uk/article/early-language-learning-europe*

65 Bruce, T *Early Childhood Education* 4th edn. (p47) Hodder Education 2011

66 Kodály, Z *The Selected Writings of Zoltán Kodály* Trans. Lily Halápy and Fred Macnicol. Boosey & Hawkes 1974 *http://www.cottageschoolofmusic.com/kod.html*

'I hear and I forget, I see and I remember, I do and I understand.'
Chinese proverb

Teaching children how to learn has discussed the rationale and theory behind learning to learn and the pedagogical principles that underpin the activities in Part B. This reflection and planning will have prepared you to put into practice these activities – so that you 'do and understand'.

You will experiment with the 'plan do review' learning cycle, in order to encourage a critical and enquiring approach to both your *teaching* and your children's *learning*.

You are encouraged to *'refer technique back to principle, testing one out against the other in a continual process of experimentation'* (as Henry Widdowson pleaded, back in 1984 [1]). While doing the activities, you will gain a clearer understanding of the principles which inform them, and adopt a theoretical orientation to your teaching.

Teaching children how to learn acknowledges children as being 'experts in their own lives' (Langsted, 1994 [2]) and active participants in their learning. They are given a voice in expressing their preferences, ideas and opinions. This is based on a 'new sociology of childhood' approach (James et al, 1998 [3]) and a children's rights perspective.

Consequently, there is a shift in the traditional teacher–pupil relationship from the role of the teacher as 'knower' to one of 'partner', where teachers are encouraged to collaborate with the children and value their involvement as contributors to their own learning and to research projects.

Teaching children how to learn uses participatory research methodologies, which empower the children not only to reflect on their learning, but also to take ownership of the learning process, manage their learning preferences and make choices about their learning. (See Pinter and Zandian, 2014 [4].)

Listening is an active process which grants the children voice and agency, where they are viewed as co-researchers. Research is conducted *with* children rather than *on* children – for example, explicitly seeking the children's views on who they consider to be an ideal teacher, their language learning rights and what learning English feels like.

Many of the activities in Part B use these participatory research methodologies, which empower the children to not only reflect on their learning, but also to take ownership of the learning process, manage their learning preferences and make choices about their learning.

You have the opportunity to reflect on, and review, your teaching and the children's learning in Part C. But, now, it's time to get started doing the activities in Part B with your learners.

Involving the children

The multimodal approach we use in this book allows the child to express their views through modes other than language – such as films, photographs, drawings, actions, stories – that reflect children's multifaceted communicative ability and their creativity in conveying meaning.

It is therefore important to ensure that the children's rights are respected and upheld and that their informed consent is given:

- Inform the children about activities and projects.
- Ask for their views.

Involving the parents

Some families may well not speak English at all, so we encourage the children to do the 'share' activities in the home language:

- This is referred to as 'translanguaging'.
- It involves the reprocessing of content, and allows the child to expand, extend and intensify what they have learned through one language in school through discussion with the family in the home language.
- It facilitates home–school connections and involvement.

For further information on translanguaging, you can consult the reference numbers [5] and [6] below.

Safeguarding the children

It is also important to follow your school's policy for obtaining written parental consent to photographing, recording, filming or involving children in research. The consent form should also state:

- the precise circumstances in which the children will be photographed, filmed or interviewed;
- how the end products (photos, films, drawings, interviews) will be stored;
- for how long;
- by whom.

These steps will mitigate any risks, and keep such activities ethical and safe.

[1] Widdowson, H 'The incentive value of theory in teacher education' *ELTJ* 38 (2) (p88) 1984

[2] Langsted, O 'Looking at quality from the child's perspective' In Moss, P and Pence, A (Eds) *Valuing Quality in Early Childhood Services: New Approaches to Defining Quality* (pp28–42) Sage Publications 2000

[3] James, A, Jenks, C and Prout, A *Theorizing Childhood* Cambridge: Polity 1998

[4] Pinter, A and Zandian, S "I don't ever want to leave this room': benefits of researching 'with' children' *ELTJ* 68 (1) (p72) 2014

[5] Garcia, O *Bilingual education in the 21st century: A global perspective* Wiley-Blackwell 2009

[6] Lewis, G, Jones, B and Baker, C 'Translanguaging: origins and development from school to street and beyond' *Educational Research and Evaluation: An International Journal on Theory and Practice* 18 (7) 2012

Part B is divided into three chapters, which are followed by Wilbur's toolkit.

Part C is followed by the Teachers' toolkit.

Before embarking on the activities in Chapter One, see page 36 for a detailed breakdown of how the activities in Part B are organised.

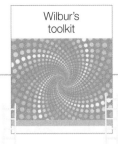
Wilbur's toolkit

Teachers' toolkit

Chapter One
Getting started

We insisted when we began *Teaching children how to learn* that a pre-requisite for successful teaching is a knowledge of oneself as a teacher, of one's class and of the resources available:

○ The first activity in Part B is therefore dedicated to knowing your pupils.

We then demonstrate how the English Language Portfolio forms an integral part of the methodology, and the second activity is therefore dedicated to the introduction and creation of a portfolio for each child:

○ The children will learn all about the purpose of using a portfolio and about the different samples of work they can organise in it.
○ A Teacher Development activity, to help you negotiate criteria with your pupils for selecting samples of work for their portfolios, is provided in Part C on page 118.

In Chapter One we then introduce the friendly class mascot, Wilbur the Worm:

○ A first activity provides earthworm facts, as presented by Wilbur. It is important not to underestimate the class: even young children will have some knowledge of earthworms, and will be curious to learn more.
○ A second activity involves the children in making their own Wilbur sock puppet, which they can use when doing the other activities in Part B.

Although the children will have learnt (or will learn) that worms do not have eyes, Wilbur, as the class mascot, has been given eyes in *Teaching children how to learn* – as well as a friendly smile! – in order to personify him, and help the children relate to him.

Wilbur's toolkit. This is in the book at the end of Part B, starting on page 96, and as downloadable worksheets on the Delta Publishing website.

Go to: *www.deltapublishing.co.uk/resources*

Wilbur's toolkit includes the following:

Activity worksheets

These are aimed to facilitate your lesson preparation:

○ They are presented in reduced format in the book.
○ They are then reproduced as A4 downloadable worksheets on the website.

My Activity Record pages

These are for the children to complete for each activity:

○ They are presented in reduced format in the book.
○ They are then provided as A4 downloadable pages on the website.

 Go to: *www.deltapublishing.co.uk/resources*
Click on the cover of the book.
Click on Wilbur's toolkit.

Teachers' toolkit. This is in the book at the end of Part C, starting on page 149, and includes all the Keys, Transcripts and Commentaries from Part C.

Teachers' toolkit on the website. This includes a number of A4 downloadable templates (see page 171 for a list of these):

Templates

○ A speech bubble template for Wilbur's learning suggestions, to display supportive phrases around the classroom.
See page 15 in Part A.
○ Templates for building a class profile and for ongoing reflection on the benefits of really knowing your class.
See page 37 in Part B.
○ A selection of templates from Part C.
See pages 171–174 for examples of these in reduced format.

Storybook recommendations

The Teachers' toolkit on the website also provides synopses of all the storybooks suggested by Wilbur in the activities in Part B.

 Go to: *www.deltapublishing.co.uk/resources*
Click on the cover of the book.
Click on Teachers' toolkit.

The activities

The activities themselves are presented across two pages as follows:
- They incorporate the pedagogical principles outlined in Part A.
- They adhere to the 'plan do review' learning cycle.

The Review activities

The review activities on the second page take the children through a series of reflection questions:
- Different interaction modes are suggested. For example: whole-class, groups, pairs or individual work. As the children become more familiar with the review activities, you can choose which interaction mode best suits your class.
- Using the children's mother tongue or shared classroom language is often more efficient for reviewing, especially in the early stages of language learning, and valorises and empowers the children's voices. There will be no loss of the learning to learn benefits if the target language is not used.

Activity titles	These aim to do the following: First, provide appeal and meaning for the child, set the context and give a point of entry. For example: *Learning English feels like ...* , *A friend is someone who ...* . Second, state the type of activity. For example: *Writing a senses poem*, *Making a friendship tree*.
Age/level	The Common European Framework of Reference (CEFR) level descriptors and ages give approximate indications, to help select activities according to the range of factors influencing children's English language learning. Many activities can span the primary age range, depending on the amount of scaffolding provided. Activities focusing on the written mode are generally more suitable for older, literate children. For further information on age/level suitability, see pages 29 and 30.
Activity type	This states the type of activity, as related to the main mode of input, For example: Verbal input: *Listen and respond*. See Chapter Two. Non-verbal input: *Read and respond*. See Chapter Three.
Response type	Response to the activities takes various forms, and the main response types are listed for each activity. For example: physical, spoken, written, creative, analytical or personal, or a combination of these.
Learning aims	The learning aims for each activity are listed: These highlight the main focus of each activity in terms of the language and skills areas developed.
Learning strategies	The learning strategies to be developed through each activity are listed, to make these explicit: A typology of learning strategies developed throughout the book can be found on page 12.
Main outcome	The main outcome is stated: The teacher can inform the children at the beginning of an activity where their work is leading.
Curricular/ cultural links	Opportunities for linking the activity to other subject areas in the curriculum or to seasonal and cultural events are suggested: in this way, content and concepts that cross subject boundaries can be consolidated.
Values	Values that can be developed through each activity are suggested: this will enable teachers to model these and to raise the children's awareness.
Assumptions	These provide general information about what we expect the children will be able to do, and what we expect they may need additional help with. They also provide general information about an activity.
Materials	To facilitate preparation for each activity, the materials required are listed: where there are downloadable materials in Wilbur's toolkit, this is indicated.
Transfer	Suggestions are provided as to how the activity type, learning strategy or language can be transferred. For example: to other activities or subject areas across the primary curriculum.
Wilbur recommends	Storybooks are suggested, to allow the children to extend and consolidate language and themes beyond the activity. There is a short synopsis for each storybook on the website, and a Teacher Development activity on page 137 in Part C to further help you select storybooks for a specific class.

Knowing your class

Creating a class profile

Aim

To create a class profile, in order to make learning more inclusive, through a better understanding of:

○ how a class is constituted;

○ the advantages and limitations of the learning context.

To learn to make informed decisions about classroom procedures and materials selection.

Plan

'Expert teachers are more context-dependent and have high situation cognition. When experts classify learning scenarios, the categories they create are more dependent on existing context, surrounding setting, or embedded in particular circumstances.'
John Hattie

Each teacher is different and each class is different, as all children are unique in what they bring to the classroom.

On page 21, we looked at some of the factors influencing children's achievements in order to better understand the background and diversity of our learners and their learning context.

Think of a particular class:

○ *How well do you know the children in your class?*

○ *What do you consider to be the benefits of a better knowledge and understanding of how your class is constituted to your teaching and your pupils' learning?*

Compare your thoughts with the 'Knowing your class' list of benefits in the Teachers' toolkit on page 171 and on the website.

See pages 149 and 171 for information on the Teachers' toolkit.

Do

● Select a class you are currently teaching.

● Complete the profile opposite, to deepen your knowledge about your class and your teaching context:

○ You will find a downloadable profile that you can complete in the Teachers' toolkit on the website.

● Compare with the completed 'class storybook profile' in the Teachers' toolkit in Part C on page 167:

○ *What are the similarities? What are the differences?*

You will see that knowing your class also has an impact on *any* materials you choose to use at *any* particular moment.

Do more

Draw up profiles for each of the classes you teach.

Class profile	
Date	
School year .... **Class**	
Age of pupils	
Number of pupils	
Gender mix (boys/girls)	
Language(s) spoken at home	
Shared classroom language	
English language level	
Cognitive ability	
School setting (urban/suburban/rural)	
Children's interests	
Classroom space/layout (fixed desks, rows, movable tables, etc)	
Resources/technology	
Other information:	

Review

As you use the activities in Part B, consider the impact this knowledge has on the following:

○ The way you teach.

○ The materials you select.

○ The language(s) you use in the classroom.

○ The routines and procedures you use.

○ The children's attitudes to their learning.

○ The children's self-concept.

○ The children's motivation.

○ Your relationship with your class.

Share

Organise a 'class profile' resource file, to share with your colleagues.

Hattie, J *Visible Learning for Teachers: Maximising Impact on Learning* Routledge 2012

My English Language Portfolio

Keeping a learning record

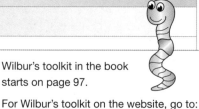

Age/level
5–11 years; A1
For younger children, the portfolio can
be created in picture form.

Activity type
Listen and do; Write and record

Response type
Spoken, written, personal and creative

Learning aims
To follow instructions
To learn key vocabulary related to the
portfolio: *folder, passport, activity record,
learning strategy, intercultural experience*
To explain the purpose of a portfolio,
using the structure: *We can* + verb

Learning strategies
Listening for specific information
Concentrating and paying attention
Following instructions
Thinking about language learning

Main outcome
Making a portfolio

Curricular/cultural links
Study skills; Critical thinking
European Day of Languages
International Mother Language Day

Values
Accountability/tolerance: respect for
individual differences and cultures

Assumptions
The children may not have had
experience of using a personal portfolio.

Materials
A ready-made portfolio;
A folder for each child;
Pages to download (see Wilbur's toolkit
on the website, and page 98)

Transfer
The children can use a portfolio for
other languages or other subjects.

I recommend ...
Why Is The Sky Blue?

Plan

Explain the learning aims of the activity:
*'We're going to learn how to listen and
follow instructions in order to make an
English Language Portfolio.'*

Give or identify the following success criteria:
○ *Listen carefully to your teacher.*
○ *Think about how a portfolio will help you
learn English.*

Show the children your ready-made portfolio. Say:
'You are going to make your own portfolio.'

Ask the children to think how a portfolio will help them
with their English language learning. Elicit:
○ *We can record what we can do in English, in our mother tongue and any other languages
we know.*
○ *We can see the progress we are making.*
○ *We can keep a record of the activities we have done to learn English.*
○ *We can organise our English language work.*
○ *We can think about how we learn English (learning strategies).*
○ *We can show our work to our parents.*

Do

◉ Give a folder to each child.

◉ Introduce the first portfolio pages indicated below:
   ○ You may prefer to do this in one lesson – or gradually, over several lessons.

◉ Distribute the My Language Passport page:
   ○ Help the children complete the page, as necessary.

◉ Distribute the My Activity Records page:
   ○ Elicit examples of work they can record in their portfolio:
   language activities, drawings, review activities, etc.

◉ Distribute the My Favourite Language Learning Strategies page:
   ○ Ask the children, for example, how they prefer to learn new vocabulary.

◉ Distribute the My Intercultural Experiences page:
   ○ Explain, and elicit examples from the children.
   ○ You will be referring to this page from time to time.
   ○ You will be encouraging the children to bring these experiences into the classroom.

Do more

The children personalise their portfolios,
and show each other.

Review

Conduct the review activities opposite.

Wilbur's toolkit in the book
starts on page 97.

For Wilbur's toolkit on the website, go to:
www.deltapublishing.co.uk/resources
 Click on the cover of the book.
Click on Wilbur's toolkit.

The English Language Portfolio was
introduced in Part A (see pages 17 and 25).
There is also a Teacher Development activity
in Part C on page 118 which encourages you
to reflect on how to help the children choose
samples of work to include.

Review activities

My English Language Portfolio

Divide the children into groups of three or four, to discuss the following questions:

 What did you do?

 What did you learn?

 How did you learn?

They discuss each question in turn.

 How well did you do?

Explain to the children how they can complete their very first My Activity Record page:

○ They colour the face which shows how well they did this activity.
○ They complete the sentence, by choosing the phrase from the signpost which is the most important for them.

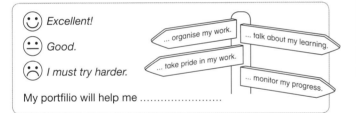

☺ *Excellent!*

😐 *Good.*

☹ *I must try harder.*

My portfilio will help me ....

... organise my work.

... talk about my learning.

... take pride in my work.

... monitor my progress.

Bring the children together for a class discussion.

 What do you need to do next?

Refer back to the success criteria, and ask the children:

'What do you need to revise?'

The children fill in their My Activity Record page.

They add the My Activity Record to their portfolio.

 Share

The children show their portfolio to their family, who write their comments on the My Activity Record page.

Make sure you always read their family's comments in the next lesson.

Using the portfolio

The English Language Portfolio is an integral part of the methodology of *Teaching children how to learn*. As Carmen Becker reports from a study by the Ministry of Education of Lower Saxony, Germany: *'Sufficient time and space for portfolio work can only be created by real tasks linked directly to the portfolio arising from concrete lessons.'*

The portfolio in *Teaching children how to learn* is therefore directly related to each lesson, and the Activity Record pages are linked to each individual activity.

What and how?

The My Activity Record pages are designed to be taken home, to support and encourage home–school connections and involve families in the portfolio process. They:
○ are first completed in class;
○ include a 'Share' activity for the children to complete with their families at home;
○ invite the families to make comments for you to read.

The children then organise the completed activity records along with other samples of their work in their portfolio.

Children are usually very happy to share their work and progress, but do respect their confidentiality as portfolios are *personal*. This will strengthen their feelings of ownership and responsibility for the portfolio. If you or other classmates want to see the portfolio, always ask for permission:
○ You may want to organise a regular 'portfolio time' to discuss and share the portfolios.
○ You may also use the portfolio at parent meetings as evidence of their child's effort and learning.

Where?

You will need to decide where the children should keep their portfolios:
○ You may allocate a shelf in your classroom so the children can access them when they wish, adding other samples of work or personally related items such as postcards, labels in English, stamps, etc.
○ This avoids carrying the portfolios home after each lesson, and ensures that the portfolios are not forgotten at home. Decide with the children how often they would like to take their portfolios home: once a week, a month, a term?
○ If you are unable to find a safe place at school, the children may need to take their portfolios home after each lesson.

Of course, if it is possible for the children to keep on-line portfolios, they'll be able to access them anywhere, anytime!

Becker, C 'Assessment and Portfolios' in *Teaching English to Young Learners: Critical Issues in Language Teaching with 3–12 Year Olds* Janice Bland (Ed) Bloomsbury Academic 2015

Wilbur the Worm: the facts

Asking and answering questions

Age/level
5+ years; A1/A2
(adapt according to age and level)

Activity type
Read/listen for information

Response type
Spoken, written, analytical, personal

Learning aims
To learn worm-related vocabulary
To ask and write questions
To make statements:
worms + verb + object, eg:
Worms have got five hearts.

Learning strategies
Using a KWL grid (see page 29 in Part A
and page 41 opposite)
Activating prior knowledge
Setting a clear focus for reading/listening
Reading/listening for specific information
Recording information

Main outcome
Using a KWL grid

Curricular/cultural links
Science

Values
Caring: respect for small creatures, and
awareness of the purpose of earthworms
for the environment

Assumptions
Children will know some facts about
worms, and will be curious to find out
more information.

Materials
Prepare a picture of an earthworm;
The Worm Facts text on page 44 and
KWL worksheet in Wilbur's toolkit

Transfer
The children can apply the KWL grid
strategy to other content-based lessons.

I recommend …
Diary of a Worm
Inch by Inch

Plan

Explain the learning aims of the activity:
'We're going to learn how to use a KWL grid, ask and write questions on the topic of worms, and make statements.'

Give or identify the following success criteria:
○ *Think what you know about worms.*
○ *Ask yourself what other information you would like to know about worms.*
○ *Review your questions, and read the text/or listen to your teacher to find the information.*

Draw an 'Earthworm' KWL grid on the board, and give the children the KWL worksheet.
Show a picture of an earthworm, and ask: What do you know about earthworms?

K	W	L
What do I **KNOW**?	What do I **WANT** to know?	What have I **LEARNT**?

Give a few minutes for the children to think and discuss with a partner. Use visual support and prompt as necessary: *Where do earthworms live? What colour are they?*

Record what they know in Column 1, and the children copy onto their worksheet.
Worms live in the earth/soil. They live in burrows.Worms are usually brown.
Worms wiggle. Worms eat soil and leaves.

Ask the children what else they would like to know about worms. For example:
○ *Can worms see?*   ○ *Do they have teeth?*   ○ *How do they breathe?*
○ *Do they have brains?*   ○ *How long do they live?*   ○ *Who are worms' enemies?*

The children write the questions in Column 2 of their worksheet.

Do

● Tell the children to look again at the questions in Column 2 and to review them, in order to focus their reading/listening.

● Give the children a copy of the Worm Facts reading text in Wilbur's toolkit on the website, or an adapted version:
   ○ They work individually or in pairs.
   ○ You can also read the text aloud (see page 44), to make it a listening activity.

● The children find the information to their questions: you monitor and help as needed.

● Ask the questions in Column 2 and elicit the information:
   ○ The children write the information in Column 3 of their worksheet.

● The children add the KWL worksheet to their portfolios, along with the Worm Facts.

Do more

Make a 'Wiggly Worm Facts' class poster for the children to illustrate:
○ Each child adds a statement to the poster, following the pattern:
   Worms … (eat soil and leaves).

Review

Conduct the review activities opposite.

Review activities

Wilbur the Worm: the facts

 What did you do?

Talk partners.

In pairs, the children discuss and share what they did in this activity with their partner.

Bring the class together and ask each pair to share one thing they did, listening carefully to ensure they do not repeat each other.

 What did you learn?

Talk partners.

Partner A says: *Tell me three things you have learnt about worms.*

Partner B says: *Tell me three things you learnt about the KWL grid.*

Discuss the children's responses, as above.

 How did you learn?

Talk partners.

Partner A says: *Tell me how you learnt about worms.*

Partner B says: *Tell me how you learnt about the KWL grid.*

Discuss the children's responses, as above.

A KWL grid

This was presented in Part A on page 29 in the 'Applying the pedagogical principles' section as a particularly useful learning strategy.

It is a valuable technique that:

○ activates the children's prior knowledge;

○ encourages personal involvement with a topic;

○ confirms the information they already know;

○ focuses their attention on what they want to find out.

 How well did you do?

Give the children the relevant My Activity Record page from Wilbur's toolkit on the website, and ask them to complete the *What have I learnt?* section.

Ask them to draw Wilbur on the ladder, as their assessment of how well they did this activity.

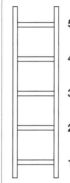

5 = *I can use a KWL grid by myself with this topic and will use it again with another topic.*

4 = *I can use a KWL grid by myself with this topic very well.*

3 = *I can use a KWL grid by myself with this topic quite well.*

2 = *I can use a KWL grid with the help of my teacher.*

1 = *I am still learning to use a KWL grid.*

Lead a discussion.

 What do you need to do next?

Refer back to the success criteria and ask the children:

'What do you need to revise?'

The children fill in their My Activity Record page.

 Share

The children show their family the KWL grid they did in class.

Give the children a copy of the KWL worksheet to use with their family, to find out how much they know about earthworms – in English or in their home language.

They keep both KWL grids together in their portfolio.

The family add their comments on the My Activity Record page:

○ The children bring the Activity Record page to the next lesson.

○ You read the family's comments.

The children add the completed activity record to their portfolio.

Wilbur the Worm: the puppet

Following instructions

Age/level
5–11 years; A1

Activity type
Listen and do

Response type
Physical, creative

Learning aims
To follow instructions
To learn key vocabulary:
sock, felt-tip pen, segment, hand, fingers, thumb, mouth, eyes
To learn a chant

Learning strategies
Listening for specific information
Concentrating and paying attention
Observing

Main outcome
Making a sock puppet

Curricular/cultural links
Art and design; Science; Music; Drama

Values
Accountability and caring: building a class learning community through a shared mascot

Assumptions
Younger children may need more time to manipulate the sock, and will need the support of the teacher.

Materials
Ready-made Wilbur puppet;
An old light brown sock for each child;
Felt-tip pens
The 'cartoon strip' worksheet – see Wilbur's toolkit on page 100 and on the website.

Transfer
The children can use their Wilbur the Worm puppet with any activity related to reviewing, reminding their classmates of learning tips, etc.

I recommend ...
Why Is The Sky Blue?

Plan

Explain the learning aims of the activity:
'We're going to learn to listen and follow instructions.'

Give or identify the following success criteria:
○ *Listen carefully to your teacher.*
○ *Watch your teacher carefully.*

Show the children your ready-made Wilbur puppet. Slip your hand into the sock.

Vary your voice, and say:
Good morning, children.
My name is Wilbur.
I'm an earthworm.

Encourage them to greet Wilbur.

Say: 'You are going to make a puppet, just like me.'
○ You ask the children to take out their sock.

Review the *Wiggly Worm facts* activity:
○ You ask, for example: *Do worms have eyes?*

No, worms don't have eyes. But I do!

Do

○ Ask the children to listen and watch your instructions, while demonstrating with your own puppet:
○ *Put your sock on the table.*
○ *Draw the segments around the body and the eyes at the end of the sock.*
○ *Put your hand in the sock, push the end of the sock between your fingers and thumb to make the mouth.*
○ *Now, your Wilbur the Worm puppet is ready!*

○ Introduce the chant opposite.

○ Get the children to repeat, using their puppet.

Hello! I'm Wilbur.
Wilbur the Worm!
I'm long and thin,
I've got brown skin.
I'm Wilbur the Worm,
To help you learn!

Do more

The children can create more verses for the chant.

Review

Conduct the review activities opposite.

Review activities

Wilbur the Worm: the puppet

 What did you do?

Give the children the cartoon strip worksheet:

○ They *draw* four things they did, to make Wilbur the Worm.

○ Older children can *write* the instructions in each frame.

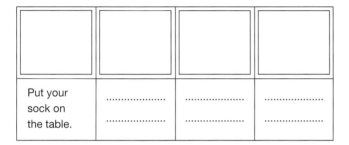

Put your sock on the table.	....	....	....

When they have completed their cartoon strip, ask the children to act it out to a partner.

They add their cartoon strip to their portfolio.

 What did you learn?

In pairs, the children identify three new things they learnt in this activity, and share them with the class using their puppet (they can vary their voice – to be Wilbur).

Encourage discussion and reflection.

 How did you learn?

In pairs, the children ask each other how they did the activity, while you monitor. For example:

○ *How did you do Wilbur's mouth?*

 How well did you do?

Give the children the relevant My Activity Record page from Wilbur's toolkit on the website, and ask them to complete the *What have I learnt?* section.

They complete the missing words from the chant with the words from the wormsearch – alone, or with a classmate.

They then colour a Wilbur speech bubble, to assess how well they did this activity.

I worked very well!

I worked quite well.

I must work harder.

Lead a discussion.

 What do you need to do next?

Refer back to the success criteria and ask the children:

'What do you need to revise?'

The children fill in their My Activity Record page.

 Share

The children show their families their Wilbur puppet, and teach them the chant.

The family add their comments on the My Activity Record page:
○ The children bring the Activity Record page to the next lesson.
○ You read the family's comments.

The children add the completed activity record to their portfolio.

Worm Facts

Worm bodies

A worm is an animal. The earthworm is one of the most common worms:

- It has a long, thin, soft body and moist brown skin.
- It can be 30 centimetres long. It does not have any bones in its body, and does not have any legs.
- Its body has many sections, called segments.
- The segments have tiny hairs, called bristles, that help the worm to grip the ground.
- The pointed end of the earthworm is the head.
- It has five hearts.
- It does not have any teeth, eyes, ears or a nose, but does have a very simple brain and can sense objects, light and vibrations.
- Its mouth is on the underside of the first few segments, and it breathes through its skin.

Worm wiggles

Earthworms wiggle through soil:

- First, the worm stretches the front half of its body forwards. This makes its body long and thin.
- Then the earthworm pulls its tail end forwards, so that its body is shorter and fatter.

Worm homes

Earthworms live in burrows in damp soil. Some burrows can be more than a metre deep.

Worm meals

Earthworms eat soil and dead leaves.

Worm usefulness

Earthworms are very useful:

- They pull pieces of leaves, grass and other living things into the soil and mix up the soil as they make their burrow. This makes the soil richer.
- Their burrows help aerate the soil and let water drain away.
- The things that go through their bodies also go back into the soil.
- Earthworms are important decomposers, and recycle soil.
- They eat garden waste in compost heaps.

Worm life cycles

Earthworms usually lay about 20 eggs at a time. These are contained inside a protective case, called a cocoon.

After about three weeks, the eggs hatch and baby worms wiggle out of the cocoon and burrow their way into the soil.

They become juvenile earthworms, and it takes about six weeks to become an adult worm.

Many earthworms live four to eight years.

Worm enemies

Worms are the favourite food of birds and small animals such as moles, shrews and hedgehogs.

Worm types

There are many different types of worms of different colours, sizes and shapes:

- Some worms are very small, and live inside other animals.
- Some worms can grow up to 40 metres long!

Websites

http://kids.nationalgeographic.com/kids/animals/creaturefeature/earthworms/

http://kids.discovery.com/tell-me/animals/bug-world/worm-world/the-earthworm

http://www.kidcyber.com.au/topics/worms.htm

http://www.bbc.co.uk/gardening/gardening_with_children/didyouknow_worms.shtml

http://www.spottygreenfrog.co.uk/10-interesting-facts-about-worms/a-46

http://urbanext.illinois.edu/worms/

Books

The Life Cycle of an Earthworm
Bobbie Kalman
Crabtree Publishing Company, 2004

Wiggling Worms at Work
Wendy Pfeffer. Illustrated by Steve Jenkins
HarperCollins, 2004

Worms
Sally Morgan
Chrysalis Children's Books, 2001

Chapter Two
Listen and respond

Chapter Two includes activities which focus on verbal input as the main mode of input:

- This input refers to any form of spoken English, such as directly from the teacher or via audio cassette, DVD, etc.

What's Fred wearing?	Doing a picture dictation
Pat-a-cake!	Saying a traditional rhyme
Everyone is different	Playing *Simon says …*
H is for Halloween	Writing a festival poem
How do you come to school?	Doing a class survey
A friend is someone who …	Making a friendship tree
A listening experiment	Identifying sounds
Sounds in a town	Identifying word stress
It's snowing!	Making a snowflake
Leisure time	Identifying collocations
At the Safari Park	Comparing descriptions
My two hands	Making a class poster
Earthworm – a poem	Listening and repeating
A royal feast	Discriminating phonemes
Our language learning rights	Creating a class convention

Chapter Three
Read and respond

Chapter Three includes activities which focus on non-verbal input as the main mode of input:

- This input refers to any form of unspoken English in the written form, as well as images, objects, movement and paralinguistic features.

English around me	Making a vocabulary diary
My school day	Reading and writing about routines
Fireworks safety	Writing instructions
Reading faces	Recognising facial expressions
Don't be a bully!	Making an anti-bullying poster
The water cycle	Reading and matching
How green am I?	Doing a quiz
The important thing about …	Reading and defining
Learning English feels like …	Writing a senses poem
My ideal English teacher	Writing a recipe

What's Fred wearing?

Doing a picture dictation

Age/level
7–9 years; A1

Activity type
Listen, draw and colour

Response type
Creative

Learning aims
To revise/learn adjectives for size and colour:
wide, long, baggy, big, black, brown, orange, blue
To revise/learn nouns for clothes:
cap, trousers, shirt, tie, shoes

Learning strategies
Listening for specific information
Concentrating and paying attention
Memorising

Main outcome
Completing a picture dictation
(see page 152)

Curricular/cultural links
Design and technology

Values
Tolerance: respect for different dress styles

Assumptions
Some of the vocabulary will already be known.

Materials
Picture dictation activity worksheet (see Wilbur's toolkit on page 100 and on the website)

Transfer
Picture dictation can be used to practise prepositions of place:
There's a pen on the table.

I recommend ...
Froggy Gets Dressed;
Meg and Mog;
The Little Old Lady Who
Was Not Afraid of Anything

Plan

Explain the learning aims of the activity:
'We're going to learn adjectives for colours and size and nouns for clothes, and how to listen carefully.'

Give or identify the following success criteria:
○ *Listen carefully to the adjectives for colours and size.*
○ *Listen carefully to the nouns for clothes.*
○ *Draw the descriptions correctly.*
○ *Ask your teacher to repeat if necessary.*

Introduce or revise vocabulary for clothes and adjectives, by referring to children in the class:
'Stand up if you are wearing a blue shirt / a red jumper / blue trousers / brown shoes …'

Do

○ Distribute the worksheet of Fred.

○ Dictate the descriptions:
　Fred's wearing a black cap.
　Fred's wearing a brown shirt.
　Fred's wearing a wide orange tie.
　Fred's wearing long baggy blue trousers.
　Fred's wearing big black shoes.

○ Repeat the descriptions at least twice, depending on the children's needs.

○ Give the children time to listen and show their understanding by drawing the clothes:
　○ They don't *colour* the clothes yet.

○ Dictate the descriptions again:
　○ The children check and colour the clothes.

○ The children show each other their picture dictations and compare:
　○ You check by asking: 'What's Fred wearing?'

○ Elicit the responses, and write them on the board:
　○ The children copy the sentences and label their pictures.

○ They put their picture dictation in their portfolio.

Do more

Write the following words on the board, for the children to make sentences by putting them in the correct order:

baggy	is	T-shirt	a
trainers	Fred	shorts	yellow
black	wearing	and	green

Review

Conduct the review activities opposite.

Wilbur's toolkit in the book starts on page 97.

For Wilbur's toolkit on the website, go to:
www.deltapublishing.co.uk/resources
Click on the cover of the book.
Click on Wilbur's toolkit.

Review activities

What's Fred wearing?

What did you do?

Copy the following sentences onto the board – without the numbers. The children sequence the sentences in the order they did the activity.

○ I drew Fred's clothes. (2)

○ I labelled my picture of Fred. (5)

○ I coloured Fred's clothes. (3)

○ I listened to my teacher describe what Fred is wearing. (1)

○ I organised my picture dictation in my portfolio. (6)

○ I revised nouns for clothes, and adjectives for colours and size. (4)

What did you learn?

Elicit which words the children learnt or revised in the following categories, and write them on the board:

'What nouns for clothes did you learn?'
○ *cap, shirt, tie, trousers*

'What adjectives for colour did you learn?'
○ *black, brown, orange, blue*

'What adjectives for size did you learn?'
○ *long, wide, baggy, big*

Ask the following questions:

'Where do adjectives go in English?'
○ *after the noun*
○ *before the noun*

'Where do adjectives of size go in English?'
○ *before the adjective of colour*
○ *after the adjective of colour*

'What about in your language?
Is it the same as in English, or different?'

How did you learn?

Ask the children to reflect on the strategies they used, to learn the nouns and adjectives. For example:

○ *I listened to the teacher.*

○ *I repeated the words.*

○ *I stood up if I was wearing the clothes the teacher described.*

○ *I listened and drew the clothes on Fred, to check I understood.*

How well did you do?

Give the children the relevant My Activity Record page from Wilbur's toolkit on the website, and ask them to complete the *What have I learnt?* section.

Ask them to colour the number of caps, as their assessment of how well they did this activity.

3 caps = *Excellent! I understood all the nouns and adjectives, and drew them correctly.*

2 caps = *Good. I understood most of the nouns and adjectives, and drew them correctly.*

1 cap = OK. *I need to revise.*

Lead a discussion.

What do you need to do next?

Refer back to the success criteria and ask:

'What do you need to revise?'

The children fill in their My Activity Record page.

Share

The children do a picture dictation with their family.

Give them the *What's Fred wearing?* picture dictation worksheet. They do the dictation at home with their family, or they can do another one of their own choice.

The family add their comments on the My Activity Record page:
○ The children bring the Activity Record page to the next lesson.
○ You read the family's comments.

The children add the completed activity record to their portfolio.

Pat-a-cake!

Saying a traditional rhyme

Age/level
5–8 years; A1

Activity type
Listen and repeat, listen and discriminate, listen and do

Response type
Spoken, physical

Learning aims
To learn vocabulary specific to the rhyme:
Nouns: *cake, man, oven, baker*
Verbs: *bake, pat, prick, put*
To distinguish between two different phonemes for the letter 'a':
/æ/ *pat, man, can;* /ei/ *cake, baker, bake*

Learning strategies
Discriminating between sounds
Listening for enjoyment
Listening intensively and repeating
Memorising and concentrating
Actions to reinforce meaning and memory

Main outcome
Reciting an action rhyme

Curricular/cultural links
Music and drama

Values
Tolerance: awareness of traditional rhymes from different cultures

Assumptions
Some of the vocabulary may be familiar.

Materials
Prepare flashcards for the nouns:
cake, man, baker (with a chef's hat), *oven, Tommy;*
A 'talking stick' (see opposite on page 49);
Pat-a-cake! worksheet (see Wilbur's toolkit)

Transfer
The children can use actions in other contexts, to reinforce meaning/memory.

I recommend …
My Book of Playtime Rhymes; Tasty Poems

Plan

Explain the learning aims of the activity:
'We are going to learn to discriminate between /æ/ and /ei/ sounds.'

Give or identify the following success criteria:
○ *Listen carefully to the teacher.*
○ *Observe your teacher carefully.*
○ *Use actions to help you understand and remember.*
○ *Repeat over and over again.*

Show your flashcards, elicit the nouns and drill them: *Tommy, baker, bake, cake, oven, man.*

Do

○ Tell the children to listen carefully and look at you while you say the rhyme – along with the actions, as explained by Wilbur:

> **Pat-a-cake, pat-a-cake, baker's man,**
> **Bake me a cake as fast as you can.**
> **Pat it and prick it and mark it with T,**
> **And put in the oven for Tommy and me.**

○ Elicit the action words in the rhyme – *pat, bake, prick, put.*

○ Repeat the rhyme: the children put up their hands every time they hear one of the words.

○ Play *Simon says …*:
Simon says … Pat the cake.
Simon says … Prick the cake …

Actions
Clap to the rhythm for the first two lines.
One hand pats the palm of the other hand.
Use the index finger of one hand to prick the palm of the other hand.
The index finger draws a T on the palm of the other hand.
The baker puts the cake in the oven.

○ Perform the action rhyme: the children listen and repeat each line with the actions.

○ Say the rhyme, replacing *Tommy* with other children's names.

○ Focus the children's attention on the different phonemes for the letter 'a' and encourage them to repeat: *cake, baker, bake* – elicit /ei/; *pat, man, can* – elicit /æ/.

○ Divide the classroom into two different 'phoneme corners':
The /ei/ corner on the left, represented by the picture of the baker.
The /æ/ corner on the right, represented by the picture of the man.

○ Read out the words: the children point to the corresponding corner.

○ Give the children a copy of the rhyme and the actions (see Wilbur's toolkit) to add to their portfolio.

Do more

Repeat other words the children may have encountered in previous lessons:
black, cat, panda, hat, jacket, family, lamp … ; *make, name, say, day, May, table …*

Review

Conduct the review activities opposite.

Review activities

Pat-a-cake!

 ### What did you do?

Ask the children to sit in a circle on the floor. Give one child the 'talking stick' and ask him/her to say one thing they did. The others listen carefully. The child then passes the talking stick to another child, who must say something different.

Try to cover the following:

○ *I repeated an action rhyme.*

○ *I performed actions to the verbs.*

○ *I discriminated between words with the sounds /æ/ and /ei/.*

○ *I clapped to the rhythm.*

 ### What did you learn?

Give one child the 'talking stick' and ask him/her to say one thing they learnt, while the others listen carefully. The child then passes the talking stick to another child who must say something different. This should prompt the children to say:

○ *I learnt an English rhyme.*

○ *I learnt the actions to the rhyme.*

○ *I learnt that the letter 'a' has different sounds: /æ/ and /ei/.*

○ *I learnt which words have these different 'a' sounds:* bake, cake, baker; man, cat, pat.

○ *I learnt to listen carefully to English words in order to pronounce them correctly.*

 ### How did you learn?

Elicit the following from the children:

○ *I listened carefully to the teacher.*

○ *I concentrated and observed the teacher.*

○ *I repeated after the teacher.*

○ *I used actions to help me remember.*

 ### How well did you do?

Give the children the relevant My Activity Record page from Wilbur's toolkit on the website, and ask them to complete the *What have I learnt?* **section.**

Ask them to colour the cakes, to assess how well they did this activity.

> Three cakes = *Very good!*
> Two cakes = *Good.*
> One cake = *I must practise more.*
> ○ *I can say a traditional English rhyme.*
> ○ *I can discriminate between /æ/ and /ei/.*
> ○ *I can perform actions while I say a rhyme.*

Lead a discussion.

 ### What do you need to do next?

Refer back to the success criteria and ask the children:

'What do you need to revise?'

The children fill in their My Activity Record page.

 ### Share

The children teach their family the action rhyme and put on a family recital.

The family add their comments on the My Activity Record page:
○ The children bring the Activity Record page to the next lesson.
○ You read the family's comments.

The children add the completed activity record to their portfolio.

> **Talking stick**
> A 'talking stick' – or other special object – is an effective classroom management tool.
> The child with the object talks. Everyone else listens:
> ○ It helps the children take turns speaking and listening.
> ○ It also helps develop concentration, and the skills of listening to each other.

Everyone is different

Playing *Simon says ...*

Age/level
8+ years; A1/A2

Activity type
Listen and identify, listen and observe

Response type
Spoken, written, physical, personal and creative

Learning aims
To explore similarities and differences, and become aware of diversity:
I have, she has; I am, he is ...
To describe people

Learning strategies
Making a mind map and categorising adjectives
Listening for specific information
Observing

Main outcome
Making an 'Everyone is different' book

Curricular/cultural links
Citizenship; Design and technology

Values
Tolerance: respecting differences and becoming aware of diversity

Assumptions
Some language for physical description and personal information may be known. The children will probably be familiar with the game *Simon says ...* .

Materials
Blank sheets of A4 paper for the 'Everyone is different' book;
Mirror board or reflective paper

Transfer
The children can use mind maps to categorise vocabulary for other themes.

I recommend ...
Hue Boy; Slowly, Slowly, Slowly, Said the Sloth; Something Else; Susan Laughs

Plan

Explain the learning aims of the activity:
'We're going to learn how to describe someone, and explore similarities and differences.'

Give or identify the following success criteria:
○ *Think of adjectives to describe someone.*
○ *Categorise the adjective.*
○ *Listen to the adjectives and nouns, to identify your classmate.*
○ *Listen and observe carefully, to identify similarities and differences.*

Draw a blank mind map on the board, elicit categories and choose the categories you wish to focus on. See an example mind map in Wilbur's toolkit which you can illustrate.

Ask two children to stand up. Ask:
'What colour are her eyes? / What colour is his skin? / What's his hair like? / Is she tall or short?'

Write the words in the mind map in the appropriate category.

Describe a child in your class:
'He's got black hair, he's got brown eyes. He is wearing blue jeans and a green T shirt. Who is it?'

Drill the language – as a whole-class activity, or in pairs or groups.

Do

- Revise parts of the body and actions – to prepare for a variation of *Simon says ...* .

- Tell the children to listen and observe carefully:
   ○ They must name one way in which they and another child are the same or different.

- Play *Simon says ...* , choosing categories appropriate for your class. For example:
   Simon says ... *Everyone with brown eyes, stand up.*
   Simon says ... *Everyone who has freckles, put your right hand on your head.*
   Simon says ... *Everyone who speaks more than one language, jump up and down.*

- The children feed back. For example:
   Pierre and I play football.
   Pierre is left-handed and I am right-handed.

- Give each child a sheet of A4 paper, which they fold in half to make their book, and ask them to write 'Everyone is different' on the cover:
   ○ On the right-hand inside page, they design a mirror (round, oval, square, rectangular). They stick reflective paper on their mirror to look at themselves.
   ○ On the left-hand page, they write descriptions of things about themselves which are the same or different to a classmate, as above.

- They store their books in their portfolios.

Do more

The children exchange books and read the descriptions.

Review

Conduct the review activities opposite.

Review activities

Everyone is different

 ### What did you do?

Play a version of *Simon says ... *.

Say the statements below: the children stand up if they did this in the lesson, and remain seated if not. You can add other statements if you wish.

○ *Simon says* ... you created a mind map.

○ *Simon says* ... you sang a song.

○ *Simon says* ... you described a classmate.

○ *Simon says* ... you played *Simon says ... *.

○ *Simon says* ... you played *Who is it?*

○ *Simon says* ... you wrote a story.

○ *Simon says* ... you identified something the same or different about a classmate.

 ### What did you learn?

Ask the children to say or write down three things they learned in this lesson.

Ask them to share their ideas, and lead a class discussion.

 ### How did you learn?

Ask the children to work in pairs, and to give instructions for another class on how to play the version of *Simon says ...* in this lesson. For example:

○ *Listen carefully to the statements.*

○ *If the statement is true about you, you do the action.*

○ *If it is not true about you, you don't do the action.*

○ *You have to listen and observe your classmates, so you can name one way in which you are the same or different.*

 ### How well did you do?

Give the children the relevant My Activity Record page from Wilbur's toolkit on the website, and ask them to complete the *What have I learnt?* section.

Ask them to draw themselves in the mirror, with the expression that assesses how well they did this activity.

Smiley face = *I did very well!*

Neutral face = *I did OK.*

Sad face = *I must practise more.*

Lead a discussion.

 ### What do you need to do next?

Refer back to the success criteria and ask the children:

'What do you need to revise?'

The children fill in their My Activity Record page.

 ### Share

The children show their *'Everyone is different'* book to their family.

They choose one family member, and write one way in which they are the same and one way in which they are different.

The family add their comments on the My Activity Record page:
○ The children bring the Activity Record page to the next lesson.
○ You read the family's comments.

The children add the completed activity record to their portfolio.

H is for Halloween

Writing a festival poem

Age/level
8+ years; A1/A2

Activity type
Listen and identify, read and complete

Response type
Spoken, creative, analytical

Learning aims
To learn Halloween-related vocabulary:
pumpkin/Jack o'lantern, ghost, cat, haunted house, witch, monster, vampire, midnight, broom, skeletons, rat
To learn to identify alliteration and rhyme

Learning strategies
Listening and repeating
Using rhyme as clues to meaning

Main outcome
Writing a poem

Curricular/cultural links
Music and drama; Citizenship; History

Values
Tolerance: awareness of different festivals around the world

Assumptions
The children will know about Halloween, but will need to revise the vocabulary.

Materials
Prepare flashcards for Halloween vocabulary;
The *H is for Halloween* poem (see the worksheet in Wilbur's toolkit and page 53 opposite)

Transfer
The children can write similar poems about other festivals.

I recommend ...
Funnybones; Meg and Mog; The Little Old Lady Who Was Not Afraid of Anything; Winnie the Witch

Plan

Explain the learning aims of the activity:
'We're going to learn how to write a poem using rhyme and alliteration.'

Give or identify the following success criteria:
○ *Learn or revise vocabulary related to Halloween.*
○ *Identify and use alliteration and rhyme to complete the poem.*
○ *Recite the poem with correct pronunciation.*

Elicit the vocabulary related to Halloween and write it on the board. Ensure you include:
haunted house
cat and *rat*

Focus on the expression **haunted house**:
○ Draw the children's attention to the fact that the two words begin with the same letter.

Tell the children this is called *alliteration*, and it is often used in poems.

Do the same for rhyme, eg:
cat / rat

Do

◉ Copy the poem in Wilbur's toolkit onto the board, or give the children the worksheet and tell them to complete the gaps with the missing words:
  ○ They use alliteration (a straight line in the Activity Worksheet) and rhyme (a dotted line).

◉ Complete the first gap with the whole class as an example of alliteration:
haunted house

◉ Complete the second gap as an example of rhyme:
broom / room

◉ The children complete the remaining gaps in groups:
  ○ You monitor as needed.

◉ Read the poem aloud, and ask the children to repeat line by line.

◉ They recite the poem.

◉ They copy the poem into, or add the worksheet to, their portfolio.

Do more

The children write a poem, using alliteration and rhyme, about a festival in their country.

Review

Conduct the review activities opposite.

Review activities

H is for Halloween

 What did you do?

In groups, the children discuss what they had to do in the activity.

Discuss as a whole class.

 What did you learn?

In groups, the children discuss what they learnt in the activity.

Discuss as a whole class.

 How did you learn?

Ask the children to reflect on the following questions:

○ *How did you learn to write a poem?*

○ *How did you learn to identify and use alliteration?*

○ *How did you learn to identify and use rhyming words?*

H is for Halloween

H is for haunted house,

And witches on a broom.

L is for lanky skeletons,

Laughing in the room.

O is for orange pumpkins,

Wailing in the night.

E is for eerie ghosts,

Evil and pale white.

N is for nasty cats, nodding at midnight.

 How well did you do?

Give the children the relevant My Activity Record page from Wilbur's toolkit on the website, and ask them to complete the *What have I learnt?* **section.**

They select and colour a pumpkin, as their assessment of how well they did this activity.

Smiley pumpkin: *Excellent! = I understood everything.*

Neutral pumpkin: *Good. = I understood most of the activity.*

Sad pumpkin: *OK. = I understood some of the activity.*

Lead a discussion.

 What do you need to do next?

Refer back to the success criteria and ask the children:

'What do you need to revise?'

The children fill in their My Activity Record page.

 **Share**

The children teach their family the poem and put on a family recital.

The family add their comments on the My Activity Record page:

○ The children bring the Activity Record page to the next lesson.

○ You read the family's comments.

The children add the completed activity record to their portfolio.

How do you come to school?

Doing a class survey

Age/level
9–10 years; A1

Activity type
Listen and do, listen and write

Response type
Physical, spoken, written, creative

Learning aims
To learn/revise transport:
car, bus, train, bicycle, foot …
To learn/revise prepositions: *by, on …*
To ask and answer:
How do you come to school every day?
How many …?
To revise numbers 1–20

Learning strategies
Listening for specific information
Using a chart and a bar graph to record, transfer and interpret information/data
Categorising

Main outcome
Completing a bar graph

Curricular/cultural links
Maths; Geography: transport

Values
Caring: awareness of forms of transport and their impact on the environment

Assumptions
Vocabulary for transport may be known. Prepositions may need to be taught. The children may need support in creating their bar graph.

Materials
Skills flashcards – see Wilbur's toolkit;
Bar graph worksheet for each child
(see the toolkit);
Prepare flashcards of transport

Transfer
The children can use bar graphs to record other types of data.

I recommend …
Mr Gumpy's Outing;
Mrs Armitage on Wheels

Plan

Explain the learning aims of the activity:
'We're going to learn how to ask questions and how to record information.'

Give or identify the following success criteria:
○ *Ask your classmates how they come to school.*
○ *Listen carefully to your classmates' responses.*
○ *Ask your classmates to repeat if necessary.*
○ *Record responses correctly on the bar graph.*

Ask the children how they come to school every day. Support their understanding with the flashcards.

Get them to repeat, using the correct preposition, eg:
I come to school by bus / on foot … .

In pairs, the children ask each other:
How do you come to school every day?

Do

○ Draw a chart on the board with five columns:
  ○ You put the means of transport at the top of each column.

By car	By bus	By train	By bicycle	On foot

○ Ask the children to repeat: *by car, by bus,* etc.

○ Going round the class, each child asks a classmate:
  Michel, how do you come to school?

○ The children listen, and write that classmate's name in the correct column.

○ Ensure the children use the complete question.

○ Ask: 'How many children come to school by bus, by car, …?'

○ Count the names on the chart in each column: *'10 children come to school on foot.'*

○ Give out the graph worksheet.

○ Tell the children to count the number of children in each column:
  ○ They transfer the information onto the bar graph.

○ The children draw and colour the bars on the graph – you help them interpret the information, by asking: 'How many children come to school by bus?'

Do more

The children conduct a survey to find out *how long they spend* travelling to school.

Review

Conduct the review activities opposite.

Review activities

How do you come to school?

 ### What did you do?

Display the skills flashcards (see Wilbur's toolkit) on the board or around the classroom. Ask the children what they represent: reading, writing, speaking, listening and counting.

Ask the children:

○ 'What reading did you do?'
  I/we read/interpreted the chart/bar graph.

○ 'What speaking did you do?'
  I/we asked and answered questions about how I/we come to school.

○ 'What listening did you do?'
  I/we listened to the teacher to know what to do, and I/we listened to my/our classmates' responses in order to complete the survey.

○ 'What writing did you do?'
  I/we wrote the names of the children in the correct column on the chart.

○ 'What counting did you do?'
  I/we counted the children who come to school by bus, by train, by car, by bicycle, on foot.

 ### What did you learn?

Ask the children to identify one thing they learnt. For example:

○ *We learnt to listen carefully to our classmates' questions/responses.*
○ *We learnt to use the correct prepositions with the means of transport.*
○ *We learnt to transfer information from a chart to a bar graph.*
○ *We learnt to interpret information on a bar graph.*

 ### How did you learn?

Elicit how the children learnt the following:

○ Means of transport
○ Prepositions
○ To ask questions
○ To understand questions and record information

 ### How well did you do?

Give the children the relevant My Activity Record page from Wilbur's toolkit on the website, and ask them to complete the *What have I learnt?* section.

They colour the bar graph, as their assessment of how well they did this activity.

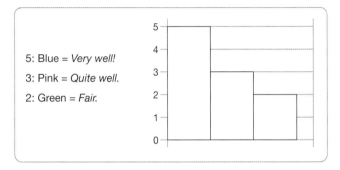

5: Blue = *Very well!*

3: Pink = *Quite well.*

2: Green = *Fair.*

Lead a discussion.

 ### What do you need to do next?

Ask the children:

'What do you need to revise?'

The children fill in their My Activity Record page.

 ### Share

The children conduct a survey at home, to record how the members of their family go to school or work.

They will need a copy of the bar graph worksheet in Wilbur's toolkit.

The family add their comments on the My Activity Record page:
○ The children bring the Activity Record page to the next lesson.
○ You read the family's comments.

The children add the completed activity record to their portfolio.

A friend is someone who …

Making a friendship tree

Age/level
8+ years; A1/A2

Activity type
Listen and write definitions and descriptions

Response type
Spoken, written, personal and creative

Learning aims
To learn/revise verbs for writing definitions of friends, eg:
A friend is someone who shares their toys.

Learning strategies
Activating prior knowledge
Using a concept web to make connections and aid memory
Recording and organising definitions visually

Main outcome
Making a Friendship Tree poster

Curricular/cultural links
Citizenship; Friendship Day; International Day of Families

Values
Caring: understanding and valuing friendship

Assumptions
Some verbs for defining friends may already be known.

Materials
Individual leaf templates for each child (see Wilbur's toolkit); The 'Family' tree worksheet for everyone (see the toolkit); A 'talking stick' or other object (see page 49)

Transfer
The children can use concept webs to develop ideas related to other topics.

I recommend …
Ping and Pong are Best Friends (mostly); Sharing a Shell; The Doorbell Rang; The Rainbow Fish

Plan

Explain the learning aims of the activity:
'We're going to learn how create a concept web.'

Give the success criteria, or involve the children in generating their own:
○ *Think about friends you know.*
○ *Use the pattern: 'A friend is someone who …'.*
○ *Use the 3rd person singular of the simple present tense.*

Draw a blank concept web on the board and write in the centre:
A friend is someone who …

Ask the children to share their ideas about a good friend, eg:
A friend is someone who cares about me.

Fill in the circles on the web with the children's ideas, drawing their attention to the 3rd person singular of the verb like in the examples opposite.

Elicit further definitions:
A friend is someone who …
answers my letters/emails / listens to me /
understands me / likes me / trusts me /
helps me with my homework / makes me happy /
keeps my secrets / wants to be with me /
respects me / asks how I am …

shares their toys, sweets with me.

cares about me.

A friend is someone who …

laughs with me.

talks with me.

plays with me.

Do

● Make a large Friendship Tree poster for your classroom wall (see the tree in Wilbur's toolkit). Distribute a leaf template to each child (see the toolkit):
   ○ They write a definition of a friend along the middle vein of the leaf.

● They stick their leaves on the tree, to record, organise and display their definitions visually. They can add other definitions in following lessons.

● Ask them to decide which definition is the most important for them, and tell them they can do this in groups.

● The children copy the concept web into their portfolio.

● Whenever there is a dispute in class, tell the children to consult the friendship tree!

Do more

Extend the concept of friendship by asking the questions below:
'How do you feel when you are with your friends?'
'Why are friends important?'

Review

Conduct the review activities opposite.

Review activities

A friend is someone who …

 ### What did you do?

Divide your class into groups. Tell each group to think about what they did. Give one group the 'talking stick' and ask them to say one thing they did. The group then gives gives the stick to another group, and that group must say another thing *they* did – without repeating the same thing.
For example:

○ *We made a concept web.*

○ *We talked about what friends do.*

○ *We wrote definitions of friends.*

○ *We made a friendship tree.*

○ *We listened to each other.*

○ *We shared our ideas.*

○ *We decided what the most important thing about a friend is.*

 ### What did you learn?

Write the following statements on the board, and ask the children to decide which was the most important/useful for them and why:

○ We learnt how to make a concept web.

○ We learnt how to write a definition.

○ We learnt about friendship.

○ We learnt to use the 3rd person singular of the present simple.

 ### How did you learn?

Elicit from the children how they did the activities, in order to focus them on the processes. For example:

○ *We thought about friends we know and what they do.*

○ *We told the teacher what our friends do.*

○ *Our teacher wrote the verbs on the concept web.*

○ *We used the 3rd person singular of the present tense.*

○ *We used the pattern 'A friend is someone who …'.*

○ *We wrote our definitions on a leaf.*

○ *We organised our definitions visually on the friendship tree*

 ### How well did you do?

Give the children the relevant My Activity Record page from Wilbur's toolkit on the website, and ask them to complete the *What have I learnt?* section.

Ask them to colour the leaf on the Friendship Tree, as their assessment of how well they did this activity.

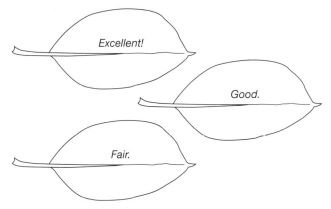

Lead a discussion.

 ### What do you need to do next?

Ask the children:

'What do you need to revise?'

The children fill in their My Activity Record page.

 ### Share

Give the children the 'Family' tree worksheet to take home, to complete a tree with their family (see Wilbur's toolkit).

They can create this in English or their home language: the aim is to use a concept web to make definitions about the family.

The family add their comments on the My Activity Record page:
○ The children bring the Activity Record page to the next lesson.
○ You read the family's comments.

The children add the completed activity record to their portfolio.

A listening experiment

Identifying sounds

Age/level
5+ years; A1

Activity type
Listen and identify

Response type
Physical, analytical

Learning aims
To learn/revise nouns for objects:
see Materials
To learn/revise verbs:
hear, listen
To ask and answer the question:
What is it? / It's a …

Learning strategies
Concentrating and listening carefully
(see 'Children and noise' on page 59
opposite)
Identifying sounds; Memorising

Main outcome
Conducting a listening experiment

Curricular/cultural links
Science: sounds and senses;
International Noise Awareness Day

Values
Resilience: awareness of the need for
quiet in order to listen and concentrate

Assumptions
Vocabulary for the face may be known.
Initially, some children may find it
difficult to identify the different sounds.

Materials
Variety of small objects for the children
to choose from: *a shell, a spoon, a nut,
some dried beans, a rubber, a pencil, a
pebble, a coin, a paper clip, a small tin,
a tangerine, a pencil sharpener, a peg*

Transfer
The children become aware of sounds
they hear in the street, in the shops …

I recommend …
Peace at Last

Plan

Explain the learning aims of the activity:
'We're going to learn how to listen carefully and identify different sounds.'

Give or identify the following success criteria:
○ *Look at the different objects and learn their names.*
○ *Concentrate and listen carefully.*
○ *Remember the sounds that objects make to help you identify them.*

Say: 'Point to your nose, point to your eyes, point to your mouth, point to your ears.'
Ask: 'What do we use our ears for?'

Elicit: *to listen, to hear.* Explain the difference between listening and hearing:
○ Listening requires concentration; hearing does not.

Demonstrate the listening experiment with the whole class:
○ Establish silence, pause and allow the children to 'listen to' the silence.
○ Show them the objects, and ask: *What is it?*
○ Elicit or teach the noun, eg: *It's a shell.*

The children repeat.

Say: 'Listen carefully' – and drop the object on a table so the children hear the sound clearly.

Write or draw the object on the board, then introduce the other objects.

Tell the children to close their eyes – you drop an object and ask: 'What is it?'
○ If they guess correctly, you put a tick next to the word. If not, you put a cross.

Continue with the other objects.

Do

● Divide the class into pairs – A and B – and draw
a chart on the board for the children to copy:
○ The children choose five objects, and draw
or write them on the chart.

Objects	✔	✗

● They now sit facing each other and put a book
between them so Partner B cannot see the objects:
○ Partner A drops each object and asks: *What is it?*
○ Partner B listens and identifies the object: *It's a coin!*
○ If B guesses correctly, A puts a tick next to the word. If not, A puts a cross.

● The children continue with the other objects:
○ They then exchange roles, and B drops the objects for A.

● Ask if there were any sounds that were more difficult to identify than others.

Do more

Make a collage of the sounds the children can hear in the classroom.

Review

Conduct the review activities opposite.

Review activities

A listening experiment

 ### What did you do?

Play a version of *Simon says ...* .

Say the following statements: the children stand up if they did this in the lesson, and remain seated if not. You can add others.

○ *Simon says ... you repeated the names of objects.*

○ *Simon says ... you sang a song.*

○ *Simon says ... you listened to different sounds.*

○ *Simon says ... you listened to a story.*

○ *Simon says ... you did a listening experiment.*

○ *Simon says ... you identified the sounds of different objects.*

 ### What did you learn?

Elicit some of the following:

○ *We learnt the names of objects.*

○ *We learnt how to ask 'What is it?' and say 'It's a ...'.*

○ *We learnt to listen and concentrate in order to identify sounds.*

○ *We learnt to memorise different sounds.*

○ *We learnt the importance of silence / quiet time.*

 ### How did you learn?

Elicit how the children learnt to listen and identify the sounds.

Encourage them to understand that they needed to concentrate 100% during the experiment and listen very carefully.

Children and noise

Children are surrounded by noise every day, which can pose a serious threat to their hearing, health, learning and behaviour – making it difficult to listen and concentrate:

○ Research suggests that 'quiet' promotes a productive learning environment: it is therefore important for children to understand the purpose of 'quiet time'.

○ Being able to listen and concentrate helps them learn how to speak, understand and communicate with others.

This activity will help the children develop this ability, by listening to and identifying specific sounds.

 ### How well did you do?

Give the children the relevant My Activity Record page from Wilbur's toolkit on the website, and ask them to complete the *What have I learnt?* section.

Ask them to colour the ears, to assess how well they did this activity – and say why.

Three ears = *I did very well!*

Two ears = *I did OK.*

One ear = *I must try harder.*

○ *I can say the names of six objects.*

○ *I can ask and answer the question 'What is it?' / 'It's a ...'.*

○ *I can concentrate, in order to listen and identify different sounds.*

Discuss as a whole class.

 ### What do you need to do next?

Refer back to the success criteria and ask the children:

'What do you need to revise?'

The children fill in their My Activity Record page.

 ### Share

The children carry out the experiment at home with their family or friends – in English!

The family add their comments on the My Activity Record page:

○ The children bring the Activity Record page to the next lesson.

○ You read the family's comments.

The children add the completed activity record to their portfolio.

Sounds in a town

Identifying word stress

Age/level
8–10 years; A1/A2

Activity type
Listen and identify

Response type
Analytical and spoken response

Learning aims
To identify stressed syllables, and number of syllables in a word
To learn or revise town-related vocabulary

Learning strategies
Listening for specific information
Concentrating and paying attention
Developing awareness of word stress
Using visual markers (stress dots) to identify word stress

Main outcome
Making a Class Sounds poster

Curricular/cultural links
Geography: the local environment;
Language awareness

Values
Tolerance: awareness that some languages are stress-timed and some are syllable-timed

Assumptions
Some of the vocabulary may already be known.

Materials
Word cards for places in a town;
A blank Class Sounds poster with word-stress columns (see Wilbur's toolkit)

Transfer
This activity can be used with any other lexical set, to develop understanding of word stress.

I recommend …
Bear About Town; Knuffle Bunny; Shark in the Park; Through the Magic Mirror

Plan

Explain the learning aims of the activity:
'We're going to learn about word stress in English.'

Give or identify the following success criteria:
○ *Identify the number of syllables in a word.*
○ *Identify the stressed syllable.*
○ *Use a big dot to mark the stressed syllable, in order to pronounce the word correctly.*
○ *Add words to the Class Sounds poster.*

Elicit vocabulary of places in a town – select them from the table in Wilbur's toolkit, and place them in columns.

Count the syllables with your fingers:
Ask: 'How many syllables are there in *cinema*?'
Answer: *Ci-ne-ma*. Three.

Repeat for the other words.

Draw a big black dot above the stressed syllable, and small dots above the other syllables.

Build up your own table on the board.

Build up a Class Sounds poster (see the toolkit).

Do

● Give out one word card between two or three children in groups.

● The groups listen to the word, hold up the card and answer the following questions:
How many syllables can you hear?
Which syllable is the stressed syllable?
Can you draw a big dot above the stressed syllable?

● Ask the children to put the word card in the correct column on the Class Sounds poster:
○ You then repeat with the other cards.

● The children copy the poster into their portfolios.

Do more

Choose five more words relevant to your town environment:
○ You write them on the board, and say them aloud.
○ The children identify the stressed syllable and add the words to their portfolio.

After every lesson, encourage the children to identify the stressed syllable of new vocabulary:
○ They add these words to the Class Sounds poster.

Review

Conduct the review activities opposite.

Review activities

Sounds in a town

 What did you do?

Copy the statements below on the board or a worksheet. The children choose the odd one out.

○ *I learnt to count syllables in English words.*

○ *I learnt to identify word stress.*

○ *I used the black dots to decorate the word.*

○ *I used the black dots to pronounce the words correctly.*

 What did you learn?

The children choose the correct statement from the pairs of statements:

○ Words in English are pronounced the same way as in my language.
○ Words in English are pronounced differently from my language.

○ One syllable in a word in English is stressed more than the other syllables.
○ All the syllables are stressed the same in English words.

○ The black dots don't help me pronounce the word correctly.
○ The black dots help me see the stressed syllable in a word and pronounce it correctly.

 How did you learn?

Ask the children what they had to do to pronounce the word correctly, and to choose the statements they agree with.

○ *I counted the dots on the words.*
○ *I counted the syllables in the words.*

○ *I listened to the teacher and put the small dot on the stressed syllable.*
○ *I listened to the teacher, identified the stressed syllable, and put the big dot on the stressed syllable.*

 How well did you do?

Give the children the relevant My Activity Record page from Wilbur's toolkit on the website, and ask them to complete the *What have I learnt?* section.

They colour the traffic lights and choose an adjective, to assess how well they did this activity.

They then mark the syllables and word stress on the adjective they chose.

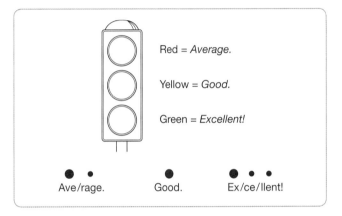

Red = *Average.*

Yellow = *Good.*

Green = *Excellent!*

Ave/rage.   Good.   Ex/ce/llent!

Discuss with the class.

 What do you need to do next?

Refer back to the success criteria and ask the children:

'What do you need to revise?'

The children fill in their My Activity Record page.

 **Share**

The children choose five 'town' words and test their family's pronunciation – and correct their word stress, if necessary.

The family add their comments on the My Activity Record page:
○ The children bring the Activity Record page to the next lesson.
○ You read the family's comments.

The children add the completed activity record to their portfolio.

It's snowing!

Making a snowflake

Age/level
8+ years; A1/A2

Activity type
Listen and make

Response type
Creative, physical, written

Learning aims
To understand how snow is formed
To listen to instructions for making a snowflake
To learn or revise nouns and verbs related to giving instructions

Learning strategies
Following instructions
Observing
Concentrating
Identifying nouns and verbs

Main outcome
Making a snowflake

Curricular/cultural links
Art and design; Natural Science; Christmas

Values
Accountability and caring: respect for the environment

Assumptions
Some children may never have seen snow.

Materials
Instructions for making snowflakes – make sure *you* practise! – and the 'snowflake search' (see Wilbur's toolkit); Sheets of white paper; scissors and pencils; 'Learning strategies' worksheet (see the toolkit)

Transfer
The children will be able to follow instructions in other contexts.

I recommend …
The Snowman;
The Snowy Day

Plan

Explain the learning aims of the activity:
'We're going to learn to listen to instructions for making a snowflake.'

Give or identify the following success criteria:
○ *Listen carefully to your teacher.*
○ *Watch your teacher carefully.*
○ *Follow your teacher's instructions.*

Ask the children to imagine being in the snow, and ask questions according to their experience of snow, eg:
Have you ever seen snow?
What colour is it?
In which countries does it snow?
Do you like snow?
What does snow feel like?

Ask: 'Do you know how snow is formed?'

Tell or remind the children how rain is formed (see *The water cycle* in Wilbur's toolkit):
○ You explain it is the same process, except that snow forms in clouds when the air temperature is below freezing.

> This activity follows on well from *The water cycle* on page 86.

Do

● Distribute the sheets of paper, scissors and pencils.

● Give step-by-step instructions (see Wilbur's toolkit). For example:
Take your paper.   *Watch me carefully.*   *Show me. Good.*
Everyone, show me.   *Fold here.*   *Now fold here …*

● Repeat the instructions several times:
○ You make sure each child has completed the step successfully before moving on.

● Get the children to show each other their finished snowflakes, and praise their efforts.

● Get the children to make another snowflake:
○ They design a more intricate pattern, this time.

● They put their snowflakes in their portfolio:
○ You can also decorate your classroom, hanging snowflakes from the ceiling.

Do more

Copy the 'How snow is formed' text at the bottom of the page opposite onto the board, leaving out the words in brackets:
○ Write the missing words in jumbled order on the board.
○ In groups, the children discuss. You check, and complete as a whole-class activity.

The children copy the text into their portfolios.

Review

Conduct the review activities opposite.

Review activities

It's snowing!

 ### What did you do?

Think-pair-share.

The children think individually about the activity. Then they discuss with a partner, then they share with the whole class.

 ### What did you learn?

Give the children the 'snowflake search' and tell them to find the word 'snowflake', and six verbs and three more nouns for instructions for making a snowflake:

make	*cut*	*paper*
open	*fold*	*scissors*
draw	*turn over*	*pencil*

Bring the class together, and check.

The children add the snowflake search to their portfolio.

 ### How did you learn?

Give out the 'Learning strategies' worksheet, or copy it onto the board:

Ask the children which strategies they used, and talk them through the strategies they did or didn't use.

How snow is formed

Snow (forms) in (clouds) when the air temperature is below (freezing). Snowflakes are (made up) of crystals of (ice). Each snowflake has (six) sides and may contain up to 200 ice (crystals).

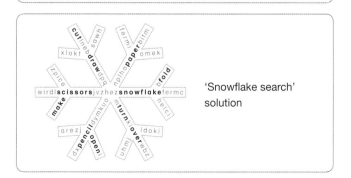

'Snowflake search' solution

 ### How well did you do?

Give the children the relevant My Activity Record page from Wilbur's toolkit on the website, and ask them to complete the *What have I learnt?* section.

Ask them to assess how well they did this activity, by selecting the number of snowflakes which best represent their performance and understanding.

Three snowflakes =	*I followed the instructions and made a beautiful snowflake. I understand how snow is formed.*
Two snowflakes =	*I followed the instructions quite well and made a snowflake. I understand a little about how snow is formed.*
One snowflake =	*I must practise listening to instructions more. I don't understand yet how snow is formed.*

Lead a discussion.

 ### What do you need to do next?

Refer back to the success criteria and ask the children:

'What do you need to revise?'

The children fill in their My Activity Record page.

 ### Share

The children show their family how to make a snowflake, by giving them instructions in English.

They demonstrate and repeat each step and use gesture, to support understanding.

The family add their comments on the My Activity Record page:
○ The children bring the Activity Record page to the next lesson.
○ You read the family's comments.

The children add the completed activity record to their portfolio.

Leisure time

Identifying collocations

Age/level
9+ years; A1/A2

Activity type
Listen and match, listen and do, watch and guess

Response type
Physical, spoken, written

Learning aims
To collate the verbs *play* and *go* with the correct noun:
play + games (*football, tennis, hopscotch, computer games, chess*)
go + activities (*rowing, dancing, swimming, mountain climbing*)
To identify other collocations (*read a book, watch TV, ride a bike, do archery*)

Learning strategies
Categorising
Developing grammatical awareness
Developing knowledge of metalanguage

Main outcome
Making a bookmark

Curricular/cultural links
Science: healthy living

Values
Accountability: awareness of the importance of sport and pastimes for a balanced and healthy life style

Assumptions
The children may know some of the vocabulary.

Materials
Prepare flashcards or pictures of sports and leisure activities, and word cards: *go*, *play*;
Bookmark templates (Wilbur's toolkit)

Transfer
The children can identify collocations in future lessons.

I recommend ...
Funnybones; You Choose

Plan

Explain the learning aims of the activity:
'*We're going to learn how to collocate verbs and nouns to talk about leisure activities.*'

Give or identify the following success criteria:
○ *Put verbs and nouns together correctly, to talk about leisure activities.*
○ *Use 'play' with games and 'go' with activities.*
○ *Identify other collocations with 'play' and 'go'.*

Display the word cards *play* and *go* around the classroom.

Elicit the nouns for games – *football, tennis,* etc – by holding up flashcards.

Place the flashcards underneath the verb 'play', eg: *play football, play tennis*.

Repeat the procedure with nouns for activities with go, and then for other pastimes.

Ask: 'Why have I placed these games and activities under 'play' or 'go'?'

Elicit and explain:
'The words go together. This is called collocation.'

Tell the children:
'We always *play* games; we use *go* with activities.'
'Some other activities have their own collocations, eg: *watch TV.*'

Ask: 'What do you do in your leisure time?'

As they say the activities on the flashcards, they place them under the correct word card.

Do

○ Divide the class into two groups:
  ○ The children stand in two rows facing each other, with enough space in between to mime an activity.
○ Tell them:
  'Mime an activity, and your team has to guess and use the correct collocation.'
○ Each team gets a point for the correct answer:
  ○ If any new collocations come up in the miming activity, add them to the list.
○ Distribute the bookmark templates.
○ Revise days of the week with the children:
  ○ They write and illustrate their leisure activities for each day, using the collocations, eg: *On Monday, I play tennis.*
○ The children add the bookmark to their portfolio – or use it as a bookmark!

Do more

Create a set of word cards and activity cards in order to play pelmanism (the 'memory game').

Review

Conduct the review activities opposite.

Review activities

Leisure time

 ### What did you do?

Ask the children to say what they did in this activity. For example:

○ *We talked about our leisure activities.*

○ *We matched the game and activity to the correct verb.*

○ *We mimed the activity for our classmates.*

○ *We wrote/drew the collocations on our bookmark.*

○ *We played pelmanism.*

 ### What did you learn?

Ask the children what they learnt with each particular activity. For example:

○ *We talked about our leisure activities.*
We learnt the words for sports, games and activities.

○ *We matched the activity to the correct verb.*
We learnt collocations: that games go with 'play', activities go with 'go', and other words have their own collocations.

○ *We mimed the activity for our classmates.*
We learnt to watch our classmates carefully and guess their actions.

○ *We wrote/drew the collocations.*
We learnt to record new vocabulary.

○ *We played pelmanism.*
We made word/picture pairs to remember collocations.

 ### How did you learn?

Remind the children of the different activities or resources they used:

How did they help them learn?

○ Flashcards/pictures – helped remember or learn new vocabulary and collocations.

○ Mime – helped learn the leisure activities and the collocations.

○ Bookmark – illustrations helped remember activities and collocations.

○ Pelmanism – helped revise the leisure activities and collocations.

 ### How well did you do?

Give the children the relevant My Activity Record page from Wilbur's toolkit on the website, and ask them to complete the *What have I learnt?* section.

They colour the archery target, following the descriptions, to assess how well they did this activity – by writing number 1, 2 or 3 in the matching circle.

Colour:

Inner circle	Yellow
Second circle	Red
Third circle	Blue

Write:

Inner circle	1 = *Excellent! I can use 'play' and 'go' with the correct nouns.*
Second circle	2 = *Good. I can use 'play' and 'go' with the correct nouns most of the time.*
Third circle	3 = *OK. I must practise more.*

Lead a discussion.

 ### What do you need to do next?

Refer back to the success criteria and ask the children:

'What do you need to revise?'

The children fill in their My Activity Record page.

 ### Share

The children show their family their bookmark, and can play the mime activity or pelmanism at home with them.

The family add their comments on the My Activity Record page:
○ The children bring the Activity Record page to the next lesson.
○ You read the family's comments.

The children add the completed activity record to their portfolio.

At the Safari Park

Using prepositions of place

Age/level:
8+ years; A1/A2

Activity type
Read and draw, read and describe, listen and draw

Response type
Spoken, creative

Learning aims
To revise/introduce:
prepositions of place
animals: *monkey, giraffe, elephant, lion, crocodile, flamingo, hippo*
safari park related vocabulary: *safari, waterhole, tree, rock*

Learning strategies
Reading and listening for specific information
Concentrating; Following instructions

Main outcome
Make a Safari Park map

Curricular/cultural links
Geography and the environment

Values
Caring: wildlife conservation and respect for animals in captivity

Assumptions
The children may already know some vocabulary for African animals

Materials
Safari Park map (see Wilbur's toolkit) for each child;
Description cards for each pair of pupils (see the toolkit);
Prepare flashcards of African animals

Transfer
Dictations can be used to teach or practise other vocabulary areas.

I recommend ...
Brown Bear, Brown Bear, What Do You See?;
The Kangaroo from Woolloomooloo; We All Went on Safari; We're Going on a Lion Hunt

Plan

Explain the learning aims of the activity:
'We're going to learn to use prepositions to describe where animals are in a safari park.'

Give or identify the following success criteria:
○ *Give and follow instructions.*
○ *Listen carefully to your partner.*
○ *Describe the picture, using the correct preposition.*
○ *Draw the animals on the map, according to the preposition you hear.*

Elicit or teach vocabulary for African animals, using flashcards.
○ Write the names of the animals on the board.

Practise the prepositions, using classroom objects (eg: the pencil is *on* the table, the pencil is *under* the table) and Total Physical Response (see page 153 in Part C for more information on TPR).

Do

○ Hand out the Safari Park map, and ask the children to copy the names of the animals on the dotted lines.

○ Divide class into pairs, A and B:
  ○ Give out the A and B description cards in Wilbur's toolkit.
  ○ Tell the children not to show them to their partner.

○ Each pupil reads their description card and draws the animals on their map.

○ Say:
  'You are now going to take turns to read your description card to your partner so he/she can complete their map.'

○ Pupil A begins by reading the first sentence, and Pupil B listens and draws the animal:
  ○ They tick off each description as they read it aloud.

○ Pupil B then reads aloud his/her first sentence:
  ○ They both listen carefully to their partner.

○ They alternate, until they have read out all four descriptions and completed their maps.

○ The children show each other their maps, and check.

Do more

The children fold their maps along the dotted lines:
○ They illustrate the front cover of their map.
○ They invent a name for their safari park.

They add the map to their portfolio.

Review

Conduct the review activities opposite.

Review activities

At the Safari Park

 What did you do?

Write the following verbs on the board, and ask the children to say what they did:

drew   read   read aloud   checked   learnt   listened to

1 I .... the names of the African animals and prepositions. (*learnt*)

2 I .... descriptions and .... the animals on my map. (*read, drew*)

3 I .... my descriptions to my partner. (*read aloud*)

4 I .... my partner and .... the animals on my map. (*listened to, drew*)

5 We .... our maps together. (*checked*)

 What did you learn?

Ask the children to look at their pictures, and say three things they learnt.

Encourage discussion.

 How did you learn?

Ask the children to complete the sentences:

1 I learnt the names of the animals by ....

2 I learnt the prepositions by ....

3 I completed the map by ....

 How well did you do?

Give the children the relevant My Activity Record page from Wilbur's toolkit on the website, and ask them to complete the *What have I learnt?* section.

The children colour the monkey on the banana tree, to assess how well they did in this activity.

Near the top of the tree = *Brilliant! I did really well.*

Near the middle of the tree = *Good. I did well.*

Near the bottom of the tree = *Fair. I did OK.*

Lead a discussion.

 What do you need to do next?

Refer back to the success criteria and ask:

'What do you need to revise?'

The children fill in their My Activity Record page.

 Share

The children show their Safari Park map to their parents.

They ask: *Where's the monkey?* etc, to test their parents' knowledge of prepositions in English.

The family add their comments on the My Activity Record page:
○ The children bring the Activity Record page to the next lesson.
○ You read the family's comments.

The children add the completed activity record to their portfolio.

My two hands

Making a class poster

Age/level
6+ years; A1

Activity types
Listen and say

Response type
Personal, spoken, creative

Learning aims
To revise/learn verbs that associate with *hands*
To complete the phrase:
My two hands can + verb

Learning strategies
Activating and building on prior knowledge
Collaborating
Categorising
Generating sentences from a model
Personalising learning

Main outcome
Making a poster

Curricular/cultural links
Science: parts of the body

Values
Tolerance: respecting individuality

Assumptions
The children will be able to give many examples, but will probably need help with vocabulary.

Materials
A large sheet of paper for the poster;
Class dictionaries (optional)

Transfer
The children can create a class poster, based on their two feet:
My two feet can …

I recommend …
Susan Laughs; You Choose

Plan

Explain the learning aims of the activity:
'We're going to learn how to say what we can do with our hands.'

Give or identify the following success criteria:
○ *Think about what you can do with your two hands.*
○ *Work together to think of ideas.*
○ *Ask your teacher for help with vocabulary, or use a dictionary.*
○ *Watch your classmates' actions carefully.*

Hold up your hands and elicit 'hands':
Say: 'My two hands can wave.' (*mime waving*)
Ask: 'What can your two hands do?' (*My two hands can draw.*)

Divide the class into groups.

Give each group a category, and ask them to think of what they can do with their hands:
○ Help with vocabulary as needed:

Pastimes	Sports	Cooking	Communicating
Play the piano/violin	Ride a bike	Cut	Write
Paint	Play table tennis	Chop	Wave
Draw	Play basketball	Wash up	Sign
Sew	Play netball	Mix	Give directions
Knit	Play handball	Stir	Type/text
Play cards		Ice cakes	Hold hands
Play computer games			Help
			Hug

Pool ideas from each group and practise the response: *My two hands can (draw).*

Do

◯ Ask the children for ideas as to how they can design their poster, eg: a border of hands, by topic … see the sample on page 69 opposite.
○ Each child writes something they can do with their hands on the poster, with their name next to it.
○ With younger children, you write the verb for them.

◯ In groups, the children mime an action, and the others guess, eg: *Noor's two hands can type.*

Do more

Once the poster is displayed on the classroom wall, the children read it, eg:
Ahmed's two hands can play table tennis.

Review

Conduct the review activities opposite.

Review activities

My two hands

 What did you do?

The children mime what they did in this lesson.

 What did you learn?

In pairs, the children say three new things they learnt this lesson.

Discuss their ideas, and encourage further reflection.

 How did you learn?

The children change pairs, and discuss how they learnt their three new things.

Discuss their comments, and encourage further reflection.

My two hands can ...

The children can draw outlines of their hands on the poster, add their names and say what their two hands can do.

Sample poster

 How well did you do?

Give the children the relevant My Activity Record page from Wilbur's toolkit on the website, and ask them to complete the *What have I learnt?* section.

Ask them to colour one of the thumb signs, as their assessment of how well they did this activity.

Thumb up = *I worked hard, and can say what my two hands can do and what my classmates' hands can do.*

Thumb level = *I worked hard, and can say what my two hands can do.*

Thumb down = *I must work harder. I can say a few things that my two hands can do.*

Lead a discussion.

 What do you need to do next?

Refer back to the success criteria and ask the children:

'What do you need to revise?'

The children fill in their My Activity Record page.

 Share

The children make a poster at home with their family:

My two hands can ...

The family add their comments on the My Activity Record page:
○ The children bring the Activity Record page to the next lesson.
○ You read the family's comments.

The children add the completed activity record to their portfolio.

Earthworm – a poem

Listening and repeating

Age/level
6+ years; A1/A2

Activity type
Listen and repeat

Response type
Spoken, creative, physical

Learning aims
To learn and recite a poem
To learn or revise nouns and verbs
related to worms and the weather

Learning strategies
Listening and repeating
Using rhyme to aid memory
Using actions, expressions and gestures
to aid memory

Main outcome
Reciting a poem

Curricular/cultural links
Music and drama

Values
Caring: respect for small creatures, and
awareness of the purpose of earthworms
for the environment

Assumptions
The children will enjoy reciting this
poem with actions.

Materials
Wilbur the worm puppets; the
Earthworm poem (see page 71 opposite)

Transfer
The children will be able to use memory
techniques to remember and recite other
poems, songs or rhymes.

I recommend ...
*Diary of a Worm;
Inch by Inch*

Plan

Explain the learning aims of the activity:
'We're going to learn to memorise and recite a poem – a poem about a worm!'

Give or identify the following success criteria:
○ *Listen carefully to your teacher.*
○ *Repeat after your teacher.*
○ *Use actions, expressions and gestures to help remember the words.*

Ask the children to recall some facts about earthworms, to review vocabulary, eg:
How do earthworms move?
Where do they live?
Why are worms useful?

Introduce or revise vocabulary items from the poem that may be new.

Do

⬤ Recite the *Earthworm* poem.

⬤ Ask the children to put up their hands each time they hear a rhyming word:
  worm / earth
  compost / frost
  wiggle / drizzle
  giggle / civil
  work / worm
  vital / recycle

⬤ Ask them which word it rhymed with.

⬤ Recite the whole poem again.

⬤ Recite each line of the poem, and get children to repeat – taking care to focus
  on pronunciation.

⬤ Repeat and demonstrate actions, expressions and gestures for:
  wiggle, rain, sun, frost, hail, snow, drizzle, giggle, respect, vital, recycle

⬤ The children can also create their own actions, etc, and practise reciting the poem
  until they have memorised it and are confident.

Do more

Copy the poem on to the board, with the following words blanked out:
earth, frost, drizzle, civil, work, useful, recycle

The children copy the poem into their portfolios, and write in the missing words.

They use their Wilbur puppets to recite the poem.

Review

Conduct the review activities opposite.

Review activities

Earthworm – a poem

 What did you do?

In groups, the children discuss what they had to do in the activity.

Bring the class together, and discuss.

 What did you learn?

Hold a class discussion around the following questions:

○ *What did you like about the poem?*

○ *Which words did you learn?*

○ *What was special about the words?*

 How did you learn?

Think-pair-share.

Ask the children to reflect on how they learnt the poem, and the techniques they used to help them remember.

Discuss.

Earthworm **poem**

Earthworm! Earthworm!

Wiggle through the earth,

Wiggle through the compost.

Rain, sun or frost.

Wiggle, wiggle,

Hail, snow or drizzle.

Giggle, giggle.

It's not civil!

Respect to the worm's work!

Useful earthworm.

It's vital

To recycle.

 How well did you do?

Give the children the relevant My Activity Record page from Wilbur's toolkit on the website, and ask them to complete the *What have I learnt?* section.

Ask the children to tick (✔) the line from the acrostic poem, as their assessment of how well they did this activity.

Wonderful work today!	☐
Only OK today.	☐
Revision time today.	☐
Must work harder tomorrow.	☐

Lead a discussion.

 What do you need to do next?

Refer back to the success criteria and ask the children:

'What do you need to revise?'

The children fill in their My Activity Record page.

 Share

The children recite the *Earthworm* poem to their family with their Wilbur puppet.

They teach their family the poem, and put on a family recital.

The family add their comments on the My Activity Record page:
○ The children bring the Activity Record page to the next lesson.
○ You read the family's comments.

The children add the completed activity record to their portfolio.

See also the poem 'Worm' by Spike Milligan, in *Unspun Socks from a Chicken's Laundry* (Puffin Books, 1982).

A royal feast

Discriminating phonemes

Age/level
8+ years; A1/A2

Activity type
Listen and discriminate, read and colour

Response type
Physical, analytical

Learning aims
To discriminate between phonemes:
/ɪ/ as in *chip*; /iː/ as in *bean*
To revise or learn vocabulary related to food and royalty

Learning strategies
Listening for general understanding
Identifying specific sounds
Using colour coding to aid visual memory and pronunciation

Main outcome
Listen and understand a story

Curricular/cultural links
Science: healthy eating; History;
World Food Day

Values
Tolerance: respect for different eating preferences; Accountability: awareness of world hunger and people's right to food.

Assumptions
Some language for royalty and food will already be known.

Materials
Prepare pictures of royal characters – real or fictional – and cards of items on the menu;
Royal Feast Story and Menu (in Wilbur's toolkit) for each child;
Template to make paper crowns (in the toolkit).

Transfer
The children listen and identify other phonemes, eg: *cap, cup*; *bag, bug* …

I recommend ...
Eat Your Peas; I will not ever NEVER eat a tomato; Ketchup on your Cornflakes

Plan

Explain the learning aims of the activity:
'We're going to learn how to discriminate between different sounds.'

Give or identify the following success criteria:
○ *Think about food that rhymes with /ɪ/ and /iː/.*
○ *Listen carefully to the different /ɪ/ and /iː/ sounds.*
○ *Watch your teacher's mouth.*
○ *Listen carefully to the story.*

Show the children pictures of royalty, and elicit: *King / Queen / crown / castle / feast.*

Ask the children what they would like to eat at a feast:
Can they think of any foods that rhyme with the sounds /ɪ/ and /iː/ as in King Jim and Queen Jean?

Elicit food vocabulary, using flashcards:
You slightly exaggerate the /ɪ/ and /iː/ sounds, and demonstrate how they are produced.

The children follow the instructions to make a crown and decide to be Queen Jean or King Jim: They colour the Queen Jean crown *green* and the King Jim crown *pink*.

Do

⊙ Read aloud Part 1 of the story in the toolkit, and tell the children to wear their crowns.

⊙ Read Part 2 of the story:
○ The King Jims put up their hands for the food with /ɪ/ sounds.
○ The Queen Jeans put up their hands for the food with /iː/ sounds.

⊙ Read Part 3 of the story:
○ The King Jims and Queen Jeans raise their hands whenever they hear the /ɪ/ or /iː/ sound.

⊙ Give the children a copy of the Royal Feast Story and Menu:
○ They read the menu, saying the words silently.

⊙ Read the menu aloud. The children listen and colour-code the food words:
○ They colour the /iː/ sounds in green; the /ɪ/ sounds in pink.

⊙ They add the story and menu to their portfolio.

Do more

In threes – waiter, King Jim and Queen Jean – the children act out the order scene at the feast. For example:

Waiter: *Good evening. Are you ready to order?*
Queen Jean: *Yes, please. I'll have roast beef and green beans, please.*
Waiter: *Roast beef and green beans* (repeats, writes down, or mimes writing down)
King Jim: *I'll have chicken and chips, please.*
Waiter: *Chicken and chips.* Etc.

Review

Conduct the review activities opposite.

Review activities

A royal feast

What did you do?

Play a version of *Simon says ... .*

The children wear their King Jim or Queen Jean crowns:
- When King Jim makes a statement, the Queen Jeans have to respond.
- When Queen Jean makes a statement, the King Jims have to respond.

For example:
King Jim says … we made a hat.
The children correct the statement:
No. Queen Jean says … we made a crown.

- *King Jim says ... we made a **hat**.*
  *No. Queen Jean says ... we made a **crown**. (✓)*

- *Queen Jean says ... we listened to a **poem**.*
  *No, King Jim says ... we listened to a **story**. (✓)*

- *King Jim says ... we **put a hand on our head** if we heard the short /ɪ/ or long /iː/ sound.*
  *No. Queen Jean says ... we **put our hands up** if we heard the short /ɪ/ or long /iː/ sound. (✓)*

- *Queen Jean says ... we **wrote** a menu.*
  *No. King Jim says ... we **read** a menu. (✓)*

- *Queen Jean says ... we coloured a **castle**.*
  *No. King Jim says ... we coloured **food words**. (✓)*

What did you learn?

In pairs of King Jim and Queen Jean, the children write down three things they learned, and then share their ideas.

Lead a class discussion.

How did you learn?

In their King Jim and Queen Jean pairs, ask the children to think about how they learnt. For example,

- *I listened carefully to the sounds in the words.*
- *I watched the teacher's mouth carefully.*
- *I listened carefully to the story.*
- *I listened and colour-coded the food words, to help me pronounce the different sounds.*

How well did you do?

Give the children the relevant My Activity Record page from Wilbur's toolkit on the website, and ask them to complete the *What have I learnt?* section.

They draw the number of crowns on the menu in the boxes under each section, to assess how well they did the activity.

Three crowns = *Excellent!*
Two crowns = *Good work today.*
One crown = *I must try harder.*

Ask them to say why, and discuss.

What do you need to do next?

Refer back to the success criteria and ask the children:

'What do you need to revise?'

The children fill in their My Activity Record page.

Share

The children show the Royal Feast Story and Menu to their family, and ask them to choose a starter, main course and dessert.

They write their names next to the dishes they choose.

They act out the 'order scene' together if they wish.

The family add their comments on the My Activity Record page:
- The children bring the Activity Record page to the next lesson.
- You read the family's comments.

The children add the completed activity record to their portfolio.

Our language learning rights

Creating a class convention

Age/level
8+ years; A1/A2

Activity type
Listen and write

Response type
Personal, spoken and written

Learning aims
To revise/learn vocabulary related to rights and responsibilities
(See the Note on page 75 opposite for more on this)
To form sentences following the patterns:
We have the right to … (+ infinitive)
We are responsible for … (+ gerund)

Learning strategies
Activating and building on prior knowledge
Collaborating
Generating sentences from a model
Personalising learning

Main outcome
Creating a class convention

Curricular/cultural links
Citizenship;
Children's Day, Universal Children's Day, European Day of Language, International Mother Language Day

Values
Accountability: understanding rights and responsibilities

Assumptions
The children will be able to think of rights and responsibilities, but will probably need help with vocabulary.

Materials
Sheets of A4 paper for the groupwork; Class dictionaries (optional)

Transfer
The children can create a class convention for another school subject.

I recommend …
Knuffle Bunny

Plan

Explain the learning aims of the activity:
'We're going to learn how to talk about your English language learning rights and responsibilities.'

Give or identify the following success criteria:
- *Think about your rights and responsibilities when learning English in class.*
- *Work together to discuss ideas.*
- *Complete the sentences:*
  We have the right to …
  We are responsible for …

Ask the children if they know what a convention is:
A convention is an agreement between countries to obey a law.
A convention contains 'rights' which are things every person should have or be able to do.

Ask the children to suggest an English language learning right, eg:
We have the right to say we don't understand.

Divide class into groups. Each group thinks of three rights, using the pattern:
We have the right to … (+ infinitive)

Do

- Draw headings for a table on the board (see the sample Class Convention in Wilbur's toolkit) and get the class's ideas.
- Ask the children to choose the five (or ten) rights they think are the most important for their own class convention. (See the examples in the toolkit).
- Divide the class into groups or pairs and give them a sheet of paper.
- Allocate one or two rights from the table on the board for each group/pair to copy.
- The children put their sheets of paper together to create their class convention poster, and display it in the classroom.
- They copy the convention into their portfolios and illustrate it (seee page 75 opposite).

Do more

Remind the children that if they have rights, they also have *responsibilities.*

Discuss, and the children add these to the portfolios as a table (see Wilbur's toolkit):
We are responsible for … (+ gerund)

Review

Conduct the review activities opposite.

Ask if the children know of the UN Convention on the Rights of the Child. For example:
You have the right to give your opinion, and for adults to listen and take it seriously. (Article 12)
You have the right to a good quality education. (Article 28)

See the Note on page 75 opposite.

Review activities

Our language learning rights

 What did you do?

In groups, the children discuss the order in which they did the different parts of the lesson.

 What did you learn?

In pairs, they say three new things they learnt this lesson.

Discuss their ideas, and encourage further reflection.

 How did you learn?

The children change pairs, and discuss how they learnt their three new things.

Discuss their comments, and encourage further reflection.

Sample class convention

> **Note**
> A child-friendly version of the UN Convention on the Rights of the Child is available here: *http://www.unicef.org/rightsite/files/ uncrcchilldfriendlylanguage.pdf*
>
> See also page 25 in Part A for more information on Children's Rights.

 How well did you do?

Give the children the relevant **My Activity Record** page from Wilbur's toolkit on the website, and ask them to complete the *What have I learnt?* section.

They choose a set of scales from Wilbur's toolkit, as their assessment of how well they did this activity.

Equal scales = *Excellent! I worked hard.*

Slightly unequal = *Good. I worked quite hard.*

Noticeably unequal = *OK. I must work harder.*

Lead a discussion.

 What do you need to do next?

Refer back to the success criteria and ask them:

'What do you need to revise?'

The children fill in their My Activity Record page.

 **Share**

The children explain the convention to their family, and write a 'My language learning rights at home' convention – either in English or their home language.

The family add their comments on the My Activity Record page:
○ The children bring the Activity Record page to the next lesson.
○ You read the family's comments.

The children add the completed activity record to their portfolio.

English around me

Making a vocabulary diary

Age/level
8+ years; A1/A2

Activity type
Read and make a vocabulary diary

Response type
Spoken, written, personal and creative

Learning aims
To develop curiosity
To find English vocabulary in the immediate environment

Learning strategies
Observing and collecting English words in the environment
Organising and recording vocabulary into meaningful groups, to aid memory
Becoming aware of English in the out-of-school context

Main outcome
Making a vocabulary diary

Curricular/cultural links
Geography; Study Skills
UN English Language Day

Values
Flexibility: being curious about how words are used

Assumptions
The children will be able to find and recognise some English words in their immediate environment.

Materials
Realia with words in English: adverts, food packets, clothes labels, stamps, etc;
Two sheets of A4 paper per child;
Copies of the 'My learning diary' (see Wilbur's toolkit)

Transfer
The children can use the concept of a vocabulary diary to record and learn other words from their lessons.

I recommend ...
Dear Diary; The World Came to My Place Today

Plan

Explain the learning aims of the activity:
'We're going to find and learn vocabulary in our environment, and learn how to organise the words.'

Give or identify the following success criteria:
○ *Look for words in English outside the classroom.*
○ *Organise and record words to help you learn and remember them.*

Ask the children:
○ *What is a diary?*   ○ *What do you write in your diary?*
○ *Do you keep a diary?* ○ *Why do you keep a diary?*

Elicit that there are two kinds of diaries:
○ One to make a note of important dates, homework, etc.
○ Another to record personal reflections.

Explain they are going to create a personal diary as part of their portfolio, to record vocabulary from their immediate environment.

Show them some examples from your realia.

Ask the children to name the places where they see the words in English, eg:
at home, on clothes labels, on food packets …

Do

● Ask the children to suggest ways of organising words in their diary. For example: by date or by place.

● Draw a table on the board and model how to complete it, by showing the children items from your realia and asking:
○ *What's the date today?*
○ *Which word do you want to record today?*
○ *Where did you find the word?*
○ *Is there anything interesting about the word that will help you remember it?*

Date	Word in English	Place found	Comments
11 November	Tin of tomatoes	Supermarket	Tomato in English is similar to *tomate* in French.

● Give the children two sheets of paper for their 'English in the Environment' vocabulary diary, and explain:
○ The left-hand page is to record their words. (Younger children can use visuals only.)
○ The right-hand page is to stick labels, photographs, etc, of the word in context.

Do more

Hold 'English in the environment' sessions regularly, for the children to 'show and tell'.

Review

Conduct the review activities opposite.

Review activities

English around me

An 'English in the Environment' diary

You will see that the review activities on this page are slightly different from the others in *Teaching children how to learn*. In keeping with the diary theme of this activity, they introduce a 'learning diary' as another strategy for monitoring progress and reflecting on and reviewing learning.

A diary is a complete set of review activities in itself:
The children will be noting all the following in their diary:

○ What they learned.
○ How they learned.
○ What they did best.
○ What they found difficult.
○ What they liked best – and why.
○ How well they did.
○ What they need to revise.

My learning diary

Date: _____

Activity title: _____

I learnt these words at school: _____

See page 108 and Wilbur's toolkit on the website for a downloadable 'My learning diary' page to complete.

A Learning Diary

The children learn how to complete a Learning Diary to review their learning.

A Learning Diary provides a framework for them to reflect on their learning, personalise their learning and make their learning memorable.

Talk them through the diary, explaining as necessary:
○ They can write in their mother tongue or shared classroom language, so as not to limit what they write. There will be no loss of the 'learning to learn' benefits.
○ You will not assess the diary – it is personal: for them to think about what they did and learnt, and to record their learning.
○ You negotiate how often they would like to complete their Learning Diary: once a week, once a month, once a term …
○ They finally add the Learning Diary to their portfolio.

If your resources allow, you could create a digital format of the diary. The children can scan in pictures or photos.

 How well did you do?

Give the children the relevant My Activity Record page from Wilbur's toolkit on the website, and ask them to complete the *What have I learnt?* section.

They choose the comment that best assesses how well they did this activity, and write it in the diary on the left. They add the date and, on the right, draw a picture that represents the day's activity.

Comment:	Date:
○	

Very good! = I can record words in the way I prefer, to help me learn and remember.

Quite good. = I can record some words in the way I prefer, to help me learn and remember.

OK. = I'm still thinking about the way I prefer to record words.

Lead a discussion.

 What do you need to do next?

Refer back to the success criteria and ask the children:

'What do you need to revise?'

The children fill in their My Activity Record page.

 Share

The children show their portfolio and 'English in the Environment' vocabulary diary to their family.

They look for words in English together – at home, at the shops, etc – and add them to the diary.

The family add their comments on the My Activity Record page:
○ The children bring the Activity Record page to the next lesson.
○ You read the family's comments.

The children add the completed activity record to their portfolio.

My school day

Reading and writing about routines

Age/level
9–10 years; A2

Activity type
Read and sequence; read, compare and write

Response type
Written, personal and analytical

Learning aims
To use time linkers as discourse markers:
first, then, next, after that, finally
To learn/revise: meal times, school subjects, days of the week, the time
To use the simple present for daily routines

Learning strategies
Sequencing
Problem solving
Reading for specific information

Main outcome
Writing about your school day

Curricular/cultural links
Maths; World Student Day

Values
Tolerance: awareness of different educational systems, and respecting differences

Materials
Sentence strips of Jane's school day for each child (see Wilbur's toolkit)

Assumptions
Some vocabulary may be known. The children will be able to talk about their own school day, but culturally-specific information may need explaining, eg: *assembly, lunch box, uniform*

Transfer
The children can use the time linkers and the concept of sequencing events in other contexts.

I recommend ...
It's a Book; Pete the Cat: Rocking in My School Shoes

Plan

Explain the learning aims of the activity:
'We're going to learn how to use time linkers to sequence events about a school day in England.'

Give or identify the following success criteria:
○ *Use clues in the text to sequence events in chronological order.*
○ *Use time linkers when writing your paragraph.*
○ *Use the first person singular of the present simple.*

Pre-teach or revise any new vocabulary.

Ask the children what they do on a typical school day.

Tell them about a typical school day in the UK. Explain:
assembly, break time/playtime, lunch box, uniform, netball

Prepare the sentence strips (see Wilbur's toolkit).

For more information on a typical school day in England and on Hillcrest Primary school in Bristol, consult the following websites:
http://www.woodlands-junior.kent.sch.uk/schday/regisassem.html
http://www.hillcrest.bristol.sch.uk/about_hillcrest.html#SchoolDay

Do

○ Hand out the sentence strips and say:
  ○ 'Work in pairs and sequence the sentences about Jane's school day in England.'

○ Check the sequence of their text, and say:
  ○ 'Read the text again and identify the time linkers in the text.'
  ○ 'How did you identify them?'
  For example:
  ○ 'Time linkers' are words that tell you that one activity follows another and create cohesion in a text.
  ○ 'Clues' are linked to times and daily routines.

○ Elicit time linkers from the children's own language, for comparison, and ask:
  ○ 'Does your school day resemble Jane's?'

○ Elicit similarities and differences, and build up a chart on the board:
  Jane's school day / Your school day

○ Tell the children to write a paragraph about their school day, referring back to the chart and using the time linkers to create a cohesive paragraph.

○ They add their paragraph to their portfolio.

Do more

Write the following jumbled words or expressions on the board. Tell the children to unscramble them, and then write them in the right sequence:
hent   nafilly   texn   tafatreth   ristf

Review

Conduct the review activities opposite.

Review activities

My school day

What did you do?

Copy the following sentences on the board, or onto strips of paper to hand out to groups, pairs or individual children: *without* **the time linkers.**

Ask the children to sequence the sentences in the order they did the activities and write in the time linkers:

1 *I read and sequenced a text about Jane's school day.* (First)

2 *I identified time linkers in English.* (Next)

3 *I discussed the purpose of time linkers.* (Then)

4 *I compared my school day with Jane's.* (After that)

5 *I wrote a paragraph about my school day, using the time linkers to create a cohesive text.* (Finally)

What did you learn?

In pairs, ask the children to identify the two most important things they learnt in this activity, and to say why.

Lead a class discussion

How did you learn?

Copy the following sentences on the board or onto strips of paper, and hand out to groups, pairs or individual children.

Ask the children to match the sentences to the sentences above that refer to what they did:

3 ... *by thinking and answering my teacher's questions.*

1 ... *by recognising clues, such as times, meal times and daily routines.*

5 ... *by using the information in the chart.*

2 ... *by associating them with the time of the day and the daily routines.*

4 ... *by drawing up a chart on the board, to highlight the similarities and differences.*

How well did you do?

Give the children the relevant My Activity Record page from Wilbur's toolkit on the website, and ask them to complete the *What have I learnt?* **section.**

Ask them to colour the stars, to assess how well they did this activity.

Gold star = *I can do this well!*

Silver star = *I can do this quite well.*

Bronze star = *I am still learning to do this.*

○ *I can use time linkers.*

○ *I can say two things that are the same about my school day and a school day in England.*

○ *I can say two things that are different about my school day and a school day in England.*

○ *I can use the simple present to talk about daily routines.*

Lead a discussion.

What do you need to do next?

Refer back to the success criteria and ask the children:

'What do you need to revise?'

The children fill in their My Activity Record page.

Share

The children tell their family about a school day in England – in English or their home language.

The family add their comments on the My Activity Record page:
○ The children bring the Activity Record page to the next lesson.
○ You read the family's comments.

The children add the completed activity record to their portfolio.

Fireworks safety

Writing instructions

Age/level
8+ years; A1/A2

Activity types
Read, think and write

Response type
Written

Learning aims
To write instructions for fireworks safety
To use the imperative: *Keep pets indoors.*
To use the auxiliary contracted negative:
don't + verb (*give, read, put, keep, throw*):
Don't throw fireworks.
To learn fireworks safety vocabulary

Learning strategies
Activating prior knowledge
Drafting
Generating instructions from a model

Main outcome
Designing a Fireworks Safety poster

Curricular/cultural links
Citizenship: health and safety; History;
Art and design; Guy Fawkes Night

Values
Accountability and caring: responsibility
for people's safety; knowledge of festivals
celebrated with fireworks

Assumptions
The children will probably have watched
a fireworks display, and will be aware of
some of the potential dangers.

Materials
Coloured paper for the final version
of the Fireworks Safety poster, plus
coloured pencils/crayons;
Copies of the template (see Wilbur's
toolkit) to make a Fountain Firework

Transfer
The children write instructions for other
situations: on the beach, in the road …

I recommend …
The Chinese New Year

Plan

Explain the learning aims of the activity:
'We're going to learn how to write instructions for fireworks safety.'

Give or identify the following success criteria:
○ *Think about when you have seen fireworks.*
○ *Think about fireworks safety.*
○ *Look carefully at each safety instruction, to understand when you must use* 'don't' + *verb.*

Ask:
○ 'Have you been to a fireworks display?'
○ 'Where was it? When was it?'
○ 'Was it to celebrate a special festival?'
○ 'Do you know of any other special festivals
  that are celebrated with fireworks?'

For example: Bonfire Night (England),
Independence Day (America), Diwali
(India), Eid (Middle East), Bastille Day
(France), Chinese New Year – or any
other time that fireworks are enjoyed.

Do

○ Explain that fireworks can be great fun, but every year people get hurt because
  they don't use fireworks safely:
  ○ Most firework accidents happen to children under the age of 16.

○ Elicit ideas about fireworks safety.

○ Give each child a sheet of A4 paper, and ask them to think about the design of their
  poster and make a draft:
  ○ They think about layout, colour and illustrations.
  ○ You discuss their ideas, and allow them to choose a coloured sheet of A4 paper
    for their poster.

○ Write the safety instructions below on the board, omitting *Don't* and capital letters:
  ○ *stand away when you are watching fireworks.*   ○ *light fireworks indoors.* (Don't)
  ○ *go near a firework that has been lit.* (Don't)   ○ *have a bucket of water and a hose*
  ○ *keep pets indoors.*   *nearby in case of accidents.*
  ○ *put fireworks in your pockets.* (Don't)   ○ *buy or light fireworks if you are*
  ○ *throw fireworks.* (Don't)   *under 18 years old.* (Don't)
  ○ *make your own fireworks.* (Don't)   ○ *wear gloves.*

○ Elicit which instructions take 'don't'. Invite the children to the board to write 'Don't'
  or give a capital letter to the first word of the instruction.

○ They copy the instructions onto their poster and you display the posters in the class.

Do more

The children write a quiz, based on their Fireworks Safety poster. For example:
○ *Where should pets be kept?*
○ *How old do you have to be, to buy fireworks?*
○ *What should you do, when you are watching fireworks?*

Review

Conduct the review activities opposite.

Review activities

Fireworks safety

 ### What did you do?

Give each child a Fountain Firework template (see Wilbur's toolkit) and demonstrate how to make the firework. The top end of the firework is cut into five strips, to represent a shower of sparks.

○ The children follow the number code and colour the pattern, cut out and roll and glue.

○ They cut the five sparks and write what they did on each one.

Discuss and encourage reflection. For example:

○ *We discussed what we know about firework displays.*

○ *We discussed what we know about fireworks safety.*

○ *We designed a Fireworks Safety poster.*

○ *We copied the safety instructions from the board onto our poster.*

 ### What did you learn?

The children read each spark on their Fountain Firework and say what they learnt. For example:

○ *We learnt about fireworks safety.*

○ *We learnt when to use the imperative and auxiliary 'Don't' in front of verbs to give instructions.*

○ *We learnt how to draft a poster and to think about layout, colour, illustrations and text, before producing our final version.*

 ### How did you learn?

Using the Fountain Firework, tell the children to say how they learnt. For example:

○ *We remembered fireworks displays we have seen.*

○ *We thought about fireworks safety.*

○ *We made a draft of our Fireworks Safety poster.*

○ *We looked at the instructions on the board, and put 'Don't' in front of the verb where necessary.*

 ### How well did you do?

Give the children the relevant My Activity Record page from Wilbur's toolkit on the website, and ask them to complete the *What have I learnt?* section.

Ask them to colour a Catherine Wheel, to assess how well they did this activity.

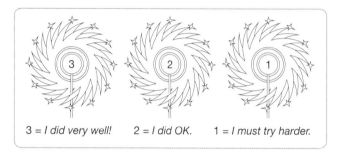

3 = *I did very well!*   2 = *I did OK.*   1 = *I must try harder.*

Lead a discussion.

 ### What do you need to do next?

Refer back to the success criteria and ask the children:

'What do you need to revise?'

The children fill in their My Activity Record page.

 ### Share

The children tell their parents about fireworks safety, in English or the home language.

They use the Fountain Firework to tell them what they did in the activity.

The family add their comments on the My Activity Record page:
○ The children bring the Activity Record page to the next lesson.
○ You read the family's comments.

The children add the completed activity record to their portfolio.

Reading faces

Recognising facial expressions

Age/level
8+ years; A1/A2

Activity type
Read and identify feelings

Response type
Physical, creative and personal

Learning aims
To learn or revise adjectives for feelings:
angry, bored, frightened, happy, sad, tired
To express feelings with the verb 'to be':
I am happy / you are happy / she is sad
To practise rhythm, via a song

Learning strategies
Concentrating and listening to each other
Recognising facial expressions, as aids
to meaning
Sorting into groups; Memorising words

Main outcomes
Making a collage
Singing a 'feelings' song

Curricular/cultural links
Music and drama

Values
Resilience: awareness of different feelings,
and how to manage feelings

Assumptions
The children may know the song, but in
this version the words have been changed.

Materials
Flashcards for facial expressions (see
Wilbur's toolkit) – you can add other
feelings if you wish; Old magazines,
newspapers, etc, for the children to cut up
for the collage; Sheets of A4 paper for the
'zigzag' book (optional); a 'talking stick'

Transfer
The children can use other visual clues
as aids to meaning.

I recommend ...
*Colour Me Happy;
Pete the Cat: I Love My
White Shoes; The Bad-
Tempered Ladybird*

Plan

Explain the learning aims of the activity:
'We're going to learn how to recognise and describe facial expressions.'

Give or identify the following success criteria:
○ *Pay attention and listen carefully.*
○ *Observe your teacher's/classmates' expressions carefully.*
○ *Sort pictures of people expressing different feelings into groups.*
○ *Listen and repeat the words of the song.*

Use the flashcards to elicit feelings, and reinforce with facial expressions.
The children repeat: *I'm happy*, etc.

Continue for each feeling, and review.

The children sit in circles and pass around a 'talking stick' (see page 49) to say
how they feel: *Today, I'm happy/tired*, etc.

Do

● Play *Teacher says …* (based on *Simon says …*):
   ○ *Teacher says … you are sad!*

● The children mime, and you repeat with other feelings.

● In groups, the children form a circle, and take turns to stand in the middle
   and mime a feeling:
   ○ They 'read the face' and identify: *You are angry.*

● Give out old magazines, newspapers, etc:
   ○ The children cut out pictures of people expressing different feelings.

● Prepare a display panel divided into six sections for each feeling:
   ○ The children sort the pictures to make a collage.
   ○ Encourage the children to say: *He's happy / she's sad*, etc.

● Introduce the song 'If you're happy and you know it':
   If you're happy and you know it, clap your hands!
   If you're happy and you know it, clap your hands!
   If you're happy and you know it, and you really want to show it,
   If you're happy and you know it, clap your hands!

● Introduce a new feeling for each verse, and discuss it. For example:
   When they are angry, what can they do to calm down?
   If you're angry … count to ten.   *If you're bored … read a book.*
   If you're sad … sing this song.   *If you're frightened … tell an adult.*

Do more

Give the children A4 paper, and show them how to fold it into a zigzag to make a book.

They draw a facial expression on each page and label the feeling.

Review

Conduct the review activities opposite.

Review activities

Reading faces

 What did you do?

Copy the following sentences on the board or hand them out to groups, pairs or individual children.

Tell the children to sequence the sentences in the order they did the activities:

○ I made a 'feelings' collage. (5)

○ I learnt/revised adjectives to describe facial expressions. (1)

○ I played *Teacher says ...* (3)

○ I identified the feeling my classmate was miming. (4)

○ I sang a song about feelings. (6)

○ I described how I feel today. (2)

 What did you learn?

Write the following statements on the board, for the children to decide what was most important for them.

Allow them to add other statements of their own.

○ *I learnt adjectives for facial expressions and to say how I feel.*

○ *I learnt to read faces, to understand feelings and meaning.*

○ *I learnt to pay attention and listen to others.*

○ *I learnt to memorise words, to sing a song about feelings.*

○ *I learnt what to do if I feel angry.*

 How did you learn?

Think-pair-share.

Together, the children discuss how they learnt. For example:

1 ... *by recognising flashcards and observing my teacher's expressions, listening to him/her and repeating the adjective.*

2 ... *by using the talking stick and saying the adjectives for feelings. I listened to other children in my group when they had the talking stick.*

3 ... *by listening carefully to the teacher and miming the facial expression when I heard 'Teacher says ...'.*

4 ... *by observing the facial expression and saying how they felt.*

5 ... *by cutting out and sorting pictures into feelings groups on a collage.*

6 ... *by listening to my teacher and singing.*

 How well did you do?

Give the children the relevant My Activity Record page from Wilbur's toolkit on the website, and ask them to complete the *What have I learnt?* section.

They assess how well they did this activity, by colouring the faces with the expression that best describes their performance.

○ *I understand adjectives to describe feelings.*

○ *I can say how I feel.*

○ *I can read faces.*

○ *I can sing a song about feelings.*

Ask them to say why, and discuss.

 What do you need to do next?

Refer back to the success criteria and ask the children:

'What do you need to revise?'

The children fill in their My Activity Record page.

 Share

The children teach their family the song *'If you're happy and you know it'* – and sing it together.

The family add their comments on the My Activity Record page:
○ The children bring the Activity Record page to the next lesson.
○ You read the family's comments.

The children add the completed activity record to their portfolio.

Don't be a bully!

Making an anti-bullying poster

Age/level
8+ years; A1/A2

Activity type
Read and categorise

Response type
Written, personal and creative

Learning aims
To develop awareness of bullying and the behaviour of a bully
To use the imperative with *Don't*
To learn vocabulary related to bullying: *hit, pinch, exclude, call names, steal, make fun of, spread rumours, frighten*

Learning strategies
Categorising
Reading for specific information

Main outcome
Making an anti-bullying poster

Curricular/cultural links
Citizenship; History; Anti-Bullying Week; Children's Day, Child Protection Day;

Values
Accountability and caring: understanding the behaviour of a bully, valuing friendship, similarities and differences

Assumptions
The language for friendship will be known, if the children did the activity *A friend is someone who …* on page 56

Materials
Action cards about bullies and friends, one set per pair (see Wilbur's toolkit); Anti-bullying images (see the toolkit); A3 paper or card for the poster

Transfer
The children can use phrases with *Don't* in other contexts – for example, classroom behaviour:
Don't shout; *Don't talk while the teacher is talking*; *Don't disturb your classmates.*

I recommend …
Is It Because?
Willy and Hugh

Plan

Explain the learning aims of the activity:
'We're going to learn about bullying, and make an anti-bullying poster.'

Give or identify the following success criteria:
○ *Think of actions that friends and bullies do.*
○ *Categorise the actions into positive (friends) and negative (bullies).*
○ *Write imperatives with 'Don't'.*
○ *Use the examples to create an anti-bullying poster.*

Write the words 'friends' and 'bullies' on the board.

Elicit what they mean: *What type of actions do friends and bullies do?*

Give out the action cards – the children work in pairs to categorise them:
○ Actions that *friends* do.
○ Actions that *bullies* do.

See the Key opposite on page 85.

Ask the children what they would say, to tell someone to stop being a bully, eg: *Don't hit me.*

Ask what form of the verb follows *Don't* (+ infinitive).

Refer the children to the action cards, and ask them to practise saying the expressions with *Don't*.

Do

● Show the children the different anti-bullying images in Wilbur's toolkit:
○ You discuss what message they are conveying.

● Tell the children to work in pairs and create their own anti-bullying poster together:
○ They use illustrations and sentences with *Don't*.
○ You monitor and help, as required.

● Display the posters on the classroom wall.

Do more

The children read each other's posters:
○ You lead a discussion on who children should speak to – if they see bullying, or are a victim of bullying.

They copy the sentences into their portfolio.

Review

Conduct the review activities opposite.

Review activities

Don't be a bully!

 ### What did you do?

Write the following sentences on the board, and ask the children to categorise them into reading and writing activities.

○ *We read the action cards about friends and bullies.*

○ *We categorised the cards into actions that friends do, and actions that bullies do.*

○ *We used the imperative 'Don't' to tell someone to stop being a bully.*

○ *We made an anti-bullying poster.*

 ### What did you learn?

Ask the children to write down three things they learned about bullying, and to share their ideas.

Lead a class discussion.

 ### How did you learn?

Ask the children to make a poster, using visual images to show how they learnt. For example:

A pen = writing.

Two children together = working in pairs and discussing.

Key

Friends ...	Bullies ...
make me feel happy.	frighten me.
help me.	hit me.
say nice things about me.	spread rumours about me.
share their things.	steal my things.
like to play with me.	exclude me from games.
respect me.	call me names.
care about me.	make fun of me.

 ### How well did you do?

Give the children the relevant My Activity Record page from Wilbur's toolkit on the website, and ask them to complete the *What have I learnt?* section.

The children ask a *friend* and their *teacher* to colour the expressions, to assess how well they did this activity, and then they assess *themselves*.

My friend says …
Fantastic!   Good effort.   OK.   Try harder next time.

My teacher says …
Fantastic!   Good effort.   OK.   Try harder next time.

I say …
Fantastic!   Good effort.   OK.   Try harder next time.

Lead a discussion.

 ### What do you need to do next?

Refer back to the success criteria and ask the children:

'What do you need to revise?'

The children fill in their My Activity Record page.

 ### Share

The children show their anti-bullying poster to their family, and tell them in English or the home language what they have learnt about bullying.

The family add their comments on the My Activity Record page:
○ The children bring the Activity Record page to the next lesson.
○ You check the family's comments.

The children add the completed activity record to their portfolio.

The water cycle

Reading and matching

Age/level
8+ years; A1/A2

Activity type
Read and match

Response type
Analytical, written, physical

Learning aims
To identify and describe the stages in a process – the water cycle – using the present simple
To learn or revise vocabulary for nouns and verbs related to the water cycle

Learning strategies
Identifying nouns and verbs
Describing and sequencing a process
Matching the stages of the water cycle to a diagram

Main outcome
Labelling a diagram to describe a process

Curricular/cultural links
Science;
World Environment Day

Values
Accountability and caring:
understanding how rain is formed, and valuing water

Assumptions
The children will know some of the vocabulary related to the water cycle, and may understand how rain is formed.

Materials
The 'water cycle' worksheet – see Wilbur's toolkit – for each child; plus the Key

Transfer
The children can match stages to other processes, eg the life cycle of the caterpillar/chicken; food cycles.

I recommend ...
Augustus and his Smile;
Cloudland; Rain;
Splish, Splash, Splosh

Plan

Explain the learning aims of the activity:
'We're going to learn to describe a process.'

Give or identify the following success criteria:
○ *Identify the nouns in the diagram.*
○ *Think about the water cycle process, to identify the verbs.*
○ *Sequence and match the stages of the water cycle to the diagram.*

Give each child a copy of the water cycle worksheet.

Ask the children to name the nouns in the diagram:
sun, sea, sky, clouds, rain, drops of water, river, land, lake, mountain, snow

Ask them if they know how rain is formed.

Elicit the process, and introduce or revise the verbs:
heats, evaporates, rises, cools, forms, makes, get heavier, fall(s), shines, begins

Use gestures and mime, to help elicit the verbs.

Focus attention on the third person present simple 's':
Why don't 'get' and 'fall' take the 's'?
(because clouds and drops of water are plural)

Do

● In pairs, the children read the stages of the water cycle on the worksheet:
　○ They sequence them 1–6. (The first has been done.)

● They then match each stage to the diagram:
　○ They write the corresponding number in the box.

● You check, and ask the children to read the stages aloud.

● They add the water cycle worksheet to their portfolios.

Do more

Create a class poster of the water cycle.

You can allocate a stage of the process to pairs of children:
○ Some children can *draw* the process.
○ Other children *write* the stages.

Review

Conduct the review activities opposite.

I recommend that this activity is completed before the *It's snowing!* activity on page 62.

Review activities

The water cycle

What did you do?

Write the statements on the board. In pairs, the children sequence the process of the lesson.

Alternatively, you could copy them onto separate strips of paper and hand them out, for the children to put them in sequence.

○ We read aloud the stages of the water cycle. (3)

○ We thought about the different stages in the water cycle and identified the verbs: *heats, evaporates, rises, cools, forms, makes, get heavier, fall(s), shines, begins.* (2)

○ We read the stages of the water cycle, and sequenced them 1–6; then matched each stage to the diagram. (4)

○ We named the nouns in the water cycle: *sun, sea, water, sky, clouds, rain, river, land, lake.* (1)

Bring the class together, and discuss the sequence.

What did you learn?

Copy these three statements onto the board. The children rank them according to the most important for them.

(3 = most important, 1 = least important.)

○ *I learnt nouns and verbs related to the water cycle.*

○ *I learnt how to describe a process.*

○ *I learnt how rain is formed.*

Bring the class together, and discuss.

How did you learn?

Write these statements on the board. The children say which are the most important for them.

○ *I identified nouns and verbs.*

○ *I used the diagram to help predict and describe the stages of the water cycle.*

○ *I used the teacher's mimes and gestures to help recall or learn the vocabulary.*

○ *I discussed the process with my classmate.*

○ *I asked my teacher if I didn't understand.*

○ *I matched the stages of the water cycle to the diagram, to show I understood.*

How well did you do?

Give the children the relevant My Activity Record page from Wilbur's toolkit on the website, and ask them to complete the *What have I learnt?* section.

The children assess how well they did this activity, by colouring the number of rain clouds which best represent their performance and understanding.

Three rain clouds = *I worked hard and can describe the water cycle. I understand how rain is formed.*

Two rain clouds = *I worked quite hard and can describe most of the water cycle. I understand a little how rain is formed.*

One rain cloud = *I must work harder. I don't understand yet how rain is formed.*

Lead a discussion.

What do you need to do next?

Refer back to the success criteria and ask the children:

'What do you need to revise?'

The children fill in their My Activity Record page.

Share

Using the water cycle worksheet, the children describe the water cycle to their family and tell them about the different stages – in English or the home language.

The family add their comments on the My Activity Record page:

○ The children bring the Activity Record page to the next lesson.

○ You check the family's comments.

The children add the completed activity record to their portfolio.

How green am I?

Doing a quiz

Age/level
9–12 years; A1/A2

Activity type
Read and answer questions

Response type
Personal response

Learning aims
To revise/learn vocabulary related to the 3Rs: *reduce*, *reuse* and *recycle*
To read and answer questions about 'green' habits
To use the simple present to describe 'green' actions
To use *will* for expressing intentions

Learning strategies
Reading for specific information
Classifying actions under the 3Rs

Main outcome
Doing a quiz

Curricular/cultural links
Geography; Science;
World Environment Day

Values
Accountability and caring: awareness of and respect for environmental protection

Assumptions
The children will have some awareness of the concept of environmental protection and of 'being green'.

Materials
A quiz worksheet for each child (see Wilbur's toolkit);
Three A4-size cards: one *bright green*, one *pale green* and one *white* – with the points on the front and comments on the back (see the toolkit).

Transfer
You can use quizzes to find out about other activities that the children do.

I recommend ...
Dinosaurs and All That Rubbish; Five Little Fiends; My Green Day; What if? A book about recycling

Plan

Explain the learning aims of the activity:
'We're going to learn how to talk about 'being green' in English.'

Give or identify the following success criteria:
○ *Read the quiz carefully, to answer the questions.*
○ *Think of ways you reduce, reuse and recycle.*

Check the children's understanding of 'being green'.

To introduce the 3R verbs, draw a table on the board with three columns:

Reduce	Reuse	Recycle

Elicit 'green' things that children do at home:
○ You help with vocabulary, and help classify their suggestions in the table.

Do

● Distribute the quiz worksheet (see Wilbur's toolkit) to all the children:
  ○ They answer the questions, add up their points and add their score to the table on the worksheet.

● Hold up the cards and elicit the colours – *bright green*, *pale green* and *white* (not green at all!).

● Put the cards in different parts of the classroom.

● You tell children to form groups, according to the number of points they scored.
  ○ One child in each group reads aloud the comments on the back.
  ○ Another child counts the number of children in their group, comes to the board and records the number.

● Ask:
  'How green is the class: bright green, pale green – or not green at all?'

● The children add their quiz to their portfolio.

Do more

Refer back to the 3Rs chart, and ask the children to suggest actions for a classroom 'Green Action Plan'. For example:
We will turn off the lights when we leave the classroom.
We will reuse old paper.

Write up their suggestions, asking the children to classify them under the 3Rs.

Display the Green Action Plan in the classroom.

Review

Conduct the review activities opposite.

Review activities

How green am I?

What did you do?

Copy the following sentences onto the board or onto strips of paper, and ask the children to sequence the sentences in the order they did the activity:

○ We answered a quiz, to find out how green we are. (3)

○ We classified the 'green' things we do under the verbs *reduce*, *reuse* and *recycle*. (2)

○ We calculated how green our class is. (5)

○ We produced a Green Action Plan for our classroom. (6)

○ We revised/learnt the verbs *reduce*, *reuse* and *recycle*. (1)

○ We added up our points, read the comments and formed groups according to our score. (4)

What did you learn?

Put the following statements on the board, and ask the children to rank them in order of importance for them.

(5 = most important, 1 = least important.)

○ *I revised/learnt new vocabulary related to the 3Rs.*

○ *I learnt how to classify my green actions under the 3Rs.*

○ *I learnt how green I am, and how green my classmates are.*

○ *I practised my reading, and understood a quiz.*

○ *I revised question forms in English in the quiz.*

○ *I learnt how I can become 'greener'.*

How did you learn?

Talk partners.

Using the statements above, ask the children to reflect on how they learnt.

Wordsearch solution

How well did you do?

Give the children the relevant My Activity Record page from Wilbur's toolkit on the website, and ask them to complete the *What have I learnt?* section.

Ask them to find and circle the three R words in the wordsearch with a *green* pen, and then to find and circle one of the adjectives with a *blue* pen, to assess how well they did this activity.

● *Excellent!*
● *Good.*
● *Terrible.*

Lead a discussion.

What do you need to do next?

Refer back to the success criteria and ask the children:

'What do you need to revise?'

The children fill in their My Activity Record page.

Share

The children do the quiz with their family, to find out how green they are.

The family add their comments on the My Activity Record page:
○ The children bring the Activity Record page to the next lesson.
○ You read the family's comments.

The children add the completed activity record to their portfolio.

The important thing about ...

Reading and defining

Age/level
8+ years; A1/A2

Activity type
Read and write

Response type
Written, personal, creative

Learning aims
To write a paragraph with a topic sentence and supporting sentences
To define and describe objects

Learning strategies
Generating paragraphs from a model
Drafting
Defining
Collaborating

Main outcome
Writing a paragraph about an object

Curricular/cultural links
English literacy; World Book Day, International Literacy Day

Values
Flexibility and caring: valuing creativity and seeing something special in day-to-day things

Assumptions
The children will need to be guided to identify the paragraph pattern, and will probably need help with vocabulary.

Materials
'The important thing about ...' example and book template from Wilbur's toolkit for each child; or copy it onto the board
(See also the example paragraph on page 91 opposite.)

Transfer
The children can write paragraphs about other objects, subjects, etc, using the same model.

I recommend ...
The Important Book

Plan

Explain the learning aims of the activity:
'We're going to learn how to write a paragraph about an object.'

Give or identify the following success criteria:
○ *Identify the pattern in the model.*
○ *Use the pattern to structure your own paragraph.*
○ *Use a dictionary, or ask your teacher if necessary.*

Hold up a ruler, and ask:
'What is the important thing about a ruler?'

Elicit responses.

Give the children a copy of 'The important thing about a ruler' example paragraph from Wilbur's toolkit, or copy it onto the board.

Ask them how the paragraph is organised.

Elicit:
It starts with a topic sentence stating the main important thing.
Then there are supporting sentences describing the object and giving details (x 3).
The final sentence repeats the main important thing.

Do

🔘 In groups, the children choose another classroom object, or an object of their own:
  ○ They draft a paragraph, using the 'The important thing about a ruler' pattern.

🔘 Tell them to be creative, and to think of details that are memorable and striking:
  ○ They can use dictionaries, if available.

🔘 The children check their drafts, and share aloud their paragraphs with the class.

🔘 They make suggestions, to improve the paragraphs.

🔘 They copy their final version onto the book template, draw a picture of the object and add it to their portfolios.

Do more

The children can collate their paragraphs into a class book – *The Important Book*.

Review

Conduct the review activities opposite.

This activity is inspired by *The Important Book* written by Margaret Wise Brown and published by HarperCollins.

Review activities

The important thing about ...

What did you do?

In pairs, the children complete the sentence:

○ *The important thing I did was* ....

Bring the class together, and each pair tells the class their important thing.

What did you learn?

In pairs, they complete the sentence:

○ *The important thing I learnt was* ....

Bring the class together, and each pair tells the class their important thing.

How did you learn?

Write these statements on the board, and ask the children to say which are the most important for them:

○ *I identified a pattern in a paragraph.*

○ *I used the pattern to organise my own paragraph.*

○ *I worked with my classmates.*

○ *I defined and described an object.*

○ *I listened to my classmates.*

○ *I used a dictionary.*

Lead a discussion.

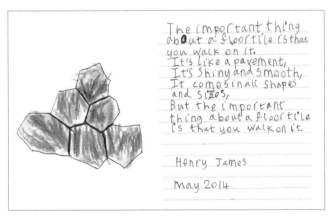

A paragraph from a 9 year old about a floor tile.

How well did you do?

Give the children the relevant My Activity Record page from Wilbur's toolkit on the website, and ask them to complete the *What have I learnt?* section.

Ask them to choose one of the comments and draw Wilbur next to it, as an assessment of how well they did this activity.

They then complete the paragraph about the activity.

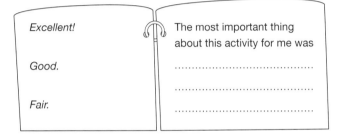

Lead a discussion.

What do you need to do next?

Refer back to the success criteria and ask the children:

'What do you need to revise?'

The children fill in their My Activity Record page.

Share

The children read their paragraphs to their family, and write a family paragraph – in English or the home language:

The important thing about learning English is ....

The family add their comments on the My Activity Record page:
○ The children bring the Activity Record page to the next lesson.
○ You read the family's comments.

The children add the completed activity record to their portfolio.

Learning English feels like ...

Writing a senses poem

Age/level
8+ years; A1/A2

Activity type
Read and write a poem

Response type
Personal, written, spoken and creative

Learning aims
To learn or revise the senses and related vocabulary
To recite a poem, using expressions and gestures

Learning strategies
Making associations
Generating a sentence from a model
Drafting
Using a dictionary

Main outcome
Writing a 'senses' poem (See examples in Wilbur's toolkit where younger children use drawings for their poem.)

Curricular/cultural links
Science: the five senses

Values
Accountability and flexibility: awareness of how to express the experience of learning English through the five senses

Assumptions
The children will have ideas for poems, but will need help with vocabulary.

Materials
Things for children to smell, taste, feel, see and hear (optional);
Sheets of A4 paper for each child, to write their senses poem;
English dictionary;
Five word cards for the Review activity (see page 93)

Transfer
The children can create senses poems on other topics: seasons, food, emotions …

I recommend ...
Rain; The Black Book of Colours

Plan

Explain the learning aims of the activity:
'We're going to learn how to write a senses poem.'

Give or identify the following success criteria:
○ *Think about what you can smell, taste, feel, see, hear.*
○ *Use your imagination, and be as creative as you can.*
○ *Ask your teacher for help with vocabulary, or use a dictionary.*
○ *Recite your poem with feeling.*

Write the five senses on the board, using mime and actions to support understanding.

Discuss, by asking the following questions:
Smell – *What can we smell?*   Sight – *What can we see?*
Taste – *What can we taste?*   Sound – *What can we hear?*
Touch – *What can we feel?*

If possible, have things for children to smell, taste, etc:
coffee, salt, something soft, something hard, colours, sounds …

Choose an object in the classroom to write a class poem. Describe it, using each sense:
A chair smells like trees in the forest.

Do

○ Tell the children they are going to write a senses poem about Learning English.

○ Write the following model on the board on separate lines:
Learning English smells like ....   *Learning English looks like ....*
Learning English tastes like ....   *Learning English sounds like ....*
Learning English feels like ....

○ The children work individually, with a partner or in small groups:
○ You give them a sheet of A4 paper to draft their poem.
○ You monitor and support with vocabulary as necessary.
○ You encourage the children to use an English dictionary.

○ They copy their final version into their portfolio, and illustrate as they wish.

○ They rehearse reciting their poems:
○ You show them how to be expressive and use gestures.

○ They recite their poems to the class:
○ The other children listen and comment.

○ You display copies of the poems in the classroom.

Do more

Using the same model, ask the children to write a senses poem about their own language:
Speaking my language (eg French) *feels like …*

Review

Conduct the review activities opposite.

Review activities

Learning English feels like ...

 ## What did you do?

Prepare cards with the following words:

○ Senses

○ Questions

○ Dictionary

○ Imagination

○ Senses poem

Give pairs of children a card and ask them to think of one thing they did, related to the word on their card. For example:

○ *We learnt/revised the senses.*

○ *We answered questions about what we can see, feel, smell, taste, hear.*

○ *We used our imagination to help us write a senses poem about 'Learning English'.*

○ *We asked our teacher to help us with words we didn't know in English, or we found them in the dictionary.*

○ *We recited our senses poems.*

Discuss the children's answers, and encourage further reflection.

 ## What did you learn?

Using the cards, ask the children what they learnt in relation to each word.

Discuss their answers, and encourage further reflection.

 ## How did you learn?

Using the cards, ask the children how they learnt in relation to each word.

Discuss their answers, and encourage further reflection.

Reviewing
The caterpillar drawing in Wilbur's toolkit on page 114 and on the website shows how drawing can also be used as an invaluable method for younger children to review their accomplishments. See also the Principle 4 activity in Part C on page 120.

 ## How well did you do?

Give the children the relevant My Activity Record page from Wilbur's toolkit on the website, and ask them to complete the *What have I learnt?* section.

They assess how well they this activity, by choosing which sense best describes the activity, and completing the sentence.

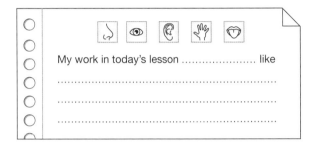

My work in today's lesson .... like
....
....
....

Lead a discussion.

 ## What do you need to do next?

Refer back to the success criteria and ask the children:

'What do you need to revise?'

The children fill in their My Activity Record page.

 ## Share

The children recite their senses poem to their family and write a senses poem together – in English or the home language:

Being a family (smells, looks, sounds, feels, tastes) like ...

The family add their comments on the My Activity Record page:
○ The children bring the Activity Record page to the next lesson.
○ You read the family's comments.

The children add the completed activity record to their portfolio.

My ideal English teacher

Writing a recipe

Age/level
9–10 years; A2

Activity type
Read and identify
Read and write from a model

Response type
Written, personal and creative

Learning aims
To learn/revise language related to recipes: *ingredients, quantities, method*
To write instructions, using the imperative: *add, bake, cool, fold in, mix, share, sprinkle, pour, pre-heat*
To learn vocabulary for personal qualities: *kind, understanding, intelligent, listening*
To understand and use metaphor

Learning strategies
Sorting
Generating recipes from a model

Main outcome
Writing a recipe using metaphor

Curricular/cultural links
Science; Maths; World Teachers' Day

Values
Accountability and caring: better understanding of the teacher's role in creating good conditions for learning.

Materials
A recipe of a typical dish from the children's culture – it can be in the mother tongue; A4 sheets of paper; A sample recipe (see Wilbur's toolkit)

Assumptions
The children probably understand the structure of a recipe, but may need the vocabulary in English.

Transfer
The children can write different recipes: *an ideal friend, mother, sister or brother …*

I recommend …
It's a Book;
Why Is The Sky Blue?

Plan

Tell children the learning aims of the activity:
'We're going to learn how to write about an ideal English teacher, using a recipe as a metaphor.'

Give or identify the following success criteria:
○ *Identify the structure of a recipe.*
○ *Use the imperative to write a recipe.*
○ *Identify qualities of an ideal English teacher.*

Ask the children to explain the purpose of a recipe.

Display a recipe from the children's culture, and identify the different sections:
○ Ingredients / Quantities / Method

Show the children the recipe from Wilbur's toolkit, and explain that the recipe is used as a metaphor for a lesson.

Ask the children to sort the vocabulary under the headings *Ingredients*, *Quantities* and *Method* – and write them on the board.

Do

- Ask the children:
  'What do they think makes an ideal English teacher?'

- Write their suggestions on the board under the heading 'Ingredients'. For example:
  500 grams of kindness
  5 kilos of interesting lessons

- Encourage the children to give more examples – and add them to the list.

- Complete the 'Method' section, using the imperative. For example:
  Mix 500 grams of kindness with 5 kilos of interesting lessons.
  Pour 1 kilo of good pronunciation …

- Give the children an A4 sheet of paper, and ask them to fold it in half to make a recipe book:
  ○ They write *Ingredients* on the left-hand inside page.
  ○ They write *Method* on the right-hand inside page.

- They write their own recipe.

- They create a cover page, and illustrate the recipes.

Do more

The children display their recipes around the classroom, and read them.

They add the recipe to their portfolio.

Review

Conduct the review activities opposite.

See Ellis, G and Read, C 'Creative recipes for planning lessons' CATS: *The IATEFL Young Learners SIG Publication*, 2006

See also 11-year-old David's recipe for a happy class in *Teaching Children to Learn* by David Fisher (Nelson Thornes, 2005)

Review activities

My ideal English teacher

Divide the class into three groups. Write the following words on the board:

Recipe   Ingredients   Method   Teacher

Ask different groups to answer Wilbur's three Review questions below.

 ### What did you do?

The children use the words above.

Group 1 say what they *did*.

 ### What did you learn?

The children use the words above.

Group 2 say what they *learnt* in this activity.

 ### How did you learn?

The children use the words above.

Group 3 say *how* they wrote the recipe about an ideal teacher.

Bring the class together, and ask for feedback from the three groups.

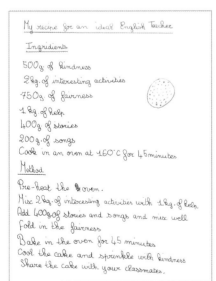

'My recipe for an ideal English teacher', from a 9 year old.

 ### How well did you do?

Give the children the relevant My Activity Record page from Wilbur's toolkit on the website, and ask them to complete the *What have I learnt?* section.

Ask them to give themselves a score out of ten, as an assessment of how well they did this activity.

10/10 = *Excellent!*

7/10 = *Good.*

5/10 = *I must work harder.*

My work today:

/10

Lead a discussion.

 ### What do you need to do next?

Refer back to the success criteria and ask the children:

'What do you need to revise?'

The children fill in their My Activity Record page.

 ### Share

The children show their families their recipe for an ideal English teacher.

They write a new recipe together. For example:

My ideal sister

The family add their comments on the My Activity Record page:
o The children bring the Activity Record page to the next lesson.
o You read the family's comments.

The children add the completed activity record to their portfolio.

Evidence of the impact of learning to learn

At the beginning of Part B, we encouraged you to reflect on your teaching and your pupils' learning as you use the activities we present in *Teaching children how to learn*.

At the end of Part B, we encourage you to look back on how teaching children how to learn has affected the teaching and learning process:

○ What impact have you noticed on your teaching and your pupils' learning?
○ What impact have your pupils noticed on your teaching and their learning?
○ What have your pupils' parents said?

Below are some comments from teachers, children and parents. You will find some further comments from teachers in Part C on page 143.

Keep a careful record of all the comments and store them in your English Teaching Portfolio. They will be invaluable evidence of the impact of integrating learning to learn into your classes.

 'What a child is able to do in collaboration today, he will be able to do independently tomorrow.'

Vygotsky, L S *Mind in Society* Cambridge, MA: Harvard Press 1978

Teachers' voices

- *'I thought it would be difficult to share information about language learning and activities, but I have realised that children are capable of a much greater level of understanding than I had given them credit for!'*

- *'When I used 'think-pair-share' time, I could see the children trying to think, and it included more of the class who would have sat back and not tried to answer.'*

- *'The children are more involved in taking responsibility for their own learning through the self-assessment techniques and through working in pairs.'*

- *'The review activities have helped my pupils to really focus not only on what they have learned, but also how they are learning. It's also helped me to reflect more on my planning and to assess my teaching.'*

- *'I have learned so much! I have become aware of how I can encourage the children to take ownership for their own learning.'*

- *'Integrating learning to learn into my classes has opened up a new area of worthwhile communication between myself and the children.'*

Children's voices

- *'I understand now what I have to do, and I feel much more sure of myself.'*

- *'It's OK if the answer isn't always right. That's how we learn.'*

- *'I like talking about my activity with my partner. We can share each other's ideas and help each other.'*

- *'I love the review activities. They really help me think about what I've enjoyed and what I'd like to do better.'*

- *'We can speak in English, we are freer and we make progress together.'*

- *'I feel as though I have learned English for myself.'*

- *'It allowed us to review lots of things, and if we had forgotten we now know what to revise.'*

Parents' voices

- *'Amine is more confident and is now able to talk to me about what he has done and learnt in his English class and takes pride in doing so.'*

- *'Katya has become much more observant, and points out words in English to me at home and in the street.'*

- *'Ricardo really enjoys using his English Language Portfolio, and I see he is becoming better organised. He also enjoys reviewing his work.'*

- *'Christophe can see he is making progress with his English and this makes him happy – and me too, of course!'*

- *'Yaroslav enjoys talking about his English lessons and showing me his work, so I feel more involved in his English language learning.'*

- *'Out of all her school subjects, she now enjoys English the most – I think she feels she has benefitted from the way the teacher tells the class what they are going to learn and why, and how to complete an activity successfully.'*

- *'We have more contact with the teacher, so we feel more involved and are able to work together.'*

Wilbur's toolkit

Activity worksheets and My Activity Record pages

Pages 98 to 114 include, in reduced format, everything that is available in Wilbur's toolkit on the website.

In the book, the pages are presented according to the order in which the activities appear in the book.

On the website, the Activity worksheets and the My Activity Record pages are presented separately.

Go to: *www.deltapublishing.co.uk/resources*
Click on the cover of the book.
Click on Wilbur's toolkit.
Click on Activity worksheets or My Activity Record pages.

My Language Passport

Put your photo
or a drawing
of yourself here.

My name is ....

I live in ....

My birthday is on .... I am .... years old.

The name of my school is ....

The languages I know are ....

I speak [ ] with my family.

I speak [ ] at school.

I speak [ ] with my friends.

I know [ ] as well.

I can read in ....

I can write in ....

My Activity Records

My Activity Records allow me to organise the activities I have done to learn English.
I can use my Activity Records to show my teachers and my parents what I have learnt.

**Examples of work I can choose
to put in my portfolio.**

....
....
....
....
....
....
....
....
....
....
....
....
....
....
....
....
....
....
....
....
....

My Favourite
Language Learning Strategies

Vocabulary:
....
....
....

Grammar:
....
....
....

Speaking:
....
....
....

Listening:
....
....
....

Reading:
....
....
....

Writing:
....
....
....

My Intercultural Experiences

Experiences or contacts I have had with people or places in or from other countries.
For example:
*holidays, postcards, people, visits, films, storybooks,
video exchanges, technology*

Experience or contact	Information	Date

My Activity Record

Activity title: **My English Language Portfolio**　　　Date: ....

What have I learnt?

....

....

What samples of work have I selected for my portfolio? Why?

....

Because ....

....

How well did I do?

Colour the face which shows how well you did this activity.

Complete the 'My portfolio will help me ...' sentence below, by choosing the phrase from the signpost which is the most important for you.

Discuss with your teacher and your classmates.

😊 *Excellent!*

😐 *Good.*

☹ *I must try harder.*

... organise my work.

... talk about my learning.

... take pride in my work.

... monitor my progress.

My portfolio will help me ....

What do I need to do next?

....

....

Sharing with my family.

Show your portfolio to your family, and tell them about it.

Ask them to write their comments on this Activity Record page.

My family's comments: ....

....

KWL grid

L — What have I **LEARNT**?

W — What do I **WANT** to know?

K — What do I **KNOW**?

Worm Facts

Hello! I'm Wilbur the worm.
I am an earthworm. I am useful.
I recycle the soil.
I'm going to help you learn English!
What do you know about me?
What else would you like to know?

Worm bodies

A worm is an animal. The earthworm is one of the most common worms:

- It has a long, thin, soft body and moist brown skin.
- It can be 30 centimetres long.
- It does not have any bones in its body, and does not have any legs.
- Its body has many sections, called segments.
- The segments have tiny hairs, called bristles, that help the worm to grip the ground.
- The pointed end of the earthworm is the head.
- It has five hearts.
- It does not have any teeth, eyes, ears or a nose.
- It does have a very simple brain and can sense objects, light and vibrations.
- Its mouth is on the underside of the first few segments, and it breathes through its skin.

Worm wiggles

Earthworms wiggle through soil:

- First, the worm stretches the front half of its body forwards.
- This makes its body long and thin.
- Then the earthworm pulls its tail end forwards, so that its body is shorter and fatter.

Worm homes

Earthworms live in burrows in damp soil. Some burrows can be more than a metre deep.

Worm meals

Earthworms eat soil and dead leaves.

Worm usefulness

Earthworms are very useful:

- They pull pieces of leaves, grass and other living things into the soil and mix up the soil as they make their burrow. This makes the soil richer.
- Their burrows help aerate the soil and let water drain away.
- The things that go through their bodies also go back into the soil.
- Earthworms are important decomposers, and recycle soil.
- They eat garden waste in compost heaps.

Worm life cycles

Earthworms usually lay about 20 eggs at a time. These are contained inside a protective case, called a cocoon.

After about three weeks, the eggs hatch and baby earthworms wiggle out of the cocoon and burrow their way into the soil.

They become juvenile earthworms, and it takes about six weeks to become an adult worm.

Many earthworms live four to eight years.

Worm enemies

Worms are the favourite food of birds and small animals such as moles, shrews and hedgehogs.

Worm types

There are many different types of worms of different colours, sizes and shapes:

- Some worms are very small, and live inside other animals.
- Some worms can grow up to 40 metres long!

My Activity Record

Activity title: **Wilbur the Worm: the facts**　　　Date: ....

What have I learnt?

....

....

What samples of work have I selected for my portfolio? Why?

....

Because ....

....

How well did I do?

Draw Wilbur on the ladder, to assess how well you did this activity.

Ask yourself why, and discuss with your teacher and your classmates.

5　*I can use a KWL grid by myself with this topic, and will use it again with another topic.*

4　*I can use a KWL grid by myself with this topic very well.*

3　*I can use a KWL grid by myself with this topic quite well.*

2　*I can use a KWL grid with the help of my teacher.*

1　*I am still learning to use a KWL grid.*

What do I need to do next?

....

....

Sharing with my family.

Use the KWL worksheet your teacher gives you, or draw one yourself.

Use it to find out how much your family knows about earthworms.

My family's comments: ....

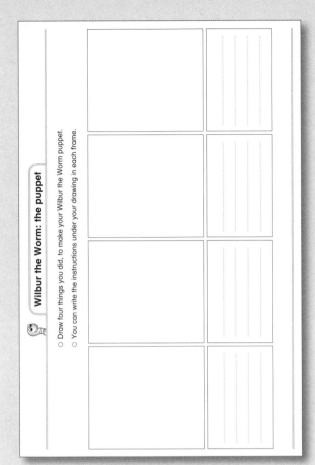

Wilbur the Worm: the puppet

○ Draw four things you did, to make your Wilbur the Worm puppet.
○ You can write the instructions under your drawing in each frame.

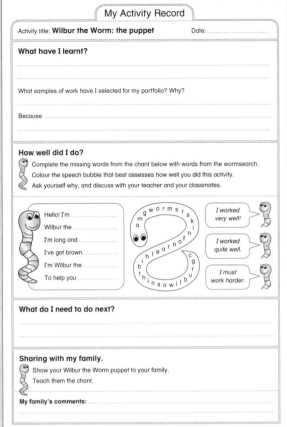

My Activity Record

Activity title: **Wilbur the Worm: the puppet**   Date: ....

What have I learnt?
....
....

What samples of work have I selected for my portfolio? Why?
....

Because ....
....

How well did I do?
Complete the missing words from the chant below with words from the wormsearch.
Colour the speech bubble that best assesses how well you did this activity.
Ask yourself why, and discuss with your teacher and your classmates.

Hello! I'm ....
Wilbur the ....
I'm long and ....
I've got brown ....
I'm Wilbur the ....
To help you ....

I worked very well!

I worked quite well.

I must work harder.

What do I need to do next?
....
....

Sharing with my family.
Show your Wilbur the Worm puppet to your family.
Teach them the chant.

My family's comments: ....
....

What's Fred wearing?

My Activity Record

Activity title: **What's Fred wearing?**   Date: ....

What have I learnt?
....
....

What samples of work have I selected for my portfolio? Why?
....

Because ....
....

How well did I do?
Colour the number of caps, to assess how well you did this activity.
Ask yourself why, and discuss with your teacher and your classmates.

Excellent! I understood all the nouns and adjectives, and drew them correctly.

Good. I understood most of the nouns and adjectives, and drew them correctly.

OK. I must try harder.

What do I need to do next?
....
....

Sharing with my family.
Prepare to do the *What's Fred wearing?* picture dictation (or another one).
Do the dictation with your family.

My family's comments: ....
....

Pat-a-cake!

Pat-a-cake, pat-a-cake, baker's man,

Bake me a cake as fast as you can.

Pat it and prick it and mark it with T,

And put in the oven for Tommy and me.

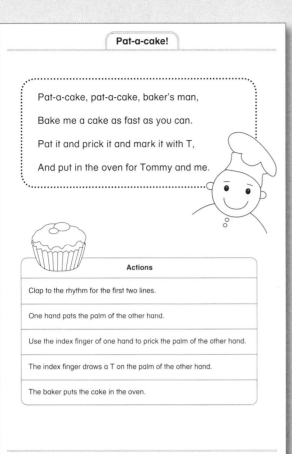

Actions
Clap to the rhythm for the first two lines.
One hand pats the palm of the other hand.
Use the index finger of one hand to prick the palm of the other hand.
The index finger draws a T on the palm of the other hand.
The baker puts the cake in the oven.

My Activity Record

Activity title: **Pat-a-cake!**   Date: ....

What have I learnt?

....

....

What samples of work have I selected for my portfolio? Why?

....

Because ....

How well did I do?

Colour the cakes, to assess how well you did this activity.

Ask yourself why, and discuss with your teacher and your classmates.

3 cakes = *Very good!*   2 cakes = *Good.*   1 cake = *I must practise more.*

I can say a traditional English rhyme.

I can discriminate between /æ/ and /ei/.

I can perform actions while I say a rhyme.

What do I need to do next?

....

....

Sharing with my family.

Teach your family the *Pat-a-cake!* action rhyme.

Recite it together.

My family's comments: ....

Everyone is different

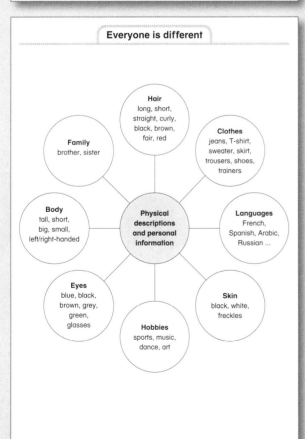

My Activity Record

Activity title: **Everyone is different**   Date: ....

What have I learnt?

....

....

What samples of work have I selected for my portfolio? Why?

....

Because ....

How well did I do?

Draw yourself in the mirror, with the expression that best shows how well you did this activity.

Ask yourself why, and discuss with your teacher and your classmates.

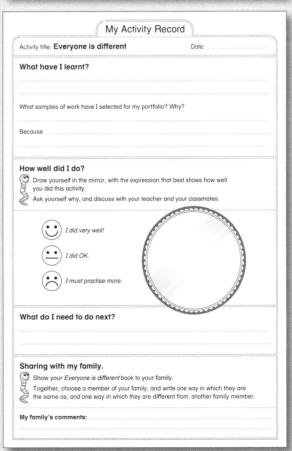

I did very well!

I did OK.

I must practise more.

What do I need to do next?

....

....

Sharing with my family.

Show your *Everyone is different* book to your family.

Together, choose a member of your family, and write one way in which they are the same as, and one way in which they are different from, another family member.

My family's comments: ....

H is for Halloween

lanky   room   eerie

white   orange

haunted   midnight   nasty

Alliteration = _____   Rhyme = ...

H is for _____ house,

And witches on a broom.

L is for _____ skeletons,

Laughing in the ....

O is for _____ pumpkins,

Wailing in the night.

E is for _____ ghosts,

Evil and pale ....

N is for _____ cats, nodding at ....

My Activity Record

Activity title: **H is for Halloween**   Date: ....

What have I learnt?

....

....

What samples of work have I selected for my portfolio? Why?

....

Because ....

....

How well did I do?

Select and colour a pumpkin, to assess how well you did this activity.

Ask yourself why, and discuss with your teacher and your classmates.

| *Excellent!*
 I understood everything. | *Good.*
 I understood most
 of the activity. | *OK.*
 I understood some
 of the activity. |

What do I need to do next?

....

....

Sharing with my family.

Teach your family the *H is for Halloween* poem.

Recite it together.

My family's comments: ....

....

How do you come to school?

Skills flashcards

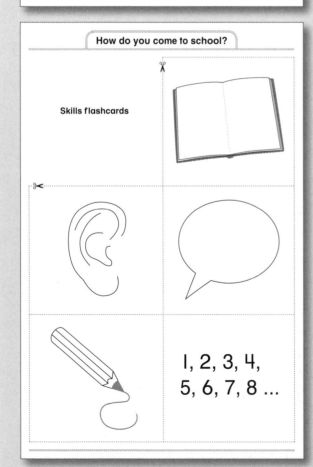

How do you come to school?

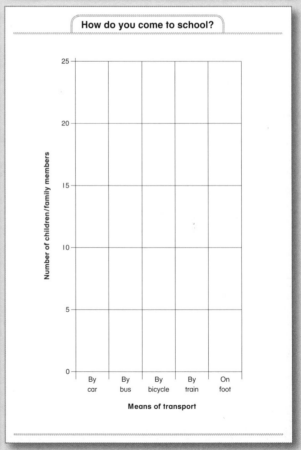

My Activity Record

Activity title: **How do you come to school?** Date: ....

What have I learnt?

....
....

What samples of work have I selected for my portfolio? Why?

....

Because ....

....

How well did I do?

Colour the bar graph, to assess how well you did this activity.

Ask yourself why, and discuss with your teacher and your classmates.

5: Blue = *Very well!*

3: Pink = *Quite well.*

2: Green = *Fair.*

	Very well!	Quite well.	Fair.
5			
4			
3			
2			
1			
0			

What do I need to do next?

....
....

Sharing with my family.

Complete a bar graph, using the worksheet your teacher gives you, to record how your family members go to school or work.

My family's comments: ....

A friend is someone who ...

Example

A family ...

- helps each other.
- plays games together.

A friend is someone who ...

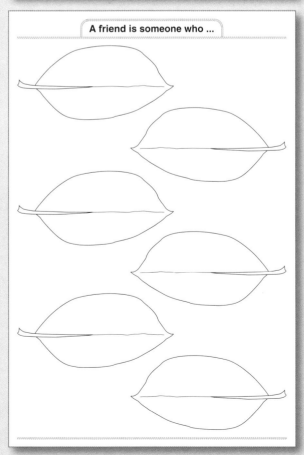

My Activity Record

Activity title: **A friend is someone who ...** Date: ....

What have I learnt?

....
....

What samples of work have I selected for my portfolio? Why?

....

Because ....

How well did I do?

Colour the leaf on the friendship tree that best describes how well you did this activity.

Discuss your assessment with your teacher and your classmates.

Excellent! Good. Fair.

What do I need to do next?

....
....

Sharing with my family.

Make a 'family tree' at home, using the tree worksheet that your teacher gives you.

Think of ideas and definitions with your family.

Write them on the tree together.

My family's comments: ....

My Activity Record

Activity title: **A listening experiment**   Date: ....

What have I learnt?

....

....

What samples of work have I selected for my portfolio? Why?

....

Because ....

How well did I do?

Colour the ears, to assess how well you did this activity.

Ask yourself why, and discuss with your teacher and your classmates.

3 ears = *I did very well!*   2 ears = *I did OK.*   I ear = *I must try harder.*

I can say the names of six objects.

I can ask and answer the question:
What is it? / It's a …

I can concentrate, in order to listen to
and identify different sounds.

What do I need to do next?

....

....

....

Sharing with my family.

Carry out the listening experiment at home with your family or friends.

Do it in English with them!

My family's comments: ....

Sounds in a town

School	Launderette	Monument
Park	Temple	Synagogue
Zoo	Baker's	Sports centre
Shop	Garage	Swimming pool
House	Hotel	Museum
Church	Café	Theatre
Mosque	Cinema	Apartments
Market	Hospital	Station
Library		

Sounds in a town

I syllable	2 syllables		3 syllables	
◯	◯◦	◦◯	◯◦◦	◦◯◯
School	Market	Hotel	Cinema	Museum
Park	Station	Launderette	Hospital	Apartments
Zoo	Temple		Library	
Shop	Baker's		Monument	
House	Garage		Synagogue	
Church	Café		Sports centre	
Mosque			Swimming pool	
			Theatre	

I syllable	2 syllables		3 syllables	
◯	◯◦	◦◯	◯◦◦	◦◯◦

My Activity Record

Activity title: **Sounds in a town**   Date: ....

What have I learnt?

....

....

What samples of work have I selected for my portfolio? Why?

....

Because ....

How well did I do?

Colour the traffic lights.

Assess how well you did this activity, and mark the syllables and word stress
on the adjective you choose.

Red = Average.

Yellow = Good.

Green = Excellent!

What do I need to do next?

....

....

Sharing with my family.

Choose five 'town' words in English, and test your family's pronunciation.

Correct their word stress, if necessary.

My family's comments: ....

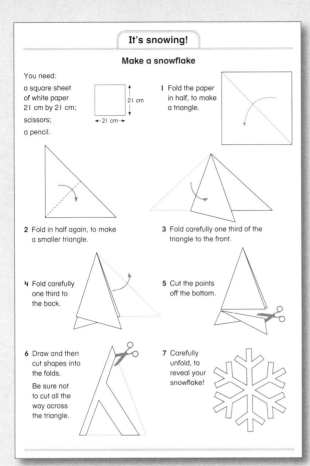

It's snowing!

Make a snowflake

You need:

a square sheet of white paper 21 cm by 21 cm; scissors; a pencil.

21 cm *←21 cm→*

I Fold the paper in half, to make a triangle.

2 Fold in half again, to make a smaller triangle.

3 Fold carefully one third of the triangle to the front.

4 Fold carefully one third to the back.

5 Cut the points off the bottom.

6 Draw and then cut shapes into the folds.

Be sure not to cut all the way across the triangle.

7 Carefully unfold, to reveal your snowflake!

It's snowing!

Snowflake search

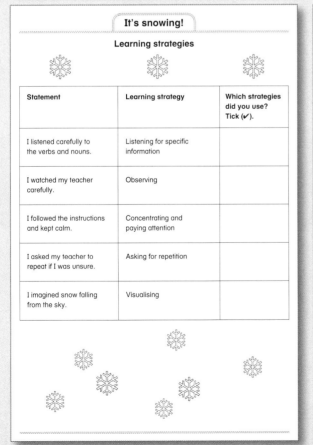

It's snowing!

Learning strategies

Statement	Learning strategy	Which strategies did you use? Tick (✔).
I listened carefully to the verbs and nouns.	Listening for specific information	
I watched my teacher carefully.	Observing	
I followed the instructions and kept calm.	Concentrating and paying attention	
I asked my teacher to repeat if I was unsure.	Asking for repetition	
I imagined snow falling from the sky.	Visualising	

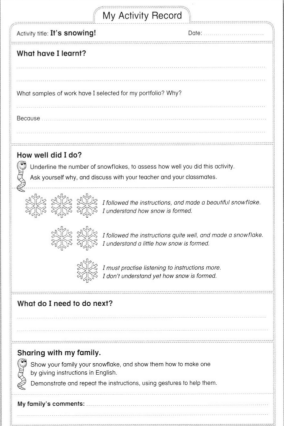

My Activity Record

Activity title: **It's snowing!**   Date: ....

What have I learnt?

....

....

What samples of work have I selected for my portfolio? Why?

....

Because ....

How well did I do?

Underline the number of snowflakes, to assess how well you did this activity.

Ask yourself why, and discuss with your teacher and your classmates.

I followed the instructions, and made a beautiful snowflake. I understand how snow is formed.

I followed the instructions quite well, and made a snowflake. I understand a little how snow is formed.

I must practise listening to instructions more. I don't understand yet how snow is formed.

What do I need to do next?

....

....

Sharing with my family.

Show your family your snowflake, and show them how to make one by giving instructions in English.

Demonstrate and repeat the instructions, using gestures to help them.

My family's comments: ....

....

105

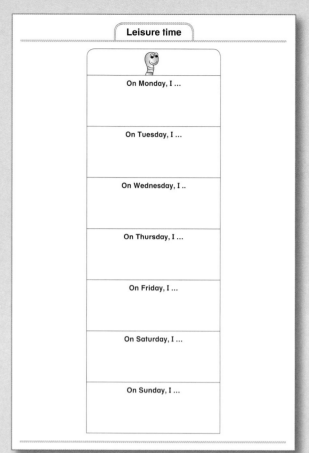

Leisure time

On Monday, I ...

On Tuesday, I ...

On Wednesday, I ..

On Thursday, I ...

On Friday, I ...

On Saturday, I ...

On Sunday, I ...

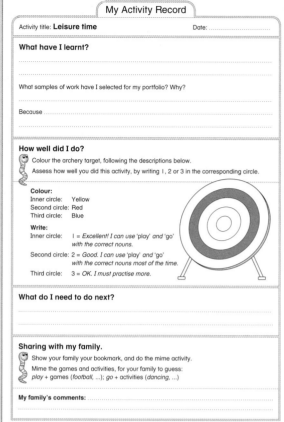

My Activity Record

Activity title: **Leisure time**   Date: ....

What have I learnt?

....
....

What samples of work have I selected for my portfolio? Why?
....

Because ....
....

How well did I do?

Colour the archery target, following the descriptions below.

Assess how well you did this activity, by writing 1, 2 or 3 in the corresponding circle.

Colour:
Inner circle: Yellow
Second circle: Red
Third circle: Blue

Write:
Inner circle: 1 = *Excellent! I can use 'play' and 'go' with the correct nouns.*

Second circle: 2 = *Good. I can use 'play' and 'go' with the correct nouns most of the time.*

Third circle: 3 = *OK. I must practise more.*

What do I need to do next?

....
....

Sharing with my family.

Show your family your bookmark, and do the mime activity.

Mime the games and activities, for your family to guess: *play* + games (*football*, ...); *go* + activities (*dancing*, ...)

My family's comments: ....
....

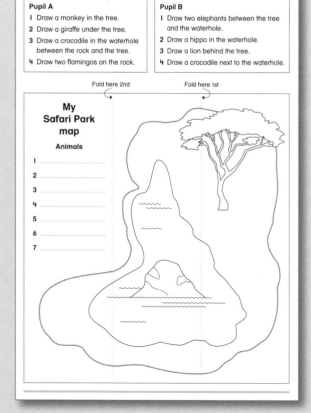

At the Safari Park

Pupil A
1 Draw a monkey in the tree.
2 Draw a giraffe under the tree.
3 Draw a crocodile in the waterhole between the rock and the tree.
4 Draw two flamingos on the rock.

Pupil B
1 Draw two elephants between the tree and the waterhole.
2 Draw a hippo in the waterhole.
3 Draw a lion behind the tree.
4 Draw a crocodile next to the waterhole.

Fold here 2nd   Fold here 1st

My Safari Park map

Animals

1 ....
2 ....
3 ....
4 ....
5 ....
6 ....
7 ....

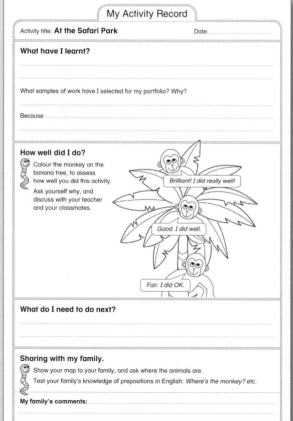

My Activity Record

Activity title: **At the Safari Park**   Date: ....

What have I learnt?

....
....

What samples of work have I selected for my portfolio? Why?
....

Because ....
....

How well did I do?

Colour the monkey on the banana tree, to assess how well you did this activity.

Ask yourself why, and discuss with your teacher and your classmates.

Brilliant! I did really well!

Good. I did well.

Fair. I did OK.

What do I need to do next?

....
....

Sharing with my family.

Show your map to your family, and ask where the animals are.

Test your family's knowledge of prepositions in English: *Where's the monkey?* etc.

My family's comments: ....
....

My Activity Record

Activity title: **My two hands**　　　Date: ....

What have I learnt?
....
....

What samples of work have I selected for my portfolio? Why?
....

Because ....

How well did I do?
Colour the thumb sign that best assesses how well you did this activity.

Ask yourself why, and discuss with your teacher and your classmates.

I worked hard, and can say what my two hands can do, and what my classmates' hands can do.

I worked hard, and can say what my two hands can do.

I must work harder. I can say a few things that my two hands can do.

What do I need to do next?
....
....

Sharing with my family.
Make a *My two hands can …* poster at home with your family.

Each family member writes on it something they can do with their hands, with their name next to it.

My family's comments: ....
....

My Activity Record

Activity title: **Earthworm – a poem**　　　Date: ....

What have I learnt?
....
....

What samples of work have I selected for my portfolio? Why?
....

Because ....

How well did I do?
Tick (✓) the line of the poem below that best assesses how well you did this activity.

Ask yourself why, and discuss with your teacher and your classmates.

Wonderful work today! ☐

Only OK today. ☐

Revision time today. ☐

Must work harder tomorrow. ☐

What do I need to do next?
....
....

Sharing with my family.
Recite the *Earthworm* poem to your family.

Teach them the poem and the actions, and put on a family recital!

My family's comments: ....
....

A royal feast

👑 Story 👑

Part 1

Once upon a time, there lived a king and queen in a big castle. King Jim and Queen Jean loved eating. One day, they decided to have a Royal Feast and invite all their friends. However, King Jim and Queen Jean could never agree about anything, and could not agree the menu. King Jim wanted food with the same sounds as *his* name, King Jim, and Queen Jean wanted food with the same sounds as *her* name, Queen Jean.

Part 2

Here is the menu their chef proposed. What food did King Jim want for the banquet and what did Queen Jean want?

👑 Royal Feast Menu 👑

Instructions
Listen and colour:
/iː/ sounds green, eg: pea
/ɪ/ sounds pink, eg: shrimp

Starters
Pea soup
Liver pâté
Cheese salad
Shrimp dip with crisps

Main courses
Grilled fish with chips
Roast beef with green beans
Roast chicken with chips
Cheese, bacon and leek pie

Desserts
Peaches and cream
Lemon whip
Peanut ice-cream
Sticky ginger biscuit

Tea or mint cordial with still or fizzy water

Part 3

But King Jim and Queen Jean could not agree the menu. Several weeks later, they were tired of arguing. 'Shall we include meat and fish?' asked King Jim. 'Yes, please,' said Queen Jean. 'Some people prefer meat and some people prefer fish.' So they included meat and fish on the menu, and everyone was happy. 'It was a delicious feast,' said King Jim. 'Yes, a very pleasing feast,' said Queen Jean.

A royal feast

How to make a crown

You need:
strips of card between 55–60 cm long and 6 cm wide for each child;
scissors;
sticky tape.

6 cm

55–60 cm

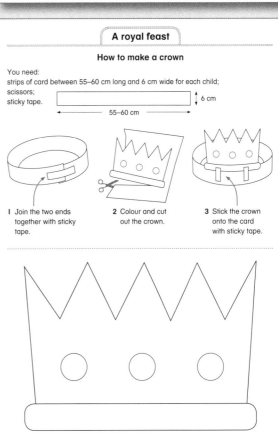

1 Join the two ends together with sticky tape.

2 Colour and cut out the crown.

3 Stick the crown onto the card with sticky tape.

My Activity Record

Activity title: **A royal feast**   Date: ....

What have I learnt?

....

....

What samples of work have I selected for my portfolio? Why?

....

Because ....

....

How well did I do?

Draw the number of crowns in the boxes on the Activity Menu below, to assess how well you did this activity.

Ask yourself why, and discuss with your teacher and your classmates.

Activity Menu

WWWW WWWW
Excellent!

| | **Starter – Plan!**
I understood the aims of the activity. | |

WWWW WWWW
Good work today.

| | **Main course – Do!**
I completed the activity. | |

WWWW
I must try harder.

| | **Dessert – Review!**
I reflected on what and how I learned. | |

What do I need to do next?

....

....

Sharing with my family.

Show the Royal Feast Menu to your family. Ask them to choose a starter, a main course and a dessert (help them with pronunciation!) and to write their name next to the dishes.

Act out the 'order scene' together if you wish.

My family's comments: ....

....

Our Language Learning Rights

Our Class Convention

Our English Language Learning Rights Convention

Class ....

Article 1
We have the right to think about how we learn English, to try out different learning strategies and review what we have learnt.

Article 2
We have the right to learn in the way we prefer, in class and at home.

Article 3
We have the right to have time before we answer a question.

Article 4
We have the right to learn together and help each other.

Article 5
We have the right to give our opinion about the activities we like doing, and to choose activities we prefer from time to time.

Article 6
We have the right to use our mother tongue or shared classroom language in the English class, to help us learn.

Article 7
We have the right to be listened to by our classmates.

Article 8
We have the right to be evaluated fairly, and not to feel silly if we make a mistake.

Article 9
We have the right to know the aims and purpose of a lesson.

Article 10
We have a right to say we don't understand, and to ask the teacher to repeat.

Our Rights and Responsibilities

Rights	Responsibilities
We have the right to …	**We are responsible for …**
have time before we answer a question.	waiting, and not shouting out the answer.
learn together, and help each other.	learning as much as we can, and sharing with each other.
give our opinion about the activities we like doing.	respecting each other's preferences.

My Activity Record

Activity title: **Our language learning rights**   Date: ....

What have I learnt?

....

....

What samples of work have I selected for my portfolio? Why?

....

Because ....

....

How well did I do?

Choose and colour the scales that best assess how well you did this activity.

Ask yourself why, and discuss with your teacher and your classmates.

Excellent!
I worked hard.   *Good.*
I worked quite hard.   *OK.*
I must work harder.

What do I need to do next?

....

....

Sharing with my family.

Show your family, and tell them about your Language Learning Rights convention.

Write together a 'My language learning rights at home' convention.

My family's comments: ....

My learning diary

Date: ....

Activity title: ....

I learnt these words at school: ....

I learnt how to: ....

The thing I did best was: ....

The thing I found difficult was: ....

Out of school, I have learnt English by: ....

My favourite word and picture is: ....

....

....

Because: ....

I need to revise: ....

My Activity Record

Activity title: **English around me**   Date: ....

What have I learnt?

....

....

What samples of work have I selected for my portfolio? Why?

....

Because ....

....

How well did I do?

Choose the comment that assesses how well you did this activity, and write it in the diary.

Add the date, and draw a picture that represents today's activity.

Discuss with your teacher and your classmates.

Very good! = I can record words in the way I prefer, to help me learn and remember.

Quite good. = I can record some words in the way I prefer, to help me learn and remember.

OK. = I'm still thinking about the way I prefer to record words.

Comment:	Date:
○	
○	

What do I need to do next?

....

....

Sharing with my family.

Show your family your portfolio and *English in the Environment* vocabulary diary.

Look for words in English together at home, at the shops, etc, and add them to your diary.

My family's comments: ....

....

My school day

Jane's school day in England

Each day, I get up at 7am, eat my breakfast, put on my school uniform, take my lunch box and school bag and walk to school.

First, I have Assembly at 8.45am.

Then I go to my first lessons in the morning, usually Maths and English.

At 10am, I have break time and I practise netball with my friends.

Lunch is at 12pm, and I take out my lunch box.

Next, I have History and Sports in the afternoon.

After that, I go home at 3.15pm and do my homework.

Finally, I have dinner at 7pm with my family, and go to bed at 9.30pm.

My Activity Record

Activity title: **My school day**   Date: ....

What have I learnt?

....

....

What samples of work have I selected for my portfolio? Why?

....

Because ....

....

How well did I do?

Colour the stars, to assess how well you did this activity.

Ask yourself why, and discuss with your teacher and your classmates.

☆ Gold
I can do this well!

☆ Silver
I can do this quite well.

☆ Bronze
I am still learning to do this.

☆☆☆ I can use time linkers.

☆☆☆ I can say two things that are the *same* about my school day and a school day in England.

☆☆☆ I can say two things that are *different* about my school day and a school day in England.

☆☆☆ I can use the simple present to talk about daily routines.

What do I need to do next?

....

....

Sharing with my family.

Tell your family about Jane's school day in England.

Discuss together what is the same as your school day, and what is different.

My family's comments: ....

....

Fireworks safety

Make a Fountain Firework

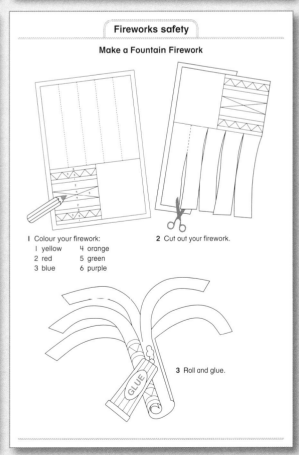

1 Colour your firework:
   1 yellow   4 orange
   2 red   5 green
   3 blue   6 purple

2 Cut out your firework.

3 Roll and glue.

Fireworks safety

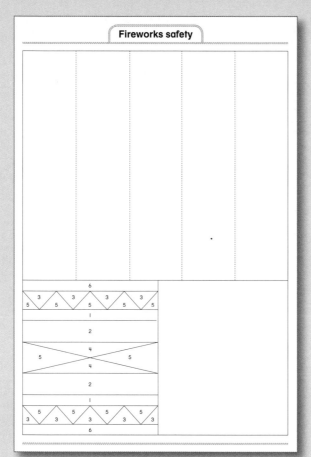

My Activity Record

Activity title: **Fireworks safety**   Date: ....

What have I learnt?

....

....

What samples of work have I selected for my portfolio? Why?

....

Because ....

....

How well did I do?

Colour a Catherine Wheel, to assess how well you did this activity.

Ask yourself why, and discuss with your teacher and your classmates.

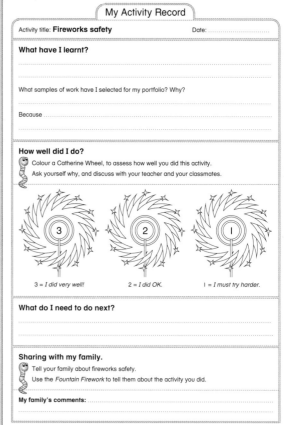

3 = I did very well!   2 = I did OK.   1 = I must try harder.

What do I need to do next?

....

....

Sharing with my family.

Tell your family about fireworks safety.

Use the *Fountain Firework* to tell them about the activity you did.

My family's comments: ....

....

Reading faces

My Activity Record

Activity title: **Reading faces**   Date: ....

What have I learnt?

....

....

What samples of work have I selected for my portfolio? Why?

....

Because ....

....

How well did I do?

Colour the face with the expression that best describes how well you did this activity.

Ask yourself why, and discuss with your teacher and your classmates.

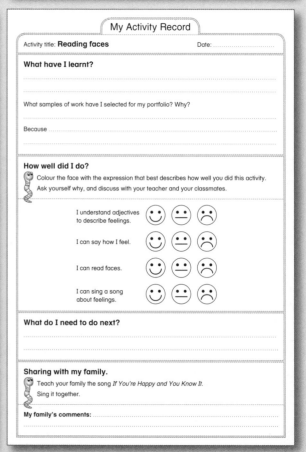

I understand adjectives to describe feelings.

I can say how I feel.

I can read faces.

I can sing a song about feelings.

What do I need to do next?

....

....

Sharing with my family.

Teach your family the song *If You're Happy and You Know It*.

Sing it together.

My family's comments: ....

....

Don't be a bully!

☺ **Friends ...**	make me feel happy.
☹ **Bullies ...**	respect me.
steal my things.	hit me.
say nice things about me.	spread rumours about me.
make fun of me.	help me.
like to play with me.	exclude me from games.
frighten me.	care about me.
call me names.	share their things.

Don't be a bully!

Anti-bullying images

Don't be a bully / Be a friend

Please don't make fun of me.

Don't pick on me

Don't make me feel sad. Be my friend!

Don't let anyone feel left out ... ... be a good friend!

Don't ignore it

My Activity Record

Activity title: **Don't be a bully!**   Date: ....

What have I learnt?

....

....

What samples of work have I selected for my portfolio? Why?

....

Because ....

How well did I do?

Ask a friend and your teacher to colour the expression that best assesses how well you did this activity.

Then assess yourself, and discuss with your teacher and your classmates.

Colour the friends.

My friend says ...

| Fantastic! | Good effort. | OK. | Try harder next time. |

My teacher says ...

| Fantastic! | Good effort. | OK. | Try harder next time. |

I say ...

| Fantastic! | Good effort. | OK. | Try harder next time. |

What do I need to do next?

....

....

Sharing with my family.

Show your portfolio and anti-bullying poster to your family.

Tell them what you have learnt about bullying.

My family's comments: ....

The water cycle

Stages of the water cycle

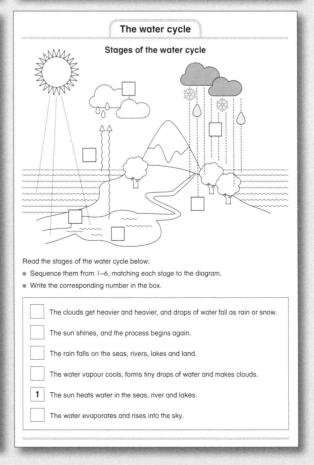

Read the stages of the water cycle below:

● Sequence them from 1–6, matching each stage to the diagram.

● Write the corresponding number in the box.

☐	The clouds get heavier and heavier, and drops of water fall as rain or snow.
☐	The sun shines, and the process begins again.
☐	The rain falls on the seas, rivers, lakes and land.
☐	The water vapour cools, forms tiny drops of water and makes clouds.
1	The sun heats water in the seas, river and lakes.
☐	The water evaporates and rises into the sky.

The water cycle

Stages of the water cycle
Key

I	The sun heats water in the seas, river and lakes.
2	The water evaporates and rises into the sky.
3	The water vapour cools, forms tiny drops of water and makes clouds.
4	The clouds get heavier and heavier, and drops of water fall as rain or snow.
5	The rain falls on the seas, rivers, lakes and land.
6	The sun shines, and the process begins again.

My Activity Record

Activity title: **The water cycle**   Date: ....

What have I learnt?

What samples of work have I selected for my portfolio? Why?

Because ....

How well did I do?

Colour the number of rain clouds, to assess how well you did this activity.
Ask yourself why, and discuss with your teacher and your classmates.

I worked hard, and can describe the water cycle. I understand how rain is formed.

I worked quite hard, and can describe most of the water cycle. I understand a little how rain is formed.

I must work harder. I don't understand yet how rain is formed.

What do I need to do next?

Sharing with my family.

Show your family the *Water cycle* worksheet.
Tell them about the different stages of the water cycle.

My family's comments: ....

How green am I?

Quiz

I What does your family recycle?
a) glass and paper
b) nothing at all
c) all glass, paper, cans, batteries, plastic

2 When you leave a room, do you turn off the lights ...
a) sometimes?
b) never?
c) always?

3 How do you go to school?
a) by bus or train
b) by car
c) by bike, or on foot

4 What do you carry the shopping home in?
a) old, used plastic bags
b) new plastic bags each time
c) our family shopping bag/basket

5 Do you usually have ...
a) a shallow bath?
b) a deep bath?
c) a shower?

6 In the street, do you put your rubbish ...
a) in your pocket/bag, to throw away at home?
b) on the ground?
c) in the bins provided?

7 Do you buy ...
a) eggs in a cardboard box?
b) eggs in a plastic box?
c) organic eggs in a cardboard box?

8 When you brush your teeth, do you ...
a) put some water in a glass?
b) keep the water tap running?
c) turn the tap off while you brush your teeth?

Now add up your points:		
a) answers	2 points	
b) answers	0 points	
c) answers	3 points	
	TOTAL points	

How green am I?

Reduce	**Reuse**	**Recycle**
• We turn off lights to reduce electricity. • We turn off electrical equipment, computer, TV, etc, to reduce electricity. • We put on an extra jumper rather than turn up the heating.	• We give our clothes that are too small to our younger brother and sister. • We give things we don't use to a charity shop. • We reuse old paper.	• We take empty bottles to the bottle bank. • We put our used paper and newspapers in the paper bin for recycling. • We make toys out of old material.

Quiz scores

Bright green card	20 points and over. Excellent! You are **bright green**! You care about the environment and look after it.
Pale green card	10 points and over. Good. You are **pale green**! You are trying to be green but you need to find out more about the things you can do.
White card	10 points and below. Terrible. You are **not green at all**! You know very little about the environment and have a lot to learn.

My Activity Record

Activity title: **How green am I?** Date: ....

What have I learnt?

....

....

What samples of work have I selected for my portfolio? Why?

....

Because ....

....

How well did I do?

Find and circle the three R words with a *green* pen:
- ○ *Reduce*
- ○ *Reuse*
- ○ *Recycle*

Look vertically, horizontally and diagonally.

Now find and circle with a *blue* pen the adjective below that assesses how well you did this activity:
- ○ *Excellent*
- ○ *Good*
- ○ *Terrible*

Ask yourself why, and discuss with your teacher and your classmates.

M	N	C	L	X	A	Y	L	U	K	E	Q
X	N	L	S	S	Z	W	C	K	A	X	H
F	B	T	E	R	R	I	B	L	E	C	F
A	R	E	D	U	C	E	O	P	D	E	R
O	T	X	O	T	E	Y	U	T	B	L	Z
S	G	W	V	D	R	T	E	S	A	L	A
D	O	W	R	E	C	Y	C	L	E	E	I
O	O	K	X	H	L	M	U	C	E	N	C
K	D	N	O	Z	W	U	X	A	J	T	I

What do I need to do next?

....

....

....

Sharing with my family.

Do the quiz with your family.

Find out how green they are!

My family's comments: ....

....

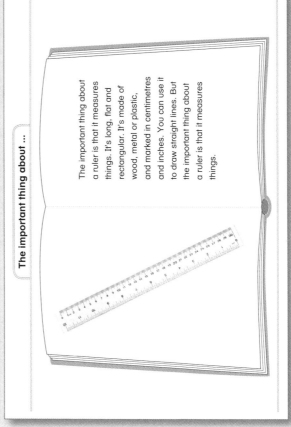

The important thing about ...

The important thing about a ruler is that it measures things. It's long, flat and rectangular. It's made of wood, metal or plastic, and marked in centimetres and inches. You can use it to draw straight lines. But the important thing about a ruler is that it measures things.

The important thing about ...

My Activity Record

Activity title: **The important thing about ...** Date: ....

What have I learnt?

....

....

What samples of work have I selected for my portfolio? Why?

....

Because ....

....

How well did I do?

Draw me, Wilbur the Worm, next to the expression on the left-hand page below that assesses how well you did this activity.

Then complete the paragraph on the right-hand page below.

Discuss with your teacher and your classmates.

Excellent!

Good.

Fair.

The most important thing about this activity for me was

....

....

....

What do I need to do next?

....

....

....

Sharing with my family.

Read the paragraph you wrote in class to your family, and explain how it is organised.

Write a paragraph together, beginning: *The important thing about learning English is ...*

My family's comments: ....

....

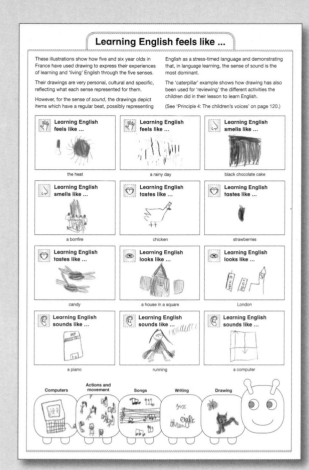

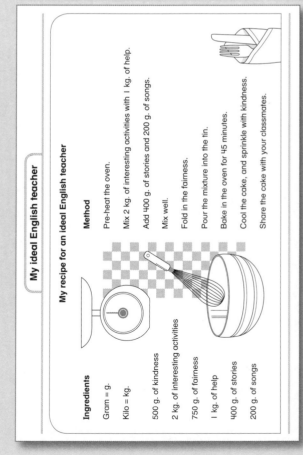

'We do not learn from experience … we learn from reflecting on experience.'
John Dewey [1]

Teaching children how to learn has so far provided the theoretical rationale to learning to learn and the pedagogical principles which underpin the activities in Part B. You may already have been able to use these activities with your classes.

In Part C, we are going to consider the importance of reflecting on your practice as part of your professional development.

Throughout this book, there is an emphasis on encouraging your *learners* to develop a spirit of enquiry by adopting a critical and enquiring approach to their learning through questioning and reflection, and also for *you* to do the same to your *teaching*.

John Hattie [2] refers to the teacher as a powerful support to and influence on learners: *'Teachers seem to be the single most powerful influence on students' learning.'*

One of the many ways teachers can provide this support and influence their learners, is to accept their responsibility to continue to grow and develop professionally in order to deliver ongoing quality teaching which impacts on their pupils' learning and achievement.

This will include actively engaging in personal and professional development, and viewing both teaching and learning as continually evolving processes.

In order to understand the relationship between theoretical principle and practical technique, we have encouraged you to follow Henry Widdowson's description of good language teachers who *'will refer technique back to principle, testing one out against the other in a continual process of experimentation'.* [3]

This reflection can empower you, by leading to more effective teaching and, consequently, greater motivation and job satisfaction, as well as improved pupil learning and progress.

Reflective practice gives a theoretical underpinning to many of the techniques and strategies you use intuitively.

Enquiry, then, is the starting point for Part C, which contains teacher development activities that will engage you systematically in reviewing and reflecting on your teaching:

○ The activities are structured around the 'plan do review' learning cycle, to enable you to experience this as applied to your own professional development.
○ The fourth stage, *Share*, encourages you to support, exchange and collaborate with your colleagues, as they can be a key source of ideas and inspiration.

The activities which explore the areas for developing professionally are first outlined on page 116.

Developing professionally

Pedagogical principles

These activities are related to each of the pedagogical principles in Part A which underpin the activities in Part B of *Teaching children how to learn*. Following your practical experimentation in Part B, the activities in Part C now give you the opportunity to further reflect on and develop awareness of how techniques relate to the principles.

You are also asked to consider the benefits and importance of the principles for your own context, as well as the impact they have had on the way you teach, on your pupils' learning and on your relationship with them.

Teaching strategies

These are related to selected teaching strategies necessary for implementing learning to learn, to other strategies which complement the activities in *Teaching children how to learn* and to your teaching in general.

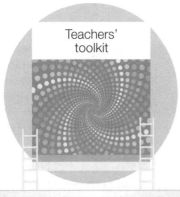

Teachers'
toolkit

The Teachers' toolkit (see page 149) contains all the Keys, Commentaries and Transcripts for the activities in Part C.

 A number of downloadable templates are available in the Teachers' toolkit on the website (see page 171).

1 Dewey, J *Democracy and Education: An Introduction to the Philosophy of Education* Simon & Brown 2011

2 Hattie, J 'Teachers make a difference. What is the research evidence?' *https://cdn.auckland.ac.nz/assets/education/hattie/docs/teachers-make-a-difference-ACER-%282003%29.pdf*

3 Widdowson, H 'The incentive value of theory in teacher education' *English Language Teaching Journal* 38 (2) 1984

Ongoing development strategies

These are in the form of longer term projects which will help you develop systematic methods and strategies for assessing the effectiveness of your teaching. The activities proposed engage you in action research and, in particular, a project on evaluating learning to learn, peer observation, and the development of an English Teaching Portfolio.

Self-assessment

We have seen the importance of helping children learn how to review and assess their performance in order to perceive a sense of progress as well as identify next steps. Self-assessment is also important to your development, and the activities in Part C involve you in this process.

In addition, there is a final overall self-assessment activity which gives you the opportunity to think about the strategies and knowledge you have acquired or improved as a result of using *Teaching children how to learn*, and what you want to improve or acquire in future.

Based on your self-assessment, you are invited to draw up your own personal action plan.

English Teaching Portfolio

An English Teaching Portfolio related to your teaching practice of learning to learn will help you reflect critically on your teaching, your pupils' learning and your own personal development and achievements. Think about what format your portfolio will take and what it will contain:
- It can adopt a paper or a digital format.
- It can contain examples of lesson plans, notes on observed lessons and examples of your pupils' work, such as completed worksheets, drawings, photos and any comments (see page 96) about their learning.
- It can contain your personal reflections, notes and worksheets from Part C, including your self-assessment and your action plan.

An English Teaching Portfolio is also useful to keep records of workshops or conferences you have attended, articles, books – including a record of storybooks you have used – and websites. Remember to organise and date all the items you collect in ways that are meaningful to you. You will be able to look back and feel pride in what you have achieved.

Principle 1
Modes of input and types of response

Aim

To become aware of the range of multimodal resources that can be used to present language and convey meaning, in order to plan and integrate these strategically into your lessons.

Plan

'Multimodal perspectives to teaching build on the basic assumption that meanings are made through many forms and resources of which language is but one – image, gesture, gaze, body posture, sound, writing, music, speech, and so on.' Carey Jewitt

1 Look at the quote above:
○ *Which resources do you currently use in your teaching, and why?*

2 When you are planning your lessons:
○ *Do you consider using a variety of resources to present language and convey meaning? Why? Why not?*

3 What types of response do the different resources generate in class?

Do

1 The following resources are commonly used to introduce or revise language and convey meaning. Do you use any others?
○ storybooks; verbal instructions, commands, explanations, eliciting, questions; songs, chants, rhymes; DVDs/films; CDs; flashcards; diagrams/charts; sound effects; dialogues; objects, realia; written descriptions; actions, gestures, expressions; apps, online language games.

2 How could the language items listed below be presented, using these multimodal resources? The first example is provided.

3 Compare your ideas with the suggestions in the Key on page 150.

Review

1 Consider the benefits of planning and integrating multimodal resources into your lessons. Evaluate how important you consider these to be for your context, on a scale of 1–5.
(1 = not very beneficial, 5 = very beneficial.)

- [ ] It allows the children to use their existing language resources to respond to input.
- [ ] It gives the children the opportunity to show their understanding, by responding in ways other than through language alone.
- [ ] It respects diversity, as it caters for the children's individual learning differences and preferences.
- [ ] It provides variety, which fosters motivation and enthusiasm.
- [ ] It makes learning more memorable and enjoyable.
- [ ] It makes learning more accessible to children with a range of needs.
- [ ] It creates more meaningful lessons.

2 Next steps: Consider how you will expand the multimodal resources you currently use, and how you will plan to integrate these into your lessons.

Share

1 Ask a colleague to observe a lesson and complete a table like the one below, in order to identify the range of multimodal resources you use and the children's responses to these.

2 After the lesson, discuss how effective they were.

3 Reciprocate the experience.

Language item	Multimodal resources	Response from children to show understanding	Type of response (see page 24)
Parts of the body	*The teacher gives verbal instructions/commands.*	*The children respond to teacher verbal input through movement.*	*Physical*
Actions			
General understanding of a story and vocabulary related to food			
Dialogue about going to the zoo			
Saying what you can do (sports)			
Saying how you come to school			
Your choice:			

Jewitt, C 'Multimodal Teaching and Learning' In *The Encyclopedia of Applied Linguistics* Chapelle, C A (Ed) Blackwell Publishing Ltd 2013

Principle 2
English Language Portfolio

Aim

To reflect on the criteria children can use, to select samples of work for their English Language Portfolio.

Plan

'Portfolios offer a child-friendly way of assessing language development and gaining insight into children's views, attitudes, and language learning strategies.'
Sophie Ioannou-Georgiou and Pavlos Pavlou

1 What systems does your school currently have in place, to encourage the children to assess their learning and organise their materials?

2 How effective are these?

Do

The English Language Portfolio is an integral part of the methodology of *Teaching children how to learn*. Introducing a portfolio is an ongoing process:
○ Children need time before they can use them effectively.
○ Children need guidance on how to choose samples of work to include in their portfolio.

1 What samples of work can the children include in an English Language Portfolio?

See Key 1 on page 150.

2 What criteria can the children use, to help them select work independently for their portfolio?

3 Ideally, the criteria should be negotiated with the children. Here is one example a child suggested:

I tried hard with this piece of work.

....

....

....

....

See Key 2 on page 150.

Review

1 As you begin to use a portfolio with children, have you noticed any changes in the following?
○ *Your relationship with the children?*
○ *The children's ability to organise their work better?*
○ *The children's confidence in taking on more responsibility for their learning?*
○ *The children's motivation?*
○ *The children's ability to assess their own performance, account for their own learning and identify the next steps?*
○ *The children's attitudes towards their English language learning?*
○ *The children's willingness to make an effort, and take pride in their work?*
○ *The children's ability to monitor their progress, and reflect on their learning?*
○ *The children's ability to select work independently for inclusion in their portfolio?*
○ *The children's ability to justify their selection of samples of work?*
○ *The parents' interest and involvement in their child's English language learning?*

2 What impact has this had on the way you teach?

3 Next steps: Consider what you need to improve, to help the children select samples of work for their portfolios independently.

Share

1 Invite the parents to comment on the use of the English Language Portfolio, and invite them to the school for a meeting to share their views.

2 Show other teachers in your school some examples of English Language Portfolios, and discuss how portfolios could be used by teachers of other subjects.

Note

If your resources allow, you may like to design a digital version of an English Language Portfolio.
See *http://eelp.gap.it/*.

Ioannou-Georgiou, S and Pavlou, P *Assessing Young Learners* (p23) OUP 2003

Principle 3
Assessment for learning

Aim

To identify and write success criteria for self-assessment.

Plan

1 Choose an activity in Part B, and look at the *Learning aims* and the *Success criteria*.

> ### Definitions
>
> ***Learning aims*** can be described as the *'What'* and the *'Why'* of the learning experience:
> - A learning aim describes what pupils should *know*, *understand* or *be able to do* by the end of the lesson – or series of lessons – as a result of the learning and teaching activities.
>
> ***Success criteria*** are the parts of the learning activity that are essential in achieving the learning aim(s) – in other words: the *'How'* of the learning experience.
>
> If learners are to take more responsibility for their own learning, then they need to know:
> - *what* they are going to learn;
> - *how* they will recognise when they have succeeded;
> - *why* they should learn it in the first place.
>
> *Success criteria* also help teachers to decide whether their pupils have, in fact, achieved the learning aim.

2 For each activity, identify the following:
- *What are the children going to do?* (activity)
- *What are the children going to learn?* (learning aims)
- *How are the children going to find out if they have been successful?* (success criteria)

3 Ask yourself:
- *How effective are the success criteria you currently provide?*

Do

1 Look at the statements below, and categorise them as follows:
Activity: *What the children are going to do.*
Learning aim(s): *What the children are going to learn.*
- Make a leaflet about healthy eating.
- Colour a picture.
- Write sentences with capital letters and full stops.
- Listen carefully and identify the different colours in English.
- Review and practise language on the topic of health and healthy eating.
- Write an email introducing yourself.

See Key 1 on page 151.

2 Write the *Success criteria* that match the *Learning aims*.

See Key 2 on page 151.

Review

1 In order to ensure that your success criteria are effective, ask yourself the following questions:
- *Are the success criteria in language the children will easily understand?*
- *Do some of the success criteria need to be explained, by modelling or showing the children examples?*
- *Do the success criteria match the initial learning aims?*
- *Do the success criteria refer to the specific skills, knowledge and understanding that you want the children to learn?*
- *Does the activity provide the opportunity for the children to demonstrate all of the success criteria?*

2 Next steps: Try out the teaching technique **Two Stars and a Wish**, to assess your response to this activity and to consider what to do as a result. See the explanatory note below.

Think about two things that you have learnt and understood in this activity. (two stars)

Think of one thing that you would *like* to know more about, or that you *need* to find out more about. (a wish)

★ ....
....
★ ....
....
☆ ....
....

Share

1 Display examples of *Learning aims* and *Success criteria* in the staff/teachers' room for your colleagues to identify.

2 Teach your pupils to use Two Stars and a Wish.

Two Stars and a Wish is a teaching technique often used to provide feedback via peer- and self-assessment:
- The children identify two positive aspects of a piece of work.
- They then identify an area where there can be improvement.

It can be used in class in the following three ways:
- Model the technique several times, by reviewing anonymous examples of work with the whole class and get all the children to provide feedback.
- Break the class up into pairs to review each other's work.
- Get each child to assess their own work.

It helps empower the children as owners of their learning. Research suggests that self-regulation of learning leads to improved performance.

Principle 4
The children's voices

Aim

To look at the child's right to be heard, and at some of the methods teachers can use to enable the children to voice their opinions and preferences about language learning, and to encourage teachers to listen to their perspectives and act on these.

Plan

'You have the right to give your opinion and for adults to listen and take it seriously.'
Article 12, UN Convention on the Rights of the Child (1989)

1 Reflect on your classroom practice:
○ *What methods do you currently use to enable the children to talk about their learning?*
○ *How do you act on what they say?*

2 Look at the examples in Wilbur's toolkit (*Learning English feels like …* on page 114 and on the website) of how young children have used drawing to express their **experience** of learning English through the five senses. The caterpillar underneath shows how children have also used drawing to **review** the activities they did during a lesson:
○ *What do you think are the benefits of using drawing?*

Do

1 The table below lists some of the methods you can use for listening to the children's interests, priorities, concerns, preferences, experiences and opinions about their English language learning.

Methods	How they can be used
Drawing.	
Filming the children doing an activity or talking about language learning.*	
The teacher or the children take photos of the main outcomes, or of the activity they are doing.*	
Interviewing or questioning the children. For example: reviewing.	
The children discussing learning together.	
Other:	

* See page 34 for information on obtaining parental consent.

2 Comment on how these can be used, and then see the Key on page 151.

3 Prepare a 'Review' stage for an activity, based on the five reflection questions used in Part B, and choose *one* method to elicit children's views on their learning.

4 List any action you will take as a result of what children said, by completing the sentence stems below:
○ *I need to do more of …*
○ *I need to do less of …*
○ *I need to review …*
○ *I need to work on …*
○ *I need to bring in …*
○ *Other …*

Review

1 Consider the benefits of listening to the children about their English language learning. Evaluate how important you consider these to be for your context, on a scale of 1–5.
(1 = not very beneficial, 5 = very beneficial.)

- [ ] Children become active participants in, and contributors to, their own learning.
- [ ] Children become more independent.
- [ ] Children become involved in decision-making, which increases motivation.
- [ ] Children become more self-aware about their English language learning.
- [ ] Children can participate through their preferred modes of communication without the need to rely on oral or written accounts.
- [ ] Teachers gain an insight into what the children think.
- [ ] Teachers are better informed to plan the next steps in learning.
- [ ] Teachers become better listeners.
- [ ] Teachers understand better the way the children learn and their learning preferences.
- [ ] Parents become more involved in their child's learning.

2 As you begin to listen to children's perspectives, have you noticed any changes in your relationship with the children?

3 Next steps: Refer back to the actions you will take in Do, Step 4, and prioritise these.

Share

1 Talk to your colleagues about your experience of encouraging the children's voices.

2 Read the comments about learning to learn on page 96 that other children have made. Ask your pupils to give *their* views and add *their* comments. Display them in your classroom.

Principle 5
Informed activities

Aim

To reflect on how and when you currently inform your pupils about the value and purpose of the activities and techniques you use in the classroom.

Plan

Consider your current teaching context:
- ○ Do your pupils understand what they are learning, and why?
- ○ Do you inform your pupils of the purpose of an activity?
- ○ Do you provide them with a good reason for what they are doing?

What do you consider are the benefits of sharing this information with the children and informing them of the value and purpose of learning activities and techniques?
- ○ Compare your thoughts with Key 1 on page 152.

How and when do you:
- ○ inform your pupils of the learning aims of an activity/lesson?
- ○ inform your pupils of the purpose of learning activities or techniques?
- ○ inform your pupils about why they are using certain strategies?
- ○ get your pupils to reflect on how they are learning?

Do

1 Here are some common activities and techniques used in the primary English language classroom:

- Singing a song in a round (see Note 1 opposite)
- Action rhyme
- Information gap
- Sequencing
- What's missing?
- Picture dictation
- Wordsearch
- Roleplay
- Total Physical Response
- Online language game
- Other:

2 Choose three, and rehearse how you will explain in child-friendly language the purpose of these activities/techniques to a class you are currently teaching. Consider the children's age, cognitive ability and the language you will use, eg:
- ○ the target language (English)
- ○ the shared classroom language
- ○ metalanguage

See Note 2 for an example of explaining a pairwork activity.

3 Compare your explanations with those in Key 2 on page 152:
- ○ *What is the same?*
- ○ *What is different?*
- ○ *Why?*

Review

1 On a scale of 1–5, rate how easy or difficult you found this activity:

1 Very easy	2 Easy	3 Neither easy nor difficult	4 Difficult	5 Very difficult

2 Explain your rating.

3 As you begin to inform the children explicitly of the value and purpose of their learning activities and techniques, have you noticed any changes in the children?
- ○ *Their attitudes to English language learning?*
- ○ *Their participation in language learning activities?*
- ○ *Their understanding of the importance and relevance of language learning activities?*
- ○ *Their awareness of themselves as language learners?*
- ○ *Their ability to work more independently?*

4 What impact has this had on your changing relationship with the class, and the way you teach?

5 Next steps: Be prepared to explain the value and purpose of your activities for each lesson you teach.

Share

Work with colleagues to build up a bank of explanations written in child-friendly language, to make primary English language activities and techniques 'informed'.

Note 1

To sing a song in a round, you divide your class into groups – for example, four groups:
- Each group starts the song at a later point.
- When each group finishes the song, they start again.
- They go 'round and round' an agreed number of times.

Frère Jacques and *London's Burning* are famous rounds.

Note 2

'Pairwork means you work together with a partner to practise speaking English by yourselves. You will learn to listen to each other, take turns and help each other. It will help you find out how well you can use English.'
- Explain your role during pairwork, to reassure the children:
  - You will not correct them during pairwork.
  - You will listen and identify any language they are having difficulties with, and will correct and help with this afterwards.
- Explain that they can ask you or another pupil for help if needed, but the main purpose is to practise speaking on their own.

Principle 6
Routines

Aim

To better understand the value of establishing effective routines in the primary English language classroom, and to become aware of the guidance and intervention techniques you can use in the review stage of the 'plan do review' routine.

Plan

1 Make a list of the routines you currently use in your classroom.

See Table 1 on page 124.

Consult the Key on page 154.

2 Now focus on the Review stage of the 'plan do review' routine. Add to the list of the guidance and intervention techniques you currently use in review sessions.

See Table 2 on page 124.

Do

1 Analyse the transcripts from the review sessions on page 123, identify the guidance and intervention techniques the teachers are using and complete the table below. An example from Transcript 1 is provided.

	Guidance/ intervention techniques	Language used	Time
1	Focusing attention Retelling the story Summarising and recapping	*OK. Our book, our book, *our story* *How the kangaroos ...* **So we talked about our book, and that helped us learn some vocabulary: colours ...*	3 mins
2			
3			
4			
5			

2 Compare the transcripts:
○ *Which teachers, in your opinion, are more successful?*
○ *Why?*

See the Transcript notes on page 155.

Review

1 Here are some of the benefits of using routines. Evaluate how important you consider them to be for your context, on a scale of 1–5. (1 = not very important, 5 = very important.)

☐ They save valuable class time.
☐ They enable the children to develop a sense of timing, and predict what is going to happen next.
☐ They facilitate classroom management.
☐ They allow the children to feel more secure and confident, as they know what is going to happen next.
☐ They help develop the class community, and promote cooperation.
☐ They provide opportunities for language acquisition.
☐ They allow the children to become more independent, as they know what is expected of them.

2 As you begin to run systematic review sessions, have you noticed any changes in the children?
○ *Their attitudes to English language learning?*
○ *Their ability to speak about their language learning and account for their learning?*
○ *Their ability to demonstrate a more informed and conscious knowledge of their learning?*
○ *Their ability to understand themselves better as language learners?*
○ *Their ability to reflect on both the content and the process of learning ?*
○ *Their ability to work more independently?*

3 What impact has this had on your changing relationship with the class, and the way you teach?

4 Next steps: Decide which routines you are going to establish in your class, and how you are going to improve the quality of your review sessions.

Share

1 Encourage your colleagues to record and transcribe some review sessions.

2 Discuss together the most effective guidance and intervention techniques used, and the language used (target language, shared classroom language, metalanguage).

Principle 6
Routines

| **Transcripts from review sessions** | *Italics* Words spoken in the target language, ie: English. | **Square brackets** Teacher's intonation, gestures, expressions, actions, use of props, etc. |
| | * **and no italics** Words translated from, or spoken in, the mother tongue or shared classroom language, eg: French. | T = Teacher Ps = Pupils |

1 5/6 year olds. Final review of the week.

Working on the story *How the kangaroos got their tails*. Told by George Mung Mung Lirrmiyarri. Compiled by Pamela Lofts. Scholastic, 1996.

T *What did you learn this week?*
Ps *We cut out some masks.*
Ps *We made a book.
T *Why did we make a book?
Ps *To write the story of the kangaroos and their tails.
T *So we spoke mainly about the kangaroos, *kangaroos.*
Ps *… the spiders.*
T *We worked on the spiders, because …*
Ps *We made some nice spiders.
T *Yes, some nice spiders, *nice spiders. OK.*
Ps *… the computers.*
T *OK. Our book, our book, *our story. How the kangaroos …*
Ps *… got their tails.*
T *Good, and there's a …* [rising intonation]
Ps *big kangaroo and a small kangaroo.* [teacher continues to elicit story mainly in English]
T *So we talked about our book and that *helped us learn some vocabulary: colours …*

2 9 year olds. End-of-lesson review.

Based on *The Snowman* by Raymond Briggs (Puffin).

T *What did you do today?
Ps *We played some games.
T *OK, we played some games, but which games?
Ps *We drew a snowman.
T *You drew a snowman.
Ps *We continued the story.
T *Wait. We're going to speak about the game, and then we'll come back to the story. OK, the game, let's speak about the game. Why did we play the game? What did you learn?
Ps *… body.
T *Good. Parts of the body. Can you tell me which parts of the body?*
Ps *Head, body, eyes, mouth, nose, neck, arms, legs.*
T *What about the clothes?*
Ps *Necklace.*
T *Necklace? Good try! Yes, it's something that goes around the neck. Look, I'm wearing a necklace* [points to own necklace]. *Is the snowman wearing a necklace? What's the snowman wearing around his neck?*

Ps *A scarf.*
T *A scarf, good. Look: necklace* [pointing to own necklace] *and scarf* [pointing to snowman's scarf]. *Both go around the neck. And a …* [rising intonation]
Ps *… a hat, and buttons.
T *A hat and buttons, good. *So we played the game … We played the game to learn the parts of the body and some clothes but also to play together, and each person had to take a turn. Very good.*

3 5/6 year olds. End-of-lesson review.

T *What song did we sing today?
Ps *Head, houlders, knees and toes. Knees and toes.*
T *Yes, good. And why did we do the movements* [mimes movements] *with the song?*
Ps *Parts of the body.*
Ps *To show where we are.
Ps *To know what we are saying.
T *Yes. *Because when we say *head* we touch *the head* and we know that *head* means head. The actions help us remember the words. Good.*

4 9 year olds. Post-activity review.

T *What did you learn in this activity?*
Ps *We put the story in order …
T *And to put the story in order, you had to …
Ps *listen …
T *listen to what …? The key words, the nouns.
Ps *Yes.*
T *Good. Tell me the nouns.*

5 7 year olds. Post-activity review.

T *What did we do?
Ps *We played bingo.
T *We played bingo. Why?
Ps *Parts of the kitchen.*
T *To learn …*
Ps *the different parts of the kitchen.
T *kitchen …*
Ps *objects.*
T *And to do the activity, what did you do? How did you learn?*
Ps *Concentrate.
T *Good. Concentrate and …
Ps *the ears
T *Ears? Listen. *Good. We played bingo to practise listening and concentrating, and to revise the vocabulary for kitchen objects.*

Principle 6

Table 1

Routine	Purpose	Form it takes	Guidance/intervention techniques	Language used	Time
Getting children's attention	To establish good learning conditions.	Teacher rings a small bell / shakes a tambourine / puts a hand up.	Using multimodal signals, eg: a bell. Giving instructions.	*Listen carefully, children.* *Quiet, everyone!*	30 seconds

Table 2

Routine	Purpose	Form it takes	Guidance/intervention techniques	Language used	Time
Reviewing	To reflect on the content and process of learning.	Class discussion.	Asking questions. Focusing the children's attention.	*What did you learn today? Wait! We're going to speak about the game and then we'll come back to the story.*	5 minutes

Principle 7

Strategies to encourage home–school connections	Accessible to parents	Manageable for the teacher	Convenience factors; culturally appropriate; meets expectations	Comments
Parent guide				
Parent meetings				
Special events, eg: story presentation, book fair, award ceremony, celebrating cultural events				
Observation of classes				
Open days				
Courses/workshops for parents				
Text messages				
E-mail				
Posters/notices				
Telephone				
Drop-off and pick-up contact				
Suggestion box				
Language learning portfolio / note book; homework book				
Other:				

Principle 7
Home involvement

Aim

To reflect on ways of planning and establishing positive and effective communication channels with parents, to facilitate home–school connections and involvement.

Plan

'The effects of teaching in the classroom and the influence of out-of-school factors need to be considered together in planning teaching programmes.' ELLiE (p6) 2011

How does your school establish home–school connections and involvement? As a starting point, consider these questions:

○ *What steps does your school take to involve parents in their children's English language learning?*
○ *How does your school inform parents about your language programme and methodology?*
○ *How effective are any systems of written communication between school and home?*
○ *Does your school arrange meetings with parents?*
○ *What efforts are made to keep in touch with parents who do not attend the meetings?*
○ *How does your school carry out the induction of children and parents who are new to the school?*
○ *How are parents encouraged to support their children's English language learning?*
○ *Is there any provision to 'train' parents to do this in the most effective way?*
○ *Are parents invited into the school or the classroom?*
○ *Are there any ways of improving what you already do?*

Do

1 In the table on page 124, there are are some strategies your school could use to encourage home–school connections. Comment on the suitability of each strategy for your context. Consider:

○ Mode of communication – face-to-face, written/visual, telephone, digital.
○ Language – target language, home language, other.

2 Choose one strategy you think your school should develop, and write a plan to implement your strategy.

Review

1 Below are some of the benefits of establishing effective home–school connections. Evaluate how important you consider them to be for your school, on a scale of 1–5.
(1 = not very beneficial, 5 = very beneficial.)

☐ It can maximise the children's learning time.
☐ Good collaboration with parents is an incentive for teachers to improve their work.
☐ Good communication has a positive effect on the children's learning.
☐ It reassures parents.
☐ It helps manage parental expectations.
☐ It contributes to a whole-school approach.
☐ It helps the parents understand the approach used to teach their children.
☐ It can help resolve issues.
☐ It allows the teachers to report on the children's progress.
☐ It builds relationships and fosters collaboration between teachers and parents.

2 Next steps: Organise a meeting with teachers in your school, to discuss your plan for implementing your strategy to encourage home–school connections.

Share

Mentor a less-experienced colleague, to help them develop the interpersonal skills and strategies to work with parents.

Enever, J 'ELLiE Early Language Learning in Europe' (p6) British Council 2011
http://www.teachingenglish.org.uk/article/early-language-learning-europe

Principle 8
Values

Aim

To reflect on techniques you can use to promote values in your teaching.

Plan

'When you quarrel with your friends, it's better if you can forgive.'
Joanne, 5 years

'I used to be in trouble a lot. But values make you think about what you're doing. Now I hardly get told off at all. And I don't get told off so much at home either.'
James, 8 years

(http://www.valuesbasededucation.com/impact.quotes.html)

1 Consider and then complete these definitions for values, before consulting Key 1 on page 156:

○ *Values are principles that* ....
   ....

○ *Values empower children to* ....
   ....

2 What are your school's values?
○ *How different or similar are they to those promoted through the activities in 'Teaching children how to learn'? (See page 28.)*

Values promoted in *Teaching children how to learn*	Values promoted in my school
Accountability	
Caring	
Flexibility	
Resilience	
Tolerance	

3 Are there any other values that you consider should be promoted in your context?
○ *Which ones, and why?*

Do

1 Below are some techniques that are used throughout this book:
○ *Which values do they help promote, and how?*

Technique	Value(s) promoted	How?
Talking stick		
English Language Portfolio		
Class discussion		
Self-assessment		
Talk partners		
Making a class convention		
Other:		

See Key 2 on page 156.

2 Choose a value that you aim to promote in your next lesson:
○ *Which technique(s) will you use to help develop this?*

Review

1 As you begin to promote values through your English language teaching, have you noticed any changes in the children?
○ *Their attitudes to collaborating and working together, to build the class community?*
○ *Their effort in their English language learning?*
○ *Their willingness to manage any difficulties in their English language learning?*
○ *Their ability to account for their English language learning?*
○ *Their resourcefulness in finding solutions to any problems?*
○ *Their understanding and respecting similarities and differences?*

2 What impact has this had on your changing relationship with the class, and the way you teach?

3 Next steps: Think about what you need to do, to promote values in your teaching.

Share

Build a bank of techniques with colleagues, to promote values in your school.

Principle 9
Cross-curricular links

Aim

To consider the benefits of creating links between English and other subject areas in the primary curriculum.

Plan

1 Think of your English language lessons, and identify an occasion when you have linked content to another area of the curriculum:
○ *What did you teach?*
○ *What area of the curriculum did it link to?*

2 Where did the content originate?
○ *In a coursebook?*
○ *A photocopiable activity?*
○ *A project you devised?*
○ *An area of the curriculum children were working on?*
○ *A topic suggested by the children?*
○ *The internet?*

3 Think about these questions:
○ *Did you need to teach the children any specific vocabulary?*
○ *Did you need to learn any specific vocabulary?*
○ *Did you need to do any additional planning for this lesson?*
○ *Did the children show greater interest in the lesson than usual? If so, why?*

Do

When planning a lesson around a content area, you need to take the following factors into account.

Write the questions you need to ask yourself at the planning stage in the table below. An example has been provided.

Factors	Questions
Content area	*What content area would interest the children?*
Language demands	
Cognitive demands	
Conceptual demands	
Activities	
Learning to learn	
Resources/technology	
Outcomes	

See Key 1 on page 157.

Review

1 What are the benefits of linking content in the primary English classroom to other areas in the curriculum? Complete the gaps in the sentences below with the words in the box.

knowledge	content	links
understanding		educational
values-based	conceptual	experience

1 It draws upon the children's everyday ....

2 It allows for .... to be made between home and school.

3 It encourages the children to bring school .... to the language class.

4 It develops and builds on the children's .... of the world.

5 It caters more clearly for the children's wider .... needs and interests.

6 It can help reinforce certain key .... areas that cross subject boundaries.

7 It allows for .... reinforcement across subject areas.

8 It includes aspects of .... education to encourage the children to think about tolerance, friendship, accountability, etc.

See Key 2 on page 158.

2 Next steps: Consider what do you need to do, to create more links between English and other subject areas in the primary curriculum.

Share

Together with a colleague, decide on a content area you would like to develop with a class and complete a bubble map like the one below.

Use the questions from this activity to help you.
See Key 1 on page 157.

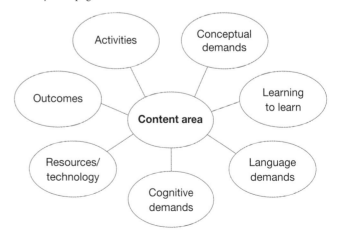

Principle 10
A main outcome

Aim

To reflect on the variety of forms main outcomes can take, to select and plan these effectively.

Plan

We have seen that the activities in *Teaching children how to learn* have a main outcome.

1 List some of the main outcomes of activities you have already used, either from this book or your own activities, and note down any comments from the children:

Activity	Main outcome	Children's comments

2 Which main outcomes were the most successful? Why?

3 Which main outcomes were less successful? Why?

Do

1 Main outcomes can take a variety of forms regarding how they are organised, how long they take and the time available and where they are carried out. Complete the table below by ticking (✓) the appropriate box.

Note: You can tick more than one box in each category, but you should justify your reasons for doing this.

See the Key on page 158.

2 How will this information assist you in your selection and planning of main outcomes?

Review

1 Rank the benefits of main outcomes in order of importance for your context. (1 = low importance, 5 = high importance.)

- [ ] They provide an incentive to the children.
- [ ] They make work more meaningful, purposeful and motivating.
- [ ] They provide opportunities for learner choice.
- [ ] They can offer opportunities for individual or collaborative work.
- [ ] They link classroom learning with the outside world and the family.
- [ ] They encourage the children to personalise their learning.
- [ ] They offer opportunities to develop creativity.
- [ ] They consolidate and extend language learning.
- [ ] They provide opportunities for integrated skills work and collaboration with other subject teachers.
- [ ] They allow the children to make use of non-linguistic skills, such as art or photography, within a language learning context.
- [ ] They can be recorded, filmed or organised in portfolios, as records of achievement.
- [ ] They provide opportunities for the children to develop social skills.
- [ ] They offer opportunities to use and integrate digital technologies.

2 Next steps: Reflect on what you need to improve, to better select and plan main outcomes.

Share

Build up a repertoire of main outcomes that have worked well in your class, and share with colleagues.

Main outcome	Organisation			Length		Place	
	Individual work	Group work	Whole-class work	1 or 2 lessons	Several lessons	In the classroom	Outside the classroom
Making a snowflake.	✓			✓		✓	
Designing a poster.							
Performing a roleplay.							
Conducting a survey.							
Giving a story presentation.							
Researching a topic.							
Creating a display.							
Conducting a quiz.							
Other – your choice:							

Teaching strategies
Using the mother tongue or shared classroom language

Aim

To identify why and when it is strategic to use the children's mother tongue or shared classroom language in the primary English language classroom.

Plan

'UNESCO supports mother tongue instruction as a means of improving educational quality by building upon the knowledge and experience of the learners and teachers.'

Teachers have different approaches to using the mother tongue, or not, in their classes:

○ This can be because of personal beliefs about the nature of language learning and teaching, or because of a school policy.
○ We have also pointed out that children should have the right to use their mother tongue in the English classroom to help them learn (Convention on the Rights of the Child: Article 30).

1 Do you ever use the mother tongue or shared classroom language in your English language lessons?

Always	Occasionally	Never

If yes, why? If no, why not?

2 Think of an occasion when and why you have used the mother tongue in an English language lesson, and consider:

○ the activity or situation;
○ the age of the children;
○ their level of English.

Did the switch to the mother tongue:

○ help you teach a particular language point?
○ help the children understand the lesson better?
○ help manage the lesson?

If yes, how?

3 Do you think you could have done this without switching to the mother tongue? If yes, how?

Do

1 Look at the classroom situations below, and match them with the use of the mother tongue, before looking at the Key on page 159.

Classroom situations	Using the mother tongue
• A child starts crying. • A lesson about the theme of friendship. • Playing a board game to practise language. • A child is chattering incessantly. • Asking the children what and how they have learnt. • The children ask you the meaning of a word. • Teaching the present perfect. • A reading text mentions 'custard' and 'high tea'.	• Translating vocabulary that may not be essential to the lesson, but will help the class understand. • Conducting review sessions. • Explaining a grammatical rule. • Explaining the meaning of an abstract concept. • Explaining a cultural reference. • Explaining a task, or giving instructions. • Disciplining. • Comforting a child.

2 Add any other examples of your own.

Review

1 Consider the statements about using the mother tongue in the primary English language classroom, and complete the table below.

2 Next steps: Plan how you are going to use the children's mother tongue or shared classroom language in your next lesson.

Share

Discuss your comments with a colleague, and compare opinions.

'Education in a Multilingual World' Education Position Paper UNESCO 2003: *http://unesdoc.unesco.org/images/0012/001297/129728e.pdf*

Using the mother tongue or shared classroom language ...	How useful is this, and why?	How could it be done differently?
... allows you to explain to the children what and how they are going to learn.		
... allows you to move from what is known to what is new, by serving as a cognitive springboard for comprehension of concepts and language in English.		
... plays an affective role and can reassure the children in the English language classroom.		
... strategically keeps the pace of the lesson fluid and prevents loss of interest.		
... is efficient for reviewing, and valorises and empowers the children's voices.		

Teaching strategies
Using the target language

Aim

To reflect on the benefits of, and techniques for, using the target language.

Plan

The strategic and appropriate use of the mother tongue or shared classroom language can improve efficiency, speed and enjoyment of learning. However, the main goal of a primary English language teacher remains English language teaching and using the target language as much as possible and encouraging learners to do so.

1 Which of the following reasons for using the target language is the most important for your context?

(1 = least important, 5 = most important.)

☐ It enables the children to see how English is used for a variety of purposes – giving instructions, praising, socialising, doing language activities, etc – as well as providing opportunities to hear and use real, natural English.

☐ It encourages the pupils to respond in English, which provides practice in listening and speaking and helps them acquire words and expressions.

☐ It helps the children become aware that English is a language used for real communication and not just a school subject.

☐ It provides valuable exposure to the language.

☐ It develops positive attitudes to the language and to the speakers of the language.

2 In the early stages of language learning, children sometimes use their mother tongue or shared classroom language.

○ *How can you respond to 'mother tongue talk'?*

Many teachers use recasting. This technique involves repeating what the children say in the mother tongue in the target language, as this shows them they are understood, they hear what they said repeated in English, and it helps them start using English.

○ *What other techniques can you use?*

3 Think how you, or someone you have observed, communicate with very young children. You have probably noticed that you modify your speech by speaking a little more slowly and clearly and using lots of paralinguistic features such as intonation, gesture, facial expression and actions. This is known as 'child-directed speech' – see the Note opposite for further information.

○ Make a list of other ways you modify your speech when communicating with very young children.

○ Compare with Key 1 on page 159.

4 Do you modify your speech like this in your English classes?

○ What do you think are the benefits of modifying your speech to help children acquire language? (See Key 2 on page 159.)

Do

Identifying child-directed speech.

On page 131 is a transcript from a storytelling session with a class of 9-year-old near-beginners in France using *The Snowman* by Raymond Briggs. Identify examples of 'child-directed speech' the teacher is using, by completing the gaps with the following words:

> expands   makes eye contact   personalises   pauses
> praises   questions   gestures   recasts   relates   repeats

See Key 3 on page 159 and the Commentary on page 160.

Review

1 As you begin to use child-directed speech to maximise the use of the target language, have you noticed any changes in the children?

○ *Attitudes to speaking more English in their lessons.*

○ *Confidence to take risks and speak more English in their lessons.*

○ *Understanding that they can communicate in English in the same way they can in their mother tongue.*

○ *Efforts to speak in English.*

○ *Ability to notice mistakes and improve.*

○ *Dependence on using the mother tongue.*

2 Next steps: Think about what you need to do, to improve your techniques for using the target language.

Share

1 Record and transcribe parts of your lessons, to identify your use of 'child-directed speech'.

2 Choose the best examples, and discuss with your colleagues.

Note

Jean Aitchison refers to **'child-directed speech'** as the speech, often used intuitively, by parents or carers to develop a child's first language. The features of child-directed speech are listed in Key 1 on page 159. It is also known as 'motherese' or 'caretaker talk'. Child-directed speech is not universal. In some societies, adults do not engage in conversation or verbal play with very young children. However, in every society, children are in situations in which they hear language that is meaningful to them in their environment in order to achieve full competence in the community language. (See Patsy Lightbown and Nina Spada.)

Aitchison, J *The Language Web* Cambridge University Press 1997

Briggs, R *The Snowman* Picture Puffins 1980

Lightbown, P M and Spada, N *How Languages are Learned* (3rd edn.) OUP 2006

Teaching strategies
Using the target language

From a storytelling session with a class of 9-year-old near-beginners using *The Snowman*.

Complete the gaps with the following words:

> expands   makes eye contact   personalises
>
> pauses   praises   questions   gestures
>
> recasts   relates   repeats

> ***Italics*** Words spoken in the target language, ie: English.
>
> *** and no italics** Words translated from, or spoken in, the mother tongue or shared classroom language, eg: French.
>
> **Square brackets** Teacher's intonation, gestures, expressions, actions, use of props, etc.
>
> T = Teacher   Ps = Pupils

T   *James said, Let's go …* [teacher uses slightly questioning intonation and pauses. She points to the picture and …….. **1** …….. in an upwards movement to prompt and elicit 'upstairs']

Ps *upstairs.*

T   *Upstairs. Let's go upstairs* [teacher smiles and nods, repeats the key word, then …….. **2** …….. by putting the key word into a complete phrase] *And James whispered at the door …*

Ps *Shhh! Be quiet!*

T   *Yes. Shhh! Be quiet! Just like I say to you!* [teacher confirms and repeats, using mime and sound effects and then …….. **3** …….. by relating it to the children] *This is my …* [she uses slightly raised intonation, pauses, points to the picture to prompt children]

P   parents' bedroom.

T   *Good. My parent's bedroom. This is my parents' bedroom.* [teacher …….. **4** …….., repeats and expands] *And in the bedroom the Snowman put on a …* [teacher pauses, points to the picture and elicits 'tie']

Ps *une cravate.

T   *Yes, a tie. A tie. Yes. Like Benjamin.* [teacher confirms, recasts and repeats. She then …….. **5** …….. it to the here and now, by referring to one of the children who is also wearing a tie]

Ben *And Mehdi.* [Benjamin points out another pupil who is wearing a tie]

T   *Oh, yes. That's right, Ben! Well observed! And Mehdi. Mehdi's wearing a tie too.* [teacher …….. **6** …….. with Ben and acknowledges his contribution and expands into a complete sentence.] *Good. And some … What are these?* [teacher brings children's attention back to the story, points to the glasses and elicits] *Lunettes [children have forgotten the word in English]. Yes, glasses. Glasses.* [teacher …….. **7** …….. in order to keep the children's attention and interest. She puts her hand to her ear to signal that she wants the children to repeat]

Ps *Glasses.*

T   *Good. And …* [teacher praises, points to the illustration, …….. **8** …….. and invites pupils to say the word]

Ps *Er. Blue jeans?*

T   *Blue jeans?* [teacher wants the children to learn 'trousers'. Pupils learnt *blue jeans* for the trousers James was wearing, and they are over-generalising the use of this word. She does not say they are wrong, but invites them to reconsider. She …….. **9** ……..] *Are they the same as James's?* [turning back the pages, and showing pupils a picture of James in his jeans. Points again at the trousers the Snowman is putting on] *What are these?* [she wants to find out if any pupils know this word]

Ps *Un pantalon.

T   *Good. Trousers. Trousers. The Snowman put on some trousers* [teacher praises, recasts, …….. **10** …….. and expands] *And a …* [points to the illustration, pauses, to elicit 'hat']

Ps *a hat.*

T   *and a hat. Good.* [teacher repeats and praises] *James said, Let's go upstairs. And James whispered at the door, Shhh! Be quiet! This is my parents' bedroom. And in the bedroom the Snowman put on a tie, some glasses, some trousers and a hat.* [teacher retells this part of the story, encouraging the children to join in]

Teaching strategies
Effective questioning

Aim

To consider the use of effective questioning techniques to encourage and scaffold reflection about learning.

Plan

The types of questions opposite are typically asked in the primary English language classroom. Match the question with the example:

See Key 1 on page 160.

Do

Teachers use a variety of questioning techniques. Complete the chart below by adding examples from your own lessons. The first example is provided.

Teacher questioning techniques	Classroom example
Pitching the language and content level of questions appropriately for the class.	Simple questions with illustrations: *What are these?*
Giving the children time to think about their response before answering questions.	
Asking the children to discuss a question with a partner before responding.	
Creating an atmosphere of trust where the children's opinions and ideas are valued, and wrong answers are not sanctioned.	
Using their responses (even incorrect ones) in a positive way.	
Planning questions in advance, in order to engage the children in thinking for themselves.	
Modelling the type of questions you want the children to ask.	
Staging and sequencing questions with increasing levels of challenge.	
Prompting and giving clues.	
Asking questions which make learning explicit and encourage the children to review.	
Other:	

Compare with Key 2 on page 161.

Type of question	Example
• Questions that require the children to give an opinion. • Questions that require the children to ask their own questions. • Questions that require the children to explain or justify. • Questions that allow for personalisation. • Questions that guide the children to the next step in learning. • Questions that make the children reflect on their learning. • Questions that encourage the children to think about language. • Questions that require the right answer.	• *What would you like to know about …?* • *What are you going to do next?* • *What colour is it?* • *Why did we play the game?* • *Why do you think that?* • *Why do you think that is true?* • *How do you come to school?* • *Where do adjectives go in English?*

Review

1 Sort the following questions into productive or unproductive questions, and justify your choice in the Comments column. (P = productive, U = unproductive.)

P/U	Question	Comments
	Did you enjoy today's lesson?	
	Is there another way you could say that?	
	Is this an apple? (Show an apple.)	
	What do you think will happen next?	
	Why can the moon not glow without the light from the sun?	
	Which poster do you think is the most interesting? Why?	
	What is it? (Show an orange.)	
	How do you know?	

See the Commentary on page 162.

2 Next steps: Reflect on what you need to do, to improve your use of questioning techniques in the primary English classroom.

Share

1 Ask a colleague to use the 'Teacher questioning techniques' chart to peer-assess your questioning techniques in your English lessons.

2 Discuss, and reciprocate the experience.

Teaching strategies
Using a class mascot

Aim

To reflect on the rationale for using a class mascot as a teaching aid.

Plan

1 There are a number of teaching aids commonly used in the primary English classroom:

○ *How many can you think of?*

See Key 1 on page 162.

2 Consider and answer these questions:

○ *How do you use these aids?*
○ *Do you use some more than others? If so, why?*
○ *Are there any others you use?*
○ *How do the children react to the different teaching aids?*

Do

In the primary English classroom, a mascot is often a soft toy or puppet that gives your class a unique identity:

○ Class mascots help build the class community and support both teacher and children in their English language teaching and learning.
○ In *Teaching children how to learn*, Wilbur the Worm is a class mascot and teaching aid.

1 Complete a bubble map:

○ *How can a class mascot help you teach?*

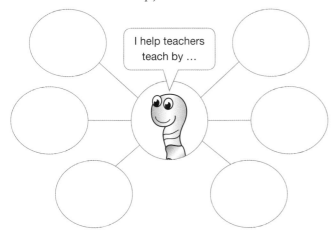

I help teachers teach by …

See Key 2 on page 162.

2 Complete a bubble map:

○ *How can a class mascot help the children learn?*

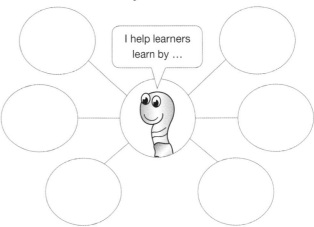

I help learners learn by …

See Key 3 on page 163.

3 Which characteristics make a class mascot attractive to children?

Review

1 A class mascot serves different purposes and plays several roles. (See page 14 in Part A.) Categorise the statements below under the four roles in the table:

Procedural role	Behavioural role
Affective role	Interactive role

○ Creates an atmosphere of trust and reassurance in the classroom.
○ Builds the class community.
○ Models language.
○ Provides information about language and content.
○ Models learning strategies.
○ Encourages the children to become independent learners.
○ Encourages the children to talk about their learning.
○ Supports the children in building their self-confidence.
○ Encourages interaction in the classroom.

See Key 4 on page 163.

2 Next steps: Consider what do you need to do, to improve your use of a class mascot.

Share

Share your ideas about using a class mascot with a colleague.

Teaching strategies
Planning lessons

Aim

To use a lesson planning template to plan lessons around the 'plan do review' learning cycle.

Plan

Throughout *Teaching children how to learn*, we have seen how 'plan do review' has been applied to activity cycles which occur within a lesson. We are now going to consider how we can use a lesson planning template to apply the 'plan do review' learning cycle to the overall structure of a lesson.

As Wilga Rivers points out: '*A lesson is not a haphazard collection of more or less interesting items, but a progression of interrelated activities which reinforce and consolidate each other in establishing the learning towards which the teacher is directing his or her efforts.*'

Do you use a lesson planning template? List what you consider are the benefits of planning lessons around a particular format.

See the Key on page 163.

Do

1 The template on page 135 shows how the 'plan do review' learning cycle has been applied to the overall lesson structure *vertically* as well as to individual activity cycles *horizontally* within the lesson, to provide clearly defined stages. This also combines the development of metacognitive and cognitive strategies through reflection, experimentation and further reflection.

A downloadable lesson plan template is provided on the website.

The three main lesson stages include a beginning, a middle – which is made up of activity cycles – and an end. The number of activity cycles included in a lesson will depend on:
○ the length of your lesson;
○ the age of your pupils;
○ their concentration spans;
○ the cognitive demands of an activity.
You can have one, two, three or even more activity cycles per lesson.

2 Use the lesson planning template to write out a plan for a lesson you are going to teach. Reflect on:
○ your aims;
○ the different stages of the lesson;
○ the sequencing of the activity cycles;
○ the timing;
○ the materials you require.

See the completed lesson plan on pages 164 and 165.

A downloadable completed lesson plan is available on the website.

3 Teach your lesson.

Review

Post-lesson personal reflection.

1 After teaching your lesson, ask yourself the following questions:
○ *How did the lesson planning template facilitate your planning?*
○ *Did you achieve the aims stated on your lesson plan? If not, why not?*
○ *Was your lesson different from your plan in any way? How and why?*
○ *How did you move from one stage of the lesson to the next? What did you say to the class?*
○ *Did you keep to your timing? If not, why not?*
○ *Were your pupils active and involved in the lesson? Why? Why not? How do you know?*
○ *Did your pupils learn what you set out to teach? How do you know?*
○ *Did your pupils respond positively to the materials and in English?*
○ *Were there any problems? If yes, why?*
○ *What would you do differently next time? Why?*
○ *What did you do better this time than ever before?*

2 Film or record your lessons from time to time, if possible, and ask your pupils to comment on your lessons. (See page 34 for information on obtaining parental consent.)

3 Analyse the transcripts of teacher-led review sessions for activity cycles 2 and 3 in the lesson on page 136. Focus on the teacher's intervention:
○ *How does the teacher guide the children into consciously stating what they did, in order to complete the activity?*
○ *What language functions does she use?*
○ *What metalanguage does she use?*
○ *How does she use the mother tongue and the target language?*
○ *What do you consider to be the benefits of reviewing the activity directly after, rather than at the end of, the lesson?*
○ *Would this be appropriate in your context?*

See the Commentary on page 163.

4 Next steps: Think about what aspects of your lesson planning you need to improve.

Share

Build up a bank of lesson plans to share with your colleagues.

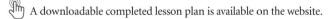

Rivers, W *Teaching Foreign Language Skills* (2nd edn.) University of Chicago Press 1981

Teaching strategies
Planning lessons

LESSON PLAN TEMPLATE

Teacher's name:		Date:	Class:	Length:	Class level:

Classroom layout/space:	Anticipated difficulties:

<table>
<tr>
<td rowspan="2">P L A N</td>
<td align="center">STAGE</td>
<td colspan="3">MAIN LESSON AIMS: In this lesson, the children will:
●
●
●</td>
<td rowspan="2">At the end of the lesson, tick off the aims achieved and add any additional aims/items that arose unexpectedly.</td>
</tr>
<tr>
<td>Beginning the lesson
● Start of lesson routine activity.
● Review work covered in previous lesson.
● Inform pupils of main lesson aims.</td>
<td colspan="3">Beginning the lesson procedures:
●
●
●</td>
<td>Time

</td>
</tr>
</table>

	Activity cycles	PROCEDURES			Materials	Time
D O	Plan / Do / Review	**PLAN** → **DO** → **REVIEW** **PLAN:** Prepare the children for the activity. Set context and inform children of aims and purpose of activity. Activate prior knowledge. Revise, introduce and practise any new language. Motivate. Negotiate success criteria.	**DO:** Children do activity and experiment and use target language. Teacher monitors and helps as necessary. **Do more** Children consolidate language by extending and personalising.	**REVIEW:** Run reflective review to evaluate activity and performance.	Plan / Do / Review	
	Activity cycle 1		**Do more**			
	Activity cycle 2		**Do more**			
	Activity cycle 3		**Do more**			

<table>
<tr>
<td>R E V I E W S H A R E</td>
<td>Ending the lesson
● Set homework and home involvement share activity.
● Round up, review and summarise lesson.
● End of lesson routine activity.</td>
<td>Ending the lesson procedures:
●
●
●

Post-lesson personal reflection: see Review questions on page 134.</td>
<td></td>
</tr>
</table>

Teaching strategies
Planning lessons

Transcripts of teacher-led review sessions for activity cycles

Italics Words spoken in the target language, ie: English.

* and no italics Words translated from, or spoken in, the mother tongue or shared classroom language, eg: French.

Square brackets Teacher's intonation, gestures, expressions, actions, use of props, etc.

T = Teacher   Ps = Pupils

Activity cycle 2

T   *OK! Good. Well done! We've done a picture dictation and have some lovely pictures of Meg!*
    *Now, what did you do in the activity?

Ps *Draw!

T   *Yes, you drew Meg, but what did you have to do in order to draw?

Ps *Listen!

T   *Yes, you had to listen. What did you have to listen to?

Ps *You!

T   *[teacher laughs] Yes, me! But what did I say?

Ps: *You were talking about Meg.

T   *Yes, I was talking about Meg. What was I saying about her?

Ps *You were telling us what she was wearing.

T   *Yes, I was describing her … [points to illustrations]

Ps *clothes.*

T   *Yes, her clothes. And what was I saying about her clothes?*

Ps *The colour, the size.*

T   *Yes, can you give me an example?*

Ps *Er …*

T   [prompts] *Meg's wearing …* [mimes hat to elicit language]

Ps *a hat*

T   *What colour it is?*

Ps *Black.*

T   *Yes, a black hat. What size is it?*

Ps *Tall.*

T   *Yes, a tall black hat. Repeat.*

Ps *A tall black hat.*

T   *Meg's wearing a tall black hat. Repeat.*

Ps *Meg's wearing a tall black hat.*

T   *But to draw, which word did you have to listen to and understand first?

Ps (uncertain what teacher is asking)

T   *Listen, Meg's wearing a tall black …*
    *Can you draw anything yet?

Ps *No

T   *Why?

Ps *Because we don't know what it is we have to draw.

T   *Good. Meg's wearing a tall black hat.*
    *Can you draw now?

Ps *Yes, because we know it's a hat!

T   *Yes, and the hat is … [rising intonation, to invite children to provide response]

Ps *tall and black.*

T   *Good. So 'tall' you know its …*

Ps *size.*

T   *'black' you know its …*

Ps *colour.*

T   *What did you learn? What are these words?

Ps *Adjectives!

T   *Good they are adjectives! What type of word is *hat*?

Ps *A noun.

T   *Good. So which type of word do you have to listen to and understand first in order to draw?

Ps *The noun.

T   *Good, the noun. So in order to do a picture dictation, you need to listen carefully to the teacher, listen for the key word, the noun, and then other adjectives, and draw what you hear.

Activity cycle 3

The teacher revises adjectives and nouns.

T   *Where do adjectives go in English?
    Meg's wearing a tall black hat!

Ps *Before the noun.

T   *Yes, and where do the adjectives of size go?

Ps *Before the adjective of colour.

T   *Good. Where do the adjectives of colour go?

Ps *Before the noun.

T   *Good. Meg's wearing a tall black hat!*

T   *Where do adjectives go in your language? Before or after the noun?

Teaching strategies
Selecting storybooks

Aim

To reflect on the criteria to use when selecting storybooks for a specific class of children.

'A picturebook has an effect on the reader not so very different from a good lesson.' Quentin Blake, First Children's Laureate 1999–2001

Plan

On page 15, we discuss how storybooks can be used to complement the activities in *Teaching children how to learn*, and the importance of selecting the right storybook for the right class.

'First catch your story. The really exciting thing is that they are all around – out there – just waiting to be caught.' Edie Garvie

However, it can be bewildering when entering a children's bookshop or library and being confronted with shelves and shelves of storybooks:
○ Where do you begin?
○ How can you 'catch' the right storybook for your class?

We provide a short synopsis for each of the storybooks Wilbur recommends in the Teachers' toolkit on the website, but you will need to apply further criteria – in order to select a storybook and evaluate its potential language learning opportunities for a specific class.

1 Think of a storybook you have already used with a class:
○ *What criteria did you use to select that storybook?*
○ *Would you select a different type of storybook as a result of that experience?*
○ *Why?*

2 Look at the list of suggested criteria opposite which you can use to select a storybook:
○ *Which questions would you ask for each criterion?*
○ *Are there any other criteria you would add to this list?*

Write your questions in the template on page 138 and then compare them with those in the Key on page 166.

Do

1 Look at the class profile on page 167 which has been completed for a class of 8 year olds in France:
○ The teacher describes why she has selected *The Chinese New Year* by Joanna Troughton (CUP, 2004).
○ For more information on *The Chinese New Year*, see Wilbur's recommendations in the Teachers' toolkit on the website.

2 Bearing in mind the criteria opposite and in the Key on page 166, and the information you have collated in your class's individual profile at the beginning of Part B, select a storybook that you think will appeal to your class.

3 Complete the class storybook profile (see page 138):
○ This will help ensure that the storybook matches your context and the interests and cognitive ability of the children, to maximise their enjoyment, involvement and learning.
○ Note that a new entry has been made to the class profile: 'Time of the year (month/season)'. Choosing *when* to tell or read a story is an important factor in its success.

🖐 A downloadable version of the profile is provided on the website.

4 Use the storybook you have selected with your class. See Ellis and Brewster for guidelines on planning lessons around a storybook.

Review

1 How did the children respond to the storybook you selected? Why?
○ *How successful was the storybook in terms of children's interest, motivation, involvement and learning?*

2 Rank the criteria below for selecting storybooks in order of importance for your context.
(1 = least important, 5 = most important.)

☐ Language level
☐ Literary devices
☐ Content
☐ Illustrations and layout
☐ Educational potential
☐ Potential for follow-up/main outcome
☐ Other

3 Next steps: As a result of your experience using the storybook, what type of storybook will you select next for the class, and why?

Share

Draw up other class storybook profiles, to share with colleagues.

Note

There are many animated versions of storybooks on YouTube which you can show your pupils as a reward for work they have done based on a storybook.

Blake, Q *Magic Pencil. Children's Book Illustration Today* British Council/British Library 2002

Ellis, G and Brewster, J *Tell it Again! The Storytelling Handbook for Primary English Language Teachers* British Council 2014 *http://www.teachingenglish.org.uk/article/tell-it-again-storytelling-handbook-primary-english-language-teachers*

Garvie, E *Story as Vehicle* Multilingual Matters 1990

Teaching strategies
Selecting storybooks

Criteria	Questions
Language level	• *Is the language (vocabulary/structures) accessible to my pupils?* • •
Literary devices	
Content	
Illustrations and layout	
Educational potential	
Potential for follow-up/main outcome	
Other:	

Class storybook profile		
School year .... **Class**		**Storybook:** ....
Age of pupils		
Number of pupils		
Gender mix (boys/girls)		
Language(s) spoken at home		
Shared classroom language		
English language level		
Cognitive ability		
School setting (urban/suburban/rural)		
Time of the year (month/season)		
Children's interests		
Classroom space/layout (fixed desks, rows, movable tables, etc)		
Resources/technology		
Other information:		

Teaching strategies
Storytelling skills

Aim

To help develop your confidence as a storyteller and identify areas for improvement.

Plan

'*The teacher is telling a story, but not in the way I, an Englishman would tell it. She is dancing it, singing it, acting it. She tells it with her face, her voice, her whole body. The class is completely caught up in the action: toes and shoulders wriggling in sympathy. There is a song involved: the whole class joins in without invitation.*'
Edie Garvie, quoting Harold Rosen's visit to an African school.

We all have our own individual storytelling styles. Some of us may be more reserved, while others may be more like the teacher above, who is able to use her eyes and voice to good effect. As long as we feel confident and at ease when reading a story aloud, the children will too. But good storytelling is a combination of several factors, and needs planning and rehearsing.

Reading a storybook aloud is usually less daunting than *telling* a story, which makes great demands on memory and linguistic skills. The beauty of a storybook is that everything is provided, as you have direct access to the text – which allows you to tell the story more confidently – and the accompanying illustrations play an important role in supporting the children's understanding.

In order to read a storybook aloud, you need to practise this skill and become aware of the techniques you can use to bring a story alive and support the children's understanding.

Use this rehearsal strategy, and assess your talents as a storyteller!

1 Select a storybook for a class you are teaching, using the criteria in the *Selecting storybooks* activity on page 137 and your class's individual profile on page 37 in Part B and on the website.

2 Familiarise youself with the storybook and prepare yourself for reading the story aloud, by looking at and applying the questions opposite.

Do

1 Imagine you are in your classroom with your pupils.

2 Read the story aloud, and record yourself.

Review

1 Replay the recording, listen, and use the self-assessment sheet on page 140 to evaluate your storytelling skills.

A downloadable evaluation sheet is provided on the website.

2 Next steps: Identify what you need to work on, to improve your storytelling skills.

Familiarise yourself with the book (story, visuals, layout, size).

- *How will you hold the book and turn the pages?*
- *When will you point to illustrations, so the children can relate what they hear to what they see and infer the meaning?*
- *Where will you pause, to invite the children to join in?*
- *Which questions will you ask, to involve the children and encourage them to predict?*
- *What extra support may you need (flashcards, props, sound effects, etc) to aid the children's understanding?*
- *How may you vary your voice – eg: speed or volume for dramatic effect – or disguise your voice for different characters?*
- *Do you anticipate any difficulties either you or the children may have?*

Practise reading the story aloud a few times.

Share

1 Invite a colleague to come into a class when you are reading a story aloud and to use the questions on the self-assessment sheet to peer-assess your storytelling skills.

2 Discuss.

3 Reciprocate the experience.

Garvie, E *Story as Vehicle* Multilingual Matters 1990

Storybooks and storytelling

The more storybooks you use, the more you will improve your storytelling skills.

But the key to successful storytelling is to have the right storybook for the right class (see page 15 in Part A).

Selecting storybooks for a specific class is one of the greatest challenges facing teachers:

- Synopses of all Wilbur's storybook recommendations are provided in the Teachers' toolkit on the website.
- Each synopsis aims to provide you with an initial overview, to guide you in your choice.

A storybook record is also included (see page 173), so you can keep track of the storybooks you have used – whether books suggested by Wilbur, or books of your own choice – and how successful they were:

- Keep an ongoing record.
- Share it with your colleagues.

Teaching strategies
Storytelling skills

Evaluating my storytelling skills

Individual sounds
- *Did I pronounce the vowels and consonants or sounds in connected speech correctly?*

....
....
....
....

Stress
- *Did I stress the syllables in individual words or in sentences correctly?*

....
....
....
....

Rhythm
- *Did I read too slowly or too quickly?*
- *Did I pause in the right places?*

....
....
....
....

Intonation
- *Did I sound interesting or boring?*
- *Did I vary my intonation, where appropriate?*
- *Did I use the appropriate intonation for questions, statements, lists, and so on?*

....
....
....
....

Variation
- *How did I vary the speed and volume of my voice, where appropriate?*
- *Did I adapt my voice for the different characters?*

....
....
....
....

Visual/audio clues
- *How did I use visual/audio clues (facial expressions and gestures, sound effects) to support the children's understanding?*

....
....
....
....

Eye contact
- *Did I retain eye contact with the children during the storytelling, to develop a shared rapport with the class?*

....
....
....
....

Pupil participation
- *Did I pause in the correct places and use appropriate intonation, to invite my pupils to join in?*
- *Did I ask appropriate questions, to encourage my pupils to predict what comes next?*
- *Did I ask the appropriate questions, to encourage the children to relate the story to their own experiences?*

....
....
....
....

General impression
- *How did I sound in general? Clear? Expressive? Lively?*

....
....
....
....

What do I need to improve?
- *What shall I focus on this week?*

....
....
....
....

Ongoing development strategies
Action research

Aim

To consider the benefits of action research, and the procedures involved.

Plan

'Gaining insights into ones' own teaching or discovering something about oneself as a professional that one didn't know before is the very essence of action research.' Michael Wallace

1 Can you describe a time when you discovered or gained an insight into something you did not know about your own teaching?
○ *What did you learn?*

2 Sequence the reasons for doing action research in order of importance for you.
(I = least important, 5 = most important.)

☐ To help me notice what I and my pupils really do, rather than what I think we do.
☐ To get feedback as to the success or failure of what I am doing.
☐ To help me tailor my teaching to the needs of my pupils and my context.
☐ To help justify the teaching and learning choices I make.
☐ To increase my knowledge of learning and teaching.
☐ To enable me to become more independent and creative in my teaching.
☐ To keep me motivated and interested in teaching.

3 Identify an area you would like to research in one of your classes.
○ *What question do you want to answer?*
○ *Try to ask this in a clear single question.*
○ *Make sure it is manageable.*
○ *Decide on a time scale, eg: a month, a term, a school year.*

See the examples opposite.

4 Investigate the area by talking to other teachers and reading about it.

5 Think about what evidence you need to collect, and how you will collect it. For example:
○ Lesson observations and note-taking.
○ Lesson plans.
○ Examples of pupils' work.
○ Audio or video recording the children doing an activity and transcribing it. (See page 34 for more information on getting parental consent.)
○ Photos of displayed work, board work, realia, portfolios.
○ Interviewing the children, other teachers, parents.
○ Keeping a diary/reflective journal.
○ Questionnaires.
○ Focus groups.

> **Example research questions:**
> - If I gather feedback from the children to find out which activities they prefer, will this result in higher levels of satisfaction and a sense of progress?
> - Which questions are the most effective to ask in teacher-led review sessions, to get the children to reflect on *how* they learn as well as *what* they learn?
> - As a result of running systematic teacher-led review sessions, are the children better able to reflect on and articulate more awareness of how they learn and account for their learning?
>   (See the activity *Evaluating learning to learn* on page 142.)
> - What impact do the classroom routines I use have on the children's developing independence and language acquisition?
> - How does an English Language Portfolio improve the children's ability to record and organise their work and encourage home involvement?

6 How will you analyse your evidence?

Do

Implement your action research.

Review

1 Analyse the evidence you gathered:
○ *What have you learnt?*

2 Next steps: Consider how this knowledge will impact on your teaching and your pupils' learning.

Share

Report your findings to your colleagues.

Wallace, M Action *Research for Language Teachers* CUP 1998

Ongoing development strategies
Action research techniques: Evaluating learning to learn

Aim

To consider different techniques for evaluating learning to learn.

Plan

In *Teaching children how to learn* we have pointed out how teachers, school heads, inspectors and parents want evidence that investment in learning to learn can be justified, in order to be convinced of its value. However, learning to learn is a complex construct and difficult to evaluate.

Consequently, there have been few empirical studies to evaluate its effects in terms of improved linguistic performance, or to investigate the rate at which a learner learns how to learn. Empirical evidence is difficult to obtain:

○ Learning to learn can lead to more than just linguistic gains, it can also offer cognitive, emotional, cultural, social and affective gains. However, these can be difficult to observe and measure.
○ Learning to learn is a long and gradual process, and there are many factors and variables affecting children's learning and motivation, which makes it difficult to compare like with like.

Despite this lack of empirical evidence, most teachers are willing to invest both the time and the effort in developing learning to learn in their classrooms and have observed valuable and justifiable benefits and outcomes.

Since using Part B, and integrating learning to learn into your English language classes, what benefits and outcomes have you observed for your pupils and for yourself? Compare these with the outcomes below:

○ *Which are the same? Which are different?*

Do

1 Look at the techniques on page 143 for obtaining evidence from learners, to support the promotion of learning to learn:
○ *What is each technique attempting to find out?*

2 Complete the research question for each technique. (A first example is given.)

See Key 1 on page 168.

3 Now consider the pros and cons of each technique.

See Key 2 on page 169.

Review

1 Which of the techniques for evaluating learning to learn are best suited for your context? Why?

2 Next steps: Conduct the action research project in the next activity, and experiment with audio- or video-recording review sessions and analysing linguistic data.

Share

Read the comments from teachers on pages 96 and 143 which show the positive outcomes they have observed since implementing learning to learn with their classes:
○ *Have you observed similar outcomes?*
○ *Add your own comments.*

Share the comments with your colleagues, to encourage them to conduct an action research project with a class. If possible, plan and conduct it together.

Outcomes for children	Outcomes for teachers
• More positive attitudes, self-esteem and confidence. • More reflective learners, through the development of the ability to review and self-assess and account for their learning. • More questioning, active and personal involvement. • More awareness of the learning process; • More collaborative learning. • More resilient and independent learners. • Better sense of progress and achievement. • Improved communication skills. • Improved concentration and memory. • Other:	• Gives an insight into what the children think by listening to their perspectives and acting on these. • Helps to plan the next steps in learning. • Helps to understand the way children learn and their learning preferences. • Facilitates lesson planning and classroom management. • Supports and improves the relationships between teacher and children. • Teacher becomes more reflective about their own practice. • Teacher gives more control to the children. • Other:

Joint outcomes
• Learning and teaching is a more enjoyable and successful experience.
• Increased motivation.
• Other:

Ongoing development strategies
Action research techniques: Evaluating learning to learn

Evaluation technique	How it can be used	Research question(s) As a result of integrating learning to learn into lessons, …
Monitoring the children's proficiency gains in English.	Traditional means of assessment.	• *Do children show greater effectiveness in English language learning?* • •
Collecting feedback and comments from teachers and children – and parents – to monitor satisfaction levels, sense of progress, views about learning to learn (see the examples below and on page 96).	Surveys, focus groups, recording teacher-led review sessions.	
Recording, logging and monitoring learner behaviour and progress.	Learning diaries, English language portfolios, self-assessment, drawings, photos, films.	
Observing the effects of strategy training.	Teacher observation of the children. Learner self-report.	
Monitoring the children's developing metacognitive awareness.	Audio- or video- recording teacher-led review sessions to collect linguistic data. Interviewing individual children.	

Teachers' comments

• *'At the beginning, the children were not very serious about the lessons. They are now more serious and they listen carefully. They say they are pleased. When they are quiet and involved, I'm also pleased and happy to see them working.'*

• *'They participate more, they ask more questions at the right time, before moving on to the next stage in the course of an activity. They feel confident and happy.'*

• *'I started to really think about the type of questions I was asking: did they really get the children to reflect on their learning, or were they just testing their knowledge or understanding?'*

• *'If I see they are having any problems, I now stop and ask if anything is wrong. I see them relaxed and calm. Most of them are now confident enough to ask or say (if they are aware of the problem).'*

• *'I now explain the purpose of the new lesson, the steps of the things we're going to do – I think this makes the children feel collected and they know what comes next.'*

• *'Now they are more aware of what they've been doing and learning. They can think of their learning strategies and develop them.'*

Your comments: ....
....
....
....

Ongoing development strategies
An action research project: Evaluating learning to learn

Aim

Research question:

As a result of running systematic teacher-led review sessions, are the children better able to reflect on and articulate more awareness of how they learn and account for their learning?

Plan

We are going to use a framework adapted from Barbara Sinclair, to evaluate learning to learn by monitoring and evaluating the children's developing metacognitive awareness. See below.

Collecting audio or video recordings of systematic teacher-led review sessions will enable you to analyse linguistic data:

○ The extent to which the children are able to respond to questions will provide clues to their developing levels of metacognitive awareness, by using appropriate metalanguage and demonstrating an informed and conscious knowledge of their learning processes.

○ The framework allows you to identify and monitor the changing nature of your guidance and intervention techniques, moving from very direct questioning and summarising to more eliciting.

The three levels of awareness on the framework refer to the following:

○ An initial stage (Level 1) where the children are largely unaware, as evidenced by little understanding of the purpose of the activities and little use, or no use, of metalanguage.

○ A transition stage (Level 2) where the children begin to show some awareness of their learning and demonstrate some understanding and rationale of what they are doing, and why, and begin to use some metalanguage.

○ A third stage (Level 3) where the children demonstrate:
  • greater confidence in talking about their learning and use of metalanguage;

• more evidence of a rationale for strategy choice;
• awareness of possible alternative strategies they could use.

Decide on the following:

○ *How often are you going to record teacher-led review sessions?*
  (For example: once a month over a school year, other.)

○ *Which language will you conduct the review sessions in?*
  (For example: target language, mother tongue, other.)

Using the mother tongue or shared classroom language to talk about language learning will provide richer data – assuming *you* can use this language, too.

Do

1 Record or film your review sessions:

○ Follow your school's policy for obtaining parental consent to record or film the children. (See page 34 for more information.)

2 Transcribe the sessions, and record the linguistic data on the framework. There is a sample completed framework on page 170.

Review

1 Analyse the data you gathered:

○ *What have you learnt?*

○ *How will this knowledge impact on your teaching and your pupils' learning?*

2 Next steps: How will the insights you have gained from your action research project help you convince all the stakeholders of the value of implementing learning to learn? Decide on your future action.

Share

Report your findings to your colleagues.

Framework for evaluating linguistic evidence of developing metacognitive awareness				
Level of metacognitive awareness	Pupil language characterised by ...	Examples of pupil language	Teacher guidance and intervention	Examples of teacher language
Level 1: Largely unaware				
Level 2: Becoming aware (transition stage)				
Level 3: Largely aware				

Sinclair, B 'More than an Act of Faith? Evaluating learner autonomy' in *Innovation and Best Practice* Chris Kennedy (Ed) Longman/British Council 1999

Ongoing development strategies
Peer observation

Aim

To consider how to implement peer observation, in order to make it a positive developmental opportunity.

Plan

'Peer observation … involve(s) colleagues – who are equal – watching and teaching together so that both may be helped in their understanding and practice.' Jeremy Harmer

1 Have you already peer-observed a colleague?
○ *If so, what did you learn?*

2 Have you already been peer-observed?
○ *Describe the experience and what you learnt.*

3 What do you consider to be the conditions that make peer observation a positive developmental opportunity?

4 Agree a time and date to observe a colleague:
○ Discuss the lesson in advance with your colleague, and how they would like you to participate – or not.
○ Ask for a lesson plan, if available, and agree:
  • the ground rules;
  • the tools you will use to gather data: photos of pupil-produced work, displayed work, board work, realia, portfolios, etc;
  • audio recording, filming (follow your school's policy to obtain parental consent to photograph, record or film their children) – see page 34;
  • the questions on the observation sheet you will focus on. For example: all, three or four only, or agree other questions of your own choice.

Do

Observe the lesson, using an observation sheet like the one opposite.

Review

1 Discuss the lesson with the teacher.

2 Were there any opportunities for learning to learn that, in your opinion, were not taken?
○ *How could they have been exploited?*

3 What have you learned about your own practice from observing this lesson?

Share

Reciprocate the lesson observation experience, by inviting the teacher to observe one of your classes.

Observation sheet

Teacher .... Number of pupils ....
Age of pupils .... Materials ....
Level of pupils .... Date ....

1 How did the teacher inform the class of the learning aims of the lesson and the purpose of the language learning activities?

2 How did the teacher move from one stage of the lesson to the next?
• *What did he/she say?*

3 Were there any opportunities for the children to personalise their work, make choices and work independently?
• *Give examples.*

4 Did the children participate actively in the lesson?
• *Was there evidence of learning?*
• *Give examples.*

5 Did the children respond positively to the materials used by the teacher?
• *How could you tell?*

6 How did the teacher review learning with the class? At what stage?
• *After each activity?*
• *At the end of the lesson?*

7 Did the teacher make use of the mother tongue or shared classroom language at any time?
• *If so, for what purpose?*

8 What routines did the teacher use?
• *For what purpose?*

9 How did the teacher make use of the classroom space?
• *To foster independence?*
• *To accommodate different learning preferences?*
• *To provide opportunities for different interaction patterns?*

10 Did the teacher keep to the timing of the lesson?
• *If not, why not?*

Further observations:

Harmer, J *The Practice of English Language Teaching* (3rd edn.) Longman 2001 (p348)

Self-assessment
Ongoing personal reflection

Aim

To think about the teaching strategies and knowledge you have acquired or improved from using *Teaching children how to learn*, and what you would like to improve or acquire at a future date.

Plan

The four core elements of effective pedagogy in *Teaching children how to learn* are:

○ **Planning interesting and stimulating learning experiences**

○ **Creating a positive classroom climate**

○ **Encouraging parental support and family involvement**

○ **Enabling children to experience success in early language learning**

The key teaching strategies related to each of these four key elements are listed on pages 147 and 148:

○ If you feel that any of the teaching strategies do not apply in your case, tick the 'Not applicable' (N/A) box.

○ You can add other areas that you would like to know more about.

 Downloadable versions of the strategies are available on the website.

Do

Assess yourself as follows:

1 = *I now feel very competent in this area.*

2 = *I now feel quite competent in this area.*

3 = *I don't feel competent yet in this area, and would like to learn more.*

Review

1 Based on your self-assessment:

○ *What do you need to do next?*

○ *What is your target development?*

2 Draw up your action plan – see opposite – and place your action plan at the front of your English Teaching Portfolio.

 A downloadable version of the action plan is provided on the website.

3 Assess yourself again in six months, to compare your progress.

Share

Your self-assessment and action plan are personal and individual activities. However, professional development does not need to be a solitary activity:

○ We have encouraged you to share your ideas, support, exchange and collaborate with your colleagues – who can be a great source of ideas and inspiration.

○ In addition to the activities we have suggested in *Teaching children how to learn*, there are many other ways that you can work with and meet other teachers.

You can join teachers' associations in your own country or international or associations like IATEFL and TESOL which organise annual conferences:

○ Many of their Special Interest Groups (SIGS) organise smaller, more regular meetings or workshops.

○ They also produce their own journals and newsletters.

There are many virtual communities and blogs where you can communicate with other teachers, such as the British Council's Teaching English site.

On a smaller scale, you can set up or join a teachers' group within your own school or district.

BRITISH COUNCIL *http://www.teachingenglish.org.uk/*
IATEFL *http://www.iatefl.org/*
TESOL *http://www.tesol.org/*

Action plan
Date ....
Action point: Describe the target development. For example: the teaching strategy you wish to try out or improve.
Link your plan to one of the core elements of effective pedagogy.
Steps you need to take, plus time frame.
Support/resources required.
Measures for impact and/or success.

Self-assessment
Ongoing personal reflection

Planning interesting and stimulating learning experiences	1	2	3	N/A
Planning challenging lessons.				
Using familiar routines.				
Providing authentic input to create an acquisition-rich learning environment.				
Making links to other areas in the primary curriculum.				
Giving opportunities for the children to relate things to their personal experience.				
Developing intercultural understanding.				
Giving meaningful exposure to the language.				
Using age-appropriate and varied activities and materials.				
Comments:				

Assess yourself as follows:

1 = *I now feel very competent in this area.*

2 = *I now feel quite competent in this area.*

3 = *I don't feel competent yet in this area, and would like to learn more.*

Creating a positive classroom climate	1	2	3	N/A
Understanding that mistakes are learning opportunities.				
Creating a climate of mutual confidence and respect in the teacher–class relationship.				
Creating an inclusive classroom, and respecting diversity.				
Recognising and praising effort, and giving constructive feedback.				
Being a positive role model, and promoting positive values.				
Establishing a learning environment where the children feel confident to take risks with the language.				
Enabling the children to voice their opinions/preferences about language learning.				
Listening to and acting on the children's perspectives.				
Building a class learning community.				
Giving the children responsibility and opportunities to work independently and make choices about activities/materials.				
Using positive behaviour and classroom management strategies.				
Providing opportunities for the children to work cooperatively.				
Making effective use of classroom space.				
Using effective questioning to create an enquiring classroom and quality dialogue.				
Comments:				

Self-assessment
Ongoing personal reflection

Encouraging parental support and family involvement	1	2	3	N/A
Creating effective communication channels between school and home.				
Enabling the children to share learning with their parents.				
Encouraging positive parental attitudes to foreign language learning.				
Fostering cooperation between teacher and parents.				
Planning activities which take the in-the-school experience into the home.				
Planning activities which take the in-the-home experience into the school.				
Supporting the parents to help their child with their English language learning.				
Comments:				

Assess yourself as follows:

1 = *I now feel very competent in this area.*

2 = *I now feel quite competent in this area.*

3 = *I don't feel competent yet in this area, and would like to learn more.*

Enabling children to experience success in early language learning	1	2	3	N/A
Planning and integrating learning to learn systematically into lessons.				
Discussing and reviewing learning.				
Encouraging the children to use the target language as much as possible, but with the right to use the mother tongue or the shared classroom language to help them learn.				
Using child-directed speech.				
Scaffolding learning.				
Discussing and negotiating success criteria.				
Giving opportunities to use language in context.				
Encouraging organised learning.				
Ensuring the children know what is expected of them, and how they are to be evaluated.				
Ensuring the children understand the purpose of what they have to do and its relevance.				
Giving the children opportunities to work at their own pace and personalise their learning.				
Comments:				

Teachers' toolkit

- Keys are provided for the activities in Part C, where appropriate. Sometimes, the Keys take the form of Commentaries, Sample responses and Transcripts.

- Note that the Keys present the authors' views: there are no 'right' or 'wrong' answers to the activities.

- The information in the toolkit is intended to encourage you to reflect on your own teaching context and come to your own conclusions.

To facilitate building your own personal profiles for some of the Teacher Development activities, a number of downloadable templates are available in the Teachers' toolkit on the website.

See page 171 for a list of these templates.

Principle 1 Modes of input and types of response

		Key	
Language item	**Multimodal resources**	**Response from children to show understanding**	**Type of responses (see page 24)**
Parts of the body	The teacher gives verbal instructions/commands.	The children respond to teacher verbal input through movement.	Physical
Actions	Flashcards.	The children mime, point to cards, walk to cards. They repeat words.	Physical Spoken
General understanding of a story and vocabulary related to food	The teacher reads a picture book aloud.	The children listen to the story, relate what they hear to what they see, and construct the gist. They participate in a story reading by repeating or predicting key words and phrases.	Analytical; personal Spoken
Dialogue about going to the zoo	Video clip.	The children repeat dialogue and act out. They complete a worksheet and follow a map.	Spoken; creative Written; analytical
Saying what you can do (sports)	Mime.	The children interpret the mime, copy and say the sport. They repeat and practise the statement *'I can swim'*, etc.	Physical; creative; spoken Spoken
Saying how you come to school	Song.	The children repeat the song, fill in missing words. They repeat and practise *'I come to school by …'* and mime.	Spoken Spoken; creative
Your choice:			

 Principle 2: English Language Portfolio

Key 1	
Songs	Recipes
Rhymes	Vocabulary banks
Samples of written work	Preferred learning strategies
Drawings	Activity record sheets
Record of storybooks	A craft activity
Realia	A main outcome from an activity
Tests	Other:
Self-assessments	

Key 2

I tried hard with this piece of work.

It is real English – eg: a stamp, a label, a postcard.

It is work I did with my parents.

It shows I can do 'xxxx'.

It shows I am making progress.

It shows what I have achieved.

I like this song/rhyme.

I did this piece of work with my classmate.

I learnt new language with this activity.

It is my best piece of work so far.

I am very proud of this activity or outcome.

Other:

Principle 3 Assessment for learning

Key 1

Activities and Learning aims	
Activities	**Learning aims**
Colour a picture.	*Listen carefully, and identify the different colours in English.*
Make a leaflet about healthy eating.	*Review and practise language on the topic of health and healthy eating.*
Write an email introducing yourself.	*Write sentences with capital letters and full stops.*

Key 2

Learning aims and Success criteria	
Learning aims	**Success criteria**
Listen carefully, and identify the different colours in English.	*Try to understand all the colours.* *Complete your picture with the correct colours.*
Review and practise language on the topic of health and healthy eating.	*Use all the words related to healthy eating.* *Use paragraphs and pictures to make your leaflet interesting.*
Write sentences with capital letters and full stops.	*Use capital letters at the beginning of sentences.* *Put a full stop at the end of each sentence.*

 Principle 4 The children's voices

Key

Methods	How they can be used
Drawing.	The children's drawings represent the different activities they did in a lesson. The drawings evaluate their performance. The drawings express their experiences or opinions about learning English.
Filming the children doing an activity, or talking about language learning.*	The children watch the film to comment on how they participated in and completed an activity.
The teacher or children take photos of the main outcomes, or of the activity they are doing.	The children use the photos to comment on the outcome of an activity and how and why they created it.
Interviewing or questioning the children. For example: reviewing	The children say how they followed the teacher's instructions or modelling. They reflect on and verbalise what and how they learn.
The children discussing learning together.	The children help each other complete a task. They evaluate each other's work.
Other:	

* See page 34 for information on obtaining parental consent.

Principle 5 Informed activities

Key 1

- The children can make use of their previous knowledge about activity types.
- The children are respected as partners in learning, feel valued and respond more positively to their English work.
- The children understand what they are learning and why, so are more willing and confident to take a risk and use English.
- The children can relate activities to their everyday experiences.
- The children are given a relevant purpose for their work.
- The children understand the outcome they are working towards.
- The children become aware of, and extend their range of, learning strategies.
- Learning English makes more sense and is more meaningful.
- Learning English becomes more inclusive.

Key 2

Activity/ technique	Child-friendly language	Teacher language
Singing a song in a round	*'Singing a song in a round will help you learn to concentrate. You will have to listen carefully to know when it's your turn to sing. It will also help you learn vocabulary and practise pronunciation and rhythm in English.'*	Singing a song in a round will help the children develop their concentration and become aware of timing. It will also develop vocabulary, pronunciation and rhythm in English.
Picture dictation	*'A picture dictation will help you improve your concentration and listening and show your understanding by drawing what your teacher says.'*	A picture dictation will develop the children's concentration and listening skills and show understanding through drawing.
Wordsearch	*'In a wordsearch, you look at letters carefully and recognise combinations of letters and spelling patterns so you can identify words in English. It will help you remember vocabulary.'*	A wordsearch will help the children recognise combinations of letters, spelling patterns and words in English. It will develop observation and memory skills.
Action rhyme	*'In an action rhyme you do actions as you say the words. The actions will help you understand and remember the words. This will help you feel confident. The rhyming words will help you predict and remember the words that come next. An action rhyme helps you learn by doing.'*	In an action rhyme, children associate actions with words to reinforce meaning and aid memory. The rhyming words provide clues to help the children predict and remember words that come next. They can do an action rhyme all together or say different parts in groups. This helps build the class community.

Key 2 (continued)

Activity/ technique	Child-friendly language	Teacher language
Roleplay	*'A roleplay will help you practise speaking so you will be prepared to use English in a real situation. This will help you develop your self-confidence. You need to imagine yourself in the real situation, and use English as much as you can.'*	A roleplay will develop the children's speaking skills in preparation for a real-life situation. This will develop their self-confidence.
Information gap	*'In an information-gap activity, you work together with a partner. One of you will have some information that your partner does not have and vice-versa. Your aim is to complete a task by talking with your partner to find the missing information. It will develop your speaking and listening as well as your vocabulary and grammar. It will help you learn to work together and help each other.'*	An information-gap activity will develop the children's speaking and listening skills, as well as vocabulary and grammar. It will help them learn to collaborate and cooperate together.
Total Physical Response (TPR)	*'Total Physical Response will help you improve your listening by following instructions and showing your understanding through actions or movement by doing what your teacher says. The actions will also help you remember vocabulary. It helps you 'learn by doing'.'*	A TPR activity will develop the children's listening skills and concentration. They show their understanding through actions and movement. It will develop their vocabulary and memory skills.
Sequencing	*'A sequencing activity will help you order numbers or colours or other items. This will help you develop your listening and remember words in English.'*	A sequencing activity will develop the children's ability to order items. It will develop their listening and memory skills.
Online language game	*'An online language game will help you practise language you have learnt in your lesson. You will learn to work on your own or with a classmate, collaborate, take turns, and develop your keyboard skills.'*	An online language game can play an important motivational role for children, and games are an important part of their social and cognitive development. It is important that children understand that using an online language game is for learning as well as playing.
What's missing?	*'What's missing? will help you look at things carefully and remember what you have seen. It will help you learn and remember English vocabulary.'*	*What's missing?* will develop the children's observation and visual memory skills, in order to better recall vocabulary.

Principle 6 Routines

Key					
Routine	Purpose	Form it takes	Guidance and intervention techniques	Language used	Time
Getting the children's attention	To establish good learning conditions.	Teacher rings a small bell / uses a tambourine / puts a hand up.	Using multimodal signals, eg: a bell. Giving instructions.	*Listen carefully, children.* *Quiet, everyone!*	30 seconds
Giving instructions to do an activity	To ensure all the children know what they have to do.	Teacher gets the children's attention, establishes silence and gives instructions.	Using multimodal signals, eg: a stop sign. Asking the children to repeat back instructions.	*Tell me what you are going to do.*	2 minutes
Moving from one activity to another	To ensure the children know that one activity has finished, and to prepare for the next.	Teacher rounds off the activity.	Using multimodal signals, eg: traffic lights, as a transition sign. Giving instructions. Giving feedback. Introducing the next activity.	*Finish now and show me your diagrams.* *Well done!* *Now we are going to use our diagrams to …*	1 minute
Giving responsibility for classroom tasks	To share classroom tasks amongst the children, to develop responsibility.	Designated pupil collects and hands out classroom materials.	Using multimodal signals, eg: materials/resources sign.	*Maria is our materials monitor this week.* *Hand out the …*	1 minute
Reviewing the lesson	To reflect on the content and process of learning.	Class discussion.	Asking questions, Focusing the children's attention.	*What did you learn today?* *How did you learn?*	5 minutes
Ending the lesson	To ensure that the children leave the lesson in an orderly, calm and happy state.	Teacher or child plays a familiar listening game.	Giving instructions.	*Everyone wearing something blue, line up.* *Everyone wearing something green, …*	1 minute

---

Transcript notes from review sessions

Italics Words spoken in the target language, ie: English.

* and no italics Words translated from, or spoken in, the mother tongue or shared classroom language, eg: French.

The words in **bold** represent guidance and intervention techniques.

Transcript 1

This transcript shows how the children reply very literally to the initial question: *'What did you learn this week?'*

- The children want to talk about everything they have done, rather than what they have learnt: *'We cut out some masks.* *We made a book, … *the spiders, … the computers.'*

- The teacher makes several attempts to **focus the pupils' attention** on the story and finally succeeds in getting the children to **retell** it: *'OK. Our book, our book,* *our story, *How the kangaroos … .'*

- She ends the review session by **summarising and recapping**: '*So we talked about our book and that *helped us learn some vocabulary: colours … .'*

Transcript 2

This transcript also shows how the children want to speak about all the things they have done.

- The teacher shows greater control than the teacher in Transcript 1. She quickly **intervenes and directs** the review by **nominating the point for discussion** and **focusing the pupils' attention** on the game: '*Wait. We're going to speak about the game.'

- She **reassures** the pupils that she will discuss the story later, '*and then we'll come back to the story'.

- She **elicits** what the children learnt from the game, and **summarises and informs** them of the social, collaborative aspect of the game: *'We played the game to learn the parts of the body and some clothes but also to play together, and each person had to take a turn.'*

Notice how the pupils give the word 'necklace' for 'scarf' – making an association with something that goes around the neck. Although incorrect, the teacher responds in a positive way, recognising their attempt to recall 'scarf'. She points to her own necklace and then to the Snowman's scarf in the illustration, to demonstrate the difference in meaning between the two words.

Transcript 3

This transcript shows how the teacher **elicits** why the children did the movements with the song.

- The children give two valid reasons.

- The teacher **focuses** on the final one: '*To know what we are saying.'

- She **emphasises** and **points out** that the corresponding movements can help the pupils understand the meaning and remember the vocabulary.

Transcript 4

This transcript shows how the teacher guides the children so they focus on, and consciously state, the process involved in the activity.

- She uses **metalanguage**: *keywords* and *nouns*.

- This transcript demonstrates a growing awareness of what the pupils are doing and why.

- The teacher introduces more metalanguage, and continues to use a **probing questioning** approach to **encourage** pupils to justify their responses.

Transcript 5

This transcript shows how the teacher **questions** the pupils' basic assumptions and **probes**, until she brings them to a conscious statement of what they have done and how they have done it.

- She **models** the types of questions the pupils can ask, so they will gradually be able to take on responsibility for this aspect of their learning by themselves: *'And to do the activity, what did you do? How did you learn?'*

- She finishes by **summarising** the language learning purpose of the bingo game: '*We played bingo to practise listening and concentrating, and to revise the vocabulary for kitchen objects.'

Principle 8 Values

Key 1

Values

- Values are the principles that guide behaviour.

- Values empower the children to become effective learners and good citizens.

Key 2

Technique	Value(s) promoted	How?
Talking stick	Caring and tolerance	Helps the children take turns speaking and to listen and respect each other's opinions.
English Language Portfolio	Accountability	Helps the children take pride in their work, learn to account for their English language learning and become responsible for informing their parents.
Class discussion	Caring and tolerance	Helps the children listen and value the ideas and opinions of others, value diversity and learn from and share with others.
Self-assessment	Accountability, flexibility and resilience	Helps the children account for their learning, become aware of strengths and weakness and identify what they need to do next and how they are going to do this.
Talk partners	Caring and tolerance	Helps the children take turns speaking and listen and respect each other's opinions.
Making a class convention*	Accountability	Helps the children understand their rights and accept their responsibilities, in order to create a class community.
Other:		

*See the activity *Our language learning rights* on page 74.

Principle 9 Cross-curricular links

	Key 1	
Factors	**Questions**	
Content area	*What content area will interest the children?* *What are they working on in other areas of the curriculum?*	
Language demands	*What vocabulary and language structures are required to teach this content?* *Do I need to teach new vocabulary or revise language the children already know?* *Do I need to simplify the language for this age group?* *Which pronunciation areas do I need to focus on?* *Are the skills mostly receptive: reading (scanning or skimming) or listening (for gist or intensely), or productive (speaking and writing)?*	
Cognitive demands	*Will the activities challenge the children?* *Are the cognitive demands appropriate for this age group? For example: can the children predict, categorise, sequence, classify, use a graphic organiser, describe a process?*	
Conceptual demands	*Are the concepts developed in this lesson/activity already familiar to the children?* *Do I need to teach or explain a concept to the children?*	
Activities	*What type of activities can I develop through this content area? For example: matching, doing a gap fill, completing a table, labelling a diagram, reading a text, listening to a story.* *Do the activities require the children to work in groups, in pairs or independently?* *How can I scaffold the activities to support the children?*	
Learning to learn	*What opportunities are there to develop learning to learn?* *How can I help the children consult different sources and extract the right information, analyse, make connections, memorise the new language?*	
Resources/technology	*What resources and technology will the children need? For example: internet, reference books, CDs and CD players, classroom material to cut and glue.* *Do the resources come from other areas of the curriculum? For example: measuring tools, tables and graphics, paints and drawing materials.* *Can I find the resources easily?*	
Outcomes	*Is the outcome related to the content area developed?* *Can the children work independently to produce the outcome, or do they need support from the teacher?* *How much time will it take?*	

Principle 9 Cross-curricular links

Key 2

1 It draws upon the children's everyday **experience**.

2 It allows for **links** to be made between home and school.

3 It encourages the children to bring school **knowledge** to the language class.

4 It develops and builds on the children's **understanding** of the world.

5 It caters more clearly for the children's wider **educational** needs and interests.

6 It can help reinforce certain key **content** areas that cross subject boundaries.

7 It allows for **conceptual** reinforcement across subject areas.

8 It includes aspects of **values-based** education, to encourage the children to think about tolerance, friendship, accountability, etc.

 ## Principle 10 A main outcome

Key

Main outcome	Organisation			Length		Place	
	Individual work	Groupwork	Whole-class work	1 or 2 lessons	Several lessons	In the classroom	Outside the classroom
Making a snowflake.	✓			✓		✓	
Designing a poster.		✓	✓	✓	✓	✓	
Performing a roleplay.		✓		✓		✓	
Conducting a survey.	✓	✓		✓		✓	✓
Acting out a story.			✓		✓	✓	✓
Researching a topic.		✓		✓	✓	✓	✓
Creating a display.			✓		✓	✓	✓
Conducting a quiz.		✓	✓	✓		✓	✓
Other – your choice:							

Teaching strategies Using the mother tongue or shared classroom language

Key

Classroom situations	Using the mother tongue
A child starts crying.	Comforting a child.
A lesson about the theme of friendship.	Explaining the meaning of an abstract concept.
Playing a board game to practise language.	Explaining a task, or giving instructions.
A child is chattering incessantly.	Disciplining.
Asking the children what and how they have learnt.	Conducting review sessions.
The children ask you the meaning of a word.	Translating vocabulary that may not be essential to the lesson, but will help the child understand.
Teaching the present perfect.	Explaining a grammatical rule.
A reading text mentions 'custard' and 'high tea'.	Explaining a cultural reference.

 Teaching strategies Using the target language

Key 1

Features of child-directed speech

Parents/carers …

talk about a concrete present situation (the here and now) and personalise language;

speak a little more slowly and clearly;

use a slightly higher-pitched voice;

articulate more, and stress key words;

use shorter, simpler sentence patterns;

vary intonation and tone of voice;

make direct eye contact;

use gesture, facial expression and actions;

use visuals, realia and sound effects to support language;

reformulate, recast or rephrase what a child says into correct English;

pause, to give children time to respond;

praise and react positively to what children say;

use a large amount of questions and imperatives to keep the children's attention;

repeat children's language;

expand and elaborate on what a child says, using the same words in simple, complete phrases.

Key 2

Benefits of using child-directed speech

- Makes language more accessible to the children.
- Retains the children's attention.
- Provides meaningful exposure to the language, by increasing the amount of target language used.
- Helps the children grasp meaning.
- Creates a secure and supportive environment.
- Gives the children confidence to try out and use the language.
- Enables the children to acquire language more naturally.
- Other:

Key 3

1	gestures	**6**	makes eye contact
2	expands	**7**	recasts
3	personalises	**8**	pauses
4	praises	**9**	questions
5	relates	**10**	repeats

Commentary

The teacher creates a secure and supportive environment in which language can develop through the interaction between herself and the children:

- She modifies her language to suit the capability of the learners.

- She recasts, repeats and expands, which allows the children to know if their own utterances are understood. The expansion provides further exposure to the language, and builds on the children's responses.

- She makes use of situations to personalise language.

- She uses illustrations from the storybook to support understanding and prompt language.

- She uses intonation, gesture, facial expression and actions to further convey meaning and elicit language.

In this transcript, the children are expanding their vocabulary around the category of clothes, which has been a recurring lexical group throughout the story.

Lynne Cameron, in her book *Teaching Languages to Young Learners* (CUP, 2001), discusses hierarchies in word learning. Generally, the middle of a general-to-specific hierarchy is particularly significant for children.

Here, the hierarchy would be as follows:

Superordinate	Clothes
Basic level	Trousers
Subordinate	Blue jeans

- The words for basic-level concepts are the most commonly-used words.

- They are usually learnt by children before words that are higher or lower in the hierarchy.

Interestingly, the children learnt *blue jeans* – the subordinate – first, as this was introduced at the beginning of the story when James gets dressed to run out into the snow. Jeans are familiar items of clothing for most children, so the word can also operate at a basic level, synonymous with trousers:

Superordinate	Clothes
Basic level	Jeans
Subordinate	Blue jeans, tight jeans, baggy jeans, designer jeans, etc

The teacher wants to find out if the children know the word *trousers*. They don't, but they show they understand the difference with *jeans* by using the French word for *trousers* – 'un pantalon' – and not 'un jean'.

The teacher recasts, repeats and continues.

 Teaching strategies Effective questioning

Key 1

Type of question	Example
Questions that require the children to give an opinion.	*Why do you think that ...?*
Questions that require the children to ask their own questions.	*What would you like to know about ...?*
Questions that require the children to explain or justify.	*Why do you think that is true?*
Questions that allow for personalisation.	*How do you come to school?*
Questions that guide the children to the next step in learning.	*Why are you going to do next?*
Questions that make the children reflect on their learning.	*Why did we play the game?*
Questions that encourage the children to think about language.	*Where do adjectives go in English?*
Questions that require the right answer.	*What colour is it?*

Teaching strategies Effective questioning

Key 2

These examples are mainly based on a storytelling session with a class of 9-year-old near-beginners:

- The focus is to support understanding of *The Snowman*, using the storybook and illustrations as an aid.

- See the Transcript on page 131 and Commentary on page 160, and Transcript 2 on page 123 and Commentary on page 155.

Teacher questioning techniques	Classroom examples
Pitching the language and content level of questions appropriately for the class.	Simple questions with illustrations, as an aid to understanding: *What are these?* Teacher points to the glasses. (See page 131, the KWL grid on page 29 and Worm Facts on page 41.)
Giving the children time to think about their response before answering questions.	'Thinking' or 'wait time' techniques (see page 17).
Asking the children to discuss a question with a partner before responding.	'Think-pair-share' time or 'talk partners' techniques (see page 17).
Creating an atmosphere of trust in which the children's opinions and ideas are valued, and wrong answers are not sanctioned.	*Necklace? Good try! Yes, it's something that goes around the neck.* Teacher acknowledges the children's attempt and the association with 'something that goes round the neck'. Praises them, and uses a rising intonation to indicate doubt. Points to her necklace, to compare: *Is the Snowman wearing a necklace?* (See page 123.)
Using their responses (even incorrect ones) in a positive way.	*Blue jeans? … Are these the same as James'? … What are these?* Teacher picks up on pupils' reply, uses a questioning intonation to convey she is looking for a different word, then invites the children to compare with the trousers the Snowman is putting on. (See page 123.)
Planning questions in advance, in order to engage the children in thinking for themselves.	*What do you think happens when the Snowman visits James' parents' bedroom?* This question, at the start of the storytelling session, encourages prediction and sets the scene for the interaction around the theme of clothes. Note: The children respond to the question in the mother tongue, and the teacher recasts as appropriate. (See the KWL grid on page 29 and Worm Facts on page 41.)
Modelling the type of questions you want the children to ask.	*What did you do? How did you learn?* (See page 123, the KWL grid on page 29 and Worm Facts on page 41.)
Staging and sequencing questions with increasing levels of challenge.	*Parts of the body? Which parts of the body? Can you tell me which parts of the body?* (See page 123.)
Prompting and giving clues.	*Necklace? … Look, I'm wearing a necklace. Is the Snowman wearing a necklace?* (points to own necklace) *What's the Snowman wearing?* Teacher compares her necklace to the Snowman's scarf, to indicate to the children that 'necklace' is incorrect, and prompts them to give her the correct word: 'scarf'. (See page 123.)
Asking questions which make learning explicit and encourage the children to review.	*What did you learn? How did you learn?* Reflection questions (see page 27 and the Review activities in Part B. See also the KWL grid on page 29 and Worm Facts on page 41.)
Other:	

Teaching strategies Effective questioning

Commentary (**U** = unproductive; **P** = productive)

U/P	Question	Comments
U	*Did you enjoy today's lesson?*	Closed question – does not encourage any reflection.
P	*Is there another way you could say that?*	Encourages the children to reflect and consider other ways of saying something.
U	*Is this an apple? (Show an apple.)*	Closed question – does not encourage any thinking and can result in boredom.
P	*What do you think will happen next?*	Challenges the children to think and to use a range of clues to make predictions.
U	*Why can the moon not glow without the light from the sun?*	Too complex and abstract – often results in silence.
P	*Which poster do you think is the most interesting? Why?*	Encourages the children to think and justify their personal opinion.
U	*What is it? (Show an orange.)*	This type of question can be useful as a memory test to remind the pupils what they know (even though they probably know the right answer). However, it is too narrow and there is no challenge to think. Can lead to boredom.
P	*How do you know?*	An open question which invites the children to reflect and justify their response.

 Teaching strategies Using a class mascot

Key 1
bell   puppets
flashcards   blackboard/IWB
CD player   realia
talking stick magazine pictures
posters   Other:

Key 2

Wilbur helps teachers teach by:

- Recommending storybooks (Wilbur's recommendations in the Teachers' toolkit);
- providing photocopiable or downloadable materials (Wilbur's toolkit);
- making links to the real world by providing cultural information (*My school day*);
- making links between activities (*It's snowing* and *The water cycle*);
- showing the teachers how to do an activity (*Pat-a-cake!*);
- helping the teacher set up routines (Wilbur's chant at the beginning and end of lessons).

Teaching strategies Using a class mascot

Key 3

Wilbur helps learners learn by:

- reassuring the children;
- encouraging them to use their imagination;
- taking the focus off the teacher, and encouraging the children to work independently;
- encouraging the children to use English as much as possible;
- helping them with activities in the classroom;
- encouraging them to work together;
- creating an affective link with the English language;
- encouraging the children to use English;
- providing learning suggestions (see the speech bubble in the Teachers' toolkit, and page 15 in Part A).

Key 4

Procedural role	Behavioural role
Encourages the children to become independent learners. Provides information about language and content.	Models language. Models learning strategies.
Affective role	**Interactive role**
Creates an atmosphere of trust and reassurance in the classroom. Builds the class community. Supports the children in building their self-confidence.	Encourages the children to talk about their learning. Encourages interaction in the classroom.

 Teaching strategies Planning lessons

Key

- A model or format represents the basis of a routine which enables the children to predict situations and the language and behaviour likely to be used.
- A lesson planning template ensures a consistent approach to lesson planning and teaching across a school.
- It makes the teacher feel more confident.
- It enables the teacher to systematically integrate learning to learn.
- It helps teachers anticipate any difficulties or special requirements.
- It helps teachers plan and manage time effectively.

- It enables teachers to prepare materials in advance, so they can give full attention to the children during the lesson.
- It helps to clearly state the aims of the lesson, and how these are to be achieved.
- It helps ensure that there is a good balance and variety of activity types, interaction patterns, content, materials and resources that suit the learning needs of the children.
- It helps ensure positive classroom management and planning classroom space effectively.
- It provides a record of learning and teaching.
- It helps see how each lesson fits into the overall syllabus, and see what has gone before and what is coming next.

Commentary

Activity cycles

- The teacher praises, asks direct questions, elicits vocabulary and information about language, commentates, summarises, repeats for consolidation.

- She uses metalanguage to describe nouns and adjectives, and encourages comparison with the children's mother tongue.

- She uses the mother tongue to talk about language learning, and the target language to reinforce key vocabulary and phrases from the story.

COMPLETED LESSON PLAN

Teacher's name:	Date:	Class: ⬤1	Length: ⬤2	Class level: ⬤3

Classroom layout/space:
⬤4

Anticipated difficulties:
⬤5

	STAGE	**MAIN LESSON AIMS:** In this lesson, the children will:	At the end of the lesson, tick off the aims achieved and add any additional aims/items that arose unexpectedly.
P L A N	**Beginning the lesson** • Start of lesson routine activity. • Review work covered in previous lesson. • Inform pupils of main lesson aims.	• • ⬤6 •	

		Beginning the lesson procedures: • • ⬤7 •	Time
			10 mins

	Activity cycles	**PROCEDURES**			**Materials**	Time
		PLAN ➜	**DO** ➜	**REVIEW**		
D O	(Plan / Do / Review cycle diagram)	Prepare the children for the activity. Set context and inform children of aims and purpose of activity. Activate prior knowledge. Revise, introduce and practise any new language. Motivate. Negotiate success criteria.	Children do activity and experiment and use target language. Teacher monitors and helps as necessary. **Do more** Children consolidate language by extending and personalising.	Run reflective review to evaluate activity and performance.	(Plan / Do / Review cycle diagram)	
	Activity cycle 1	⬤8	⬤9 **Do more** ⬤10	⬤11	Meg and Mog,	10 mins
	Activity cycle 2	⬤12	⬤13 **Do more** ⬤14	⬤15	Meg and Mog. Picture dictation worksheet. Clothes flashcards.	15 mins
	Activity cycle 3	⬤16	⬤17 **Do more** ⬤18	⬤19	Enlarged pictures of 3rd double spread from Meg and Mog + word cards.	10 mins

		Ending the lesson procedures:	Time
R E V I E W / **S H A R E**	**Ending the lesson** • Set homework and home involvement share activity. • Round up, review and summarise lesson. • End of lesson routine activity.	• • ⬤20 • **Post-lesson personal reflection: see Review questions on page 134.**	10 mins

Key

1 Class:
CM1/9 year olds

2 Length:
1 hour

3 Level:
Working towards A1

4 Classroom layout/space:
Desks in rows

5 Anticipated difficulties:
The children have listened to the story several times and understand, but some may have difficulty retelling it in English. They will need plenty of support.

6 Main lesson aims:
In this lesson, the children will:
- retell the story of Meg and Mog (Puffin Books);
- learn how to describe what people are wearing;
- think about word order in English.

7 Beginning the lesson procedures:
- Greet the children and comment on the clothes they are wearing.
- Clothes song.
- Revision of 'What's this?/What are these?' + clothes vocabulary.

Activity cycle 1

8 Plan
'We are going to retell the story of Meg and Mog so we can revise vocabulary.' Encourage the children to retell the story. Support by using picture prompts from the story and guided questioning, to elicit key vocabulary/phrases.

9 Do
Re-read story aloud for the children to listen and check.

10 Do more
Read again, encourage the children to participate by predicting and repeating key vocabulary/phrases.

11 Review
Random checking of vocabulary: 'What's this/are these? Show me … Point to … How many? … What colour is …?' etc.

Activity cycle 2

12 Plan
'Now we're going to do a picture dictation to check your understanding of clothes vocabulary, colours and sizes.' Re-read 3rd double-page spread of Meg and Mog. Revise vocab by asking 'What's Meg wearing?'

13 Do
Dictate descriptions 2 or 3 times, giving the children time to draw. Check. The children show each other their pictures.

14 Do more
Revise clothes vocabulary again. Play guessing game: Describe and guess.

15 Review
Run review of picture dictation activity (see the Transcript on page 136).

Activity cycle 3

16 Plan
'We're going to describe what Meg's wearing and think about the order of adjectives and nouns in English.' The children listen and sequence 3rd double-spread pictures on board. Hold up word cards and invite the children to read out. Stick word cards randomly on the board.

17 Do
The children make descriptions, using the word cards to label each picture, eg: 'She's wearing big black shoes.'

18 Do more
The children copy the phrases.

19 Review
Teacher uses guided questioning to get the children to reflect on word order in English and compare to mother tongue. 'Which words are adjectives?/Which words are nouns?/Where do adjectives go in English?/Where do adjectives for colour/size go?/Where do they go in your language?' (See the Transcript on page 136.)

20 Ending the lesson procedures:
- Homework: Clothes crossword and gap fill, to share with family.
- Plenary: Round up and review overall lesson.
- End lesson by describing a child. *'She's wearing a green jumper.'* As the children recognise themselves, they line up, ready to go.

Teaching strategies Selecting storybooks

	Key	
Criteria	**Questions**	
Language level	Is the language (vocabulary/structures) accessible to my pupils? Is the language authentic/appropriate? Is there an appropriate level of challenge for my pupils? Is the length of the story appropriate for my class?	
Literary devices	Does the use of repetition encourage the children to participate in the story, encourage prediction and memorisation? Does the use of rhyme and rhythm help the children predict and memorise? Does the use of dialogue provide examples of language that the children can use and transfer?	
Content	Does the genre (type of storybook: fairytale, everyday life, special occasions, animals, information books, etc) appeal to my class? Is the story relevant to the children's interests? Is the story motivating and memorable? Does the story promote positive values and attitudes? Are there opportunities for the children to relate the story to their own personal experiences? Will the story provide a positive learning experience?	
Illustrations and layout	Do the illustrations synchronise with text to support children's understanding? Are the illustrations large enough for all the children in the class to see? Are the colours used in the illustrations easy to see by the children? Do the illustrations depict the target culture?	
Educational potential	Does the story provide opportunities to develop learning strategies: predicting, sequencing, understanding general meaning, etc? Does the story develop concepts? Does the story develop knowledge of other subjects or the world? Can the story be linked to other subjects in the curriculum?	
Potential for follow-up/ main outcome	Does the story lend itself to further language learning work? Does the story lend itself to a main outcome – making a book, acting out, creating a poster, etc?	
Other:		

Completed class storybook profile

School year: 2014/15	Class: CE2, 3rd year	Storybook: The Chinese New Year
Age of pupils	8 years	This story will appeal to children of this age – they will understand the values of fairness and inclusion and be able to relate to the quarrel and competition between the animals.
Number of pupils	25	I will need to ensure that all the children remain focused and do not lose concentration, by keeping a good pace, involving them all and giving each child a chance to participate.
Gender mix (boys/ girls)	18 boys, 7 girls	The story will appeal to both boys and girls. They like animals and will like the competitive element. They will identify with the clever and caring princess. Each child will be able to personalise the story and calculate which animal they are named after.
Language(s) spoken at home	French, plus various other mother tongues	Two children have a Chinese family background and have some knowledge of Chinese languages and cultural events.
Shared classroom language	French	All the children can communicate competently in French.
English language level	Working towards and within A1	The language in the story is accessible to the children, with additional support via visuals and gestures, etc. The children already know some of the animals in English, so they will be able to add new animals to this lexical set. They will be able to transfer phrases from the story, such as: *'Me too. 1,2,3, go! I am the winner! Well done!'*
Cognitive ability	Children can predict with help from teacher, can memorise and sequence with visual support	The children will enjoy predicting and remembering the animals. They will quickly learn the names of the animals, with the support of the flashcards. The games will focus their attention and help them learn and recall the names of the animals.
School setting (urban/suburban/ rural)	State school in urban setting – capital city of Paris	This story takes place in a rural setting where there is wide river. This is in contrast to the children's urban setting, but they can relate to the river Seine.
Time of the year (month/season)	January	This is an ideal book to use in January as it will prepare the children for the Chinese New Year celebrations – a major event in the cultural calendar in Paris. Some children will be familiar with the celebrations, but not all of them with the story. The Chinese-speaking children can tell us how they celebrate Chinese New Year with their families.

Completed class storybook profile (continued)

Children's interests	Animals	This story will appeal to the interests of the children in my class. They like learning about animals. They will relate to the quarrel between the animals, the crafty rat and the fair resolution. They will enjoy acting out the story and making their own Chinese Lanterns.
Classroom space/ layout eg: fixed desks, rows, movable tables, etc	Fixed desks in rows	The illustrations are quite small and detailed, so I will need to move around the classroom as I read the story aloud so all the children can see them. This repetition will give them time to relate what they hear to what they see and construct meaning.
Resources/ technology	Blackboard; class computer	I will show the children an animated version of the story, using shadow puppets to finish off our work: *https://www.youtube.com/watch?v=f5aY11Mpvsl*

 ## Ongoing development strategies Techniques for evaluating learning to learn

Key 1

Evaluation technique	Research question(s) As a result of integrating learning to learn into classes, …
Traditional means of assessment – ie, testing – to monitor the children's proficiency gains in English.	• *Do the children show greater effectiveness in their English language learning?* • *Do the children show improved linguistic performance, by getting better results in English language tests?*
Surveys, focus groups or recordings of review sessions, to collect feedback and monitor satisfaction levels, sense of progress, increased confidence, views about learning to learn (see the teachers' comments on pages 96 and 143 and the children's comments on page 96).	• *Do the children report increased levels of satisfaction and motivation, and more positive attitudes to language learning?* • *Do the children report a sense of progress and improvement?* • *Do the children report increased confidence in their learning?* • *Do the teachers report positive outcomes as a result of implementing learning to learn?*
Learning diaries, English language portfolios and self-assessments, to log and monitor learner behaviour.	• *Do the children show evidence of reflecting on their learning, monitoring their learning and improved organisation of their learning?*
Teacher observations of the children or learner self-reports, to monitor the effects of strategy training.	• *Are the children using a wider variety of strategies than before?* • *Are the children more aware of the strategies they are using?* • *Are the children transferring strategies to other activities?*
Audio- or video-recording of teacher-led review sessions or interviewing individual children, to collect and analyse linguistic data to monitor the children's developing metacognitive awareness.	• *Are the children able to reflect on and articulate more awareness of how they learn and account for their learning?*

Key 2		
Evaluation technique	**Pros**	**Cons**
Traditional means of assessment – ie, testing – to monitor the children's proficiency gains in English.	Tests are a familiar way of assessing learning. Testing often corresponds to teacher, pupil and parent expectations of how they think they should be assessed. Tests are relatively easy to administer.	It is difficult to identify whether improved test results are a result of learning to learn or regular teaching. Tests only measure one or two aspects of linguistic performance, eg: listening, vocabulary, grammar. Tests do not take other aspects of children's learning into account, eg: cognitive, emotional, cultural, social and affective gains.
Surveys, focus groups or review sessions, to monitor satisfaction levels, sense of progress, increased confidence, views about learning to learn (see the teachers' comments on pages 96 and 143 and the children's comments on page 96).	Provide data on satisfaction levels, attitudes, motivation and sense of progress. Relate to learners/teachers personally.	Subjective. Do not always provide evidence of linguistic gains or increased independence. Risk that the children may say what they think their teacher wants to hear.
Learning diaries, English language portfolios and self-assessments, to log and monitor learner behaviour.	Relate to the learners personally, and provide data on personal preferences and learning strategies. The children develop awareness of themselves as language learners and of their personal preferences and differences.	Reflections tend to be minimal and not always very focused. Reflections need to be interpreted with care, and often require individual probing.
Teacher observations of the children or learner self-reports, to monitor the effects of strategy training.	Show increased awareness of learning strategies.	Strategy use is very personal – what may work for one learner may not work for another. Strategy use is difficult to observe as some strategies are not visible. It is difficult to ascertain if strategies are being used consciously or unconsciously. Strategy use is affected by many variables.
Audio- or video-recording of teacher-led review sessions or interviewing individual children, to collect and analyse linguistic data to monitor the children's developing metacognitive awareness.	Relate to the learners personally. Provide linguistic evidence which can be analysed according to the levels of metacognitive awareness demonstrated.	Risk that not all children will participate actively in review sessions.

Ongoing development strategies An action research project: Evaluating learning to learn

Completed sample framework, using data from the transcripts of review sessions
on page 123 in the activity in Principle 6: Routines.

Level of metacognitive awareness	Pupil language characterised by ...	Examples of pupil language	Teacher guidance and intervention	Examples of teacher language
Level 1: Largely unaware	Factual description with little or no understanding/ rationale. Little or no use of metalanguage. Few or no questions.	*We cut out some masks.* *We played some games.* *We drew a snowman.* *Parts of the kitchen.*	Nominating point for discussion and directing and focussing children's attention. Probing children's responses. Seeking responses. Initiating most exchanges. Controlling turn taking. Repeating. Informing, explaining. Introducing metalanguage. Praising, evaluating. Summarising, recapping	*Wait! We're going to speak about the game and then we'll come back to the story.* *And why did we do the movements with the song?* *Tell me the nouns.* *What did you learn in this activity?* *Wait! We played bingo.* *Good. Concentrate and …* *To know what we are saying.* *Listen to … the key words, the nouns …* *Very good.* *So we played the the game …*
Level 2: Becoming aware (transition stage)	Description with some understanding/ rationale. Questions. Beginning to use some metalanguage.	*To learn the parts of the body.* *To show where we are.* *To know what we are saying.* *We put the story in order.* *Concentrate.*	All of the above, and ... Eliciting Prompting Modelling Summarising	 *Why did we play the game? What did you learn?* *Good. Tell me the nouns.* *Because when we say 'head' we touch the head and we know that 'head' means head.* *We played bingo to practise listening and concentrating, and to revise the vocabulary.*
Level 3: Largely aware	Confident and competent use of metalanguage. Asking lots of questions.			

The following templates are reproduced as A4 downloadable templates on the website as a complement to the Teachers' toolkit:

- Wilbur's learning suggestions (see page 15)

- Knowing your class 1 – Benefits (see page 37)

- Knowing your class 2 – Class profile (see page 37)

- Lesson plan template (see page 135)

- Completed lesson plan (see pages 164–165)

- Class storybook profile (see page 138)

- Evaluating my storytelling skills (see page 140)

- Storybook record (see page 139)

- Self-assessments 1, 2, 3, 4 (see pages 147–148)

- Action plan (see page 146)

Go to: *www.deltapublishing.co.uk/resources*
Click on the cover of the book.
Click on Teachers' toolkit.

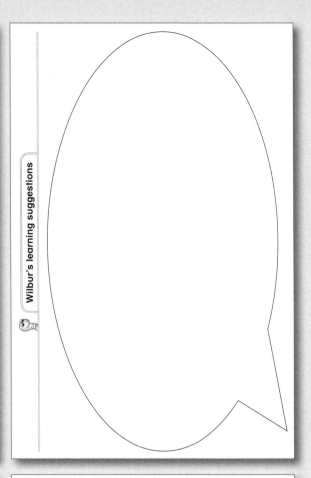

Wilbur's learning suggestions

Knowing your class 1

Benefits

Benefits to your teaching:

A better understanding of your class will enable you to:

- build on the experience and knowledge that the children bring to the classroom;

- better prepare schemes of work, select appropriate resources and make learning more meaningful and more holistic;

- initiate dialogue with parents, and encourage parental involvement;

- make your teaching more inclusive.

Benefits to your pupils' learning:

A better understanding of your class will enable you to:

- valorise the children's languages and cultures;

- recognise and promote the children's abilities and talents;

- encourage the children to participate more actively and confidently in classroom instruction;

- help the children develop more positive attitudes to English language instruction;

- meet the children's affective learning needs.

Keep a record of other benefits you notice, and write your observations below.
Add your observations to your English Teaching Portfolio.

Other benefits:

Observations:

Knowing your class 2

Class profile

School year .... Class ....

Age of pupils	
Number of pupils	
Gender mix (boys/girls)	
Language(s) spoken at home	
Shared classroom language	
English language level	
Cognitive ability	
School setting (urban/suburban/rural)	
Children's interests	
Classroom space/layout (fixed desks, rows, movable tables, etc)	
Resources/technology	
Other information:	

LESSON PLAN TEMPLATE

Teacher's name:	Date:	Class:	Length:	Class level:

Classroom layout/space:	Anticipated difficulties:

	STAGE	MAIN LESSON AIMS: In this lesson, the children will:		
P L A N	**Beginning the lesson** • Start of lesson routine activity. • Review work covered in previous lesson. • Inform pupils of main lesson aims.	• • •	At the end of the lesson, tick off the aims achieved and add any additional aims/items that arose unexpectedly.	

	Beginning the lesson procedures: • • •		Time

Activity cycles	PROCEDURES			Materials	Time
	**PLAN** ➡	**DO** ➡	**REVIEW**		
Plan / Review / Do (cycle)	Prepare the children for the activity. Set context and inform children of aims and purpose of activity. Activate prior knowledge. Revise, introduce and practise any new language. Motivate. Negotiate success criteria.	Children do activity and experiment and use target language. Teacher monitors and helps as necessary. **Do more** Children consolidate language by extending and personalising.	Run reflective review to evaluate activity and performance.	Plan / Review / Do (cycle)	
Activity cycle 1		Do more			
Activity cycle 2		Do more			
Activity cycle 3		Do more			

	Ending the lesson • Set homework and home involvement share activity. • Round up, review and summarise lesson. • End of lesson routine activity.	Ending the lesson procedures: • • • **Post-lesson personal reflection: see Review questions on page 134.**

(Left margin stage labels: **D O** for the activity cycles section; **R E V I E W** / **S H A R E** for the ending section.)

COMPLETED LESSON PLAN

Teacher's name:	Date:	Class: *CM1/9 year olds*	Length: *1 hour*	Class level: *Working towards A1*

Classroom layout/space: *Desks in rows*	Anticipated difficulties: *The children have listened to the story several times and understand, but some may have difficulty retelling it in English. They will need plenty of support.*

	STAGE	MAIN LESSON AIMS: In this lesson, the children will:	
P L A N	**Beginning the lesson** • Start of lesson routine activity. • Review work covered in previous lesson. • Inform pupils of main lesson aims.	• *retell the story of Meg and Mog (Puffin Books);* • *learn how to describe what people are wearing;* • *think about word order in English.*	At the end of the lesson, tick off the aims achieved and add any additional aims/items that arose unexpectedly.

Beginning the lesson procedures: • *Greet the children and comment on the clothes they are wearing.* • *Clothes song.* • *Revision of 'What's this?/What are these?' + clothes vocabulary.*	Time
	10 mins

Activity cycles	PROCEDURES			Materials	Time
	**PLAN** ➡	**DO** ➡	**REVIEW**		
Plan / Review / Do (cycle)	Prepare the children for the activity. Set context and inform children of aims and purpose of activity. Activate prior knowledge. Revise, introduce and practise any new language. Motivate. Negotiate success criteria.	Children do activity and experiment and use target language. Teacher monitors and helps as necessary. **Do more** Children consolidate language by extending and personalising.	Run reflective review to evaluate activity and performance.	Plan / Review / Do (cycle)	
Activity cycle 1	*'We are going to retell the story of Meg and Mog so we can revise vocabulary.' Encourage the children to retell the story. Support by using picture prompts from the story and guided questioning, to elicit key vocab/phrases.*	*Re-read story aloud for the children to listen and check.* **Do more** *Read again, encourage the children to participate by predicting and repeating key vocab/phrases.*	*Random checking of vocabulary: 'What's this/are these? Show me … Point to … How many? … What colour is …?' etc.*	*Meg and Mog.*	*10 mins*
Activity cycle 2	*'Now we're going to do a picture dictation to check your understanding of clothes vocabulary, colours and sizes.' Re-read 3rd double-page spread of Meg and Mog. Revise vocab by asking 'What's Meg wearing?'*	*Dictate descriptions 2 or 3 times, giving the children time to draw. Check. The children show each other their pictures.* **Do more** *Revise clothes vocabulary again. Play guessing game: Describe and guess.*	*Run review of picture dictation activity (see transcript on page 136).*	*Meg and Mog. Picture dictation worksheet. Clothes flashcards.*	*15 mins*
Activity cycle 3	*'We're going to describe what Meg's wearing and think about the order of adjectives and nouns in English.' The children listen and sequence 3rd double spread pictures on board. Hold up word cards and invite the children to read out. Stick word cards randomly on the board.*	*The children make descriptions, using the word cards to label each picture, eg: 'She's wearing big black shoes.'* **Do more** *The children copy the phrases.*	*Teacher uses guided questioning to get the children to reflect on word order in English and compare to mother tongue. 'Which words are adjectives?/Which words are nouns?/Where do adjectives go in English?/ Where do adjectives for colour/size go?/Where do they go in your language?' (See transcript on page 136.)*	*Enlarged pictures of 3rd double spread from Meg and Mog + word cards.*	*10 mins*

	Ending the lesson • Set homework and home involvement share activity. • Round up, review and summarise lesson. • End of lesson routine activity.	Ending the lesson procedures: • *Homework: Clothes crossword and gap fill, to share with family.* • *Plenary: Round up and review overall lesson.* • *End lesson by describing a child. 'She's wearing a green jumper.' As the children recognise themselves, they line up, ready to go.* **Post-lesson personal reflection: see Review questions on page 134.**	Time
			10 mins

(Left margin stage labels: **D O** for the activity cycles section; **R E V I E W** / **S H A R E** for the ending section.)

Class storybook profile

School year .... Class .... Storybook ....

Age of pupils		
Number of pupils		
Gender mix (boys/girls)		
Language(s) spoken at home		
Shared classroom language		
English language level		
Cognitive ability		
School setting (urban/suburban/rural)		
Time of the year (month/season)		
Children's interests		
Classroom space/layout (fixed desks, rows, movable tables, etc)		
Resources/technology		
Other information:		

Evaluating my storytelling skills

Individual sounds
- *Did I pronounce the vowels and consonants or sounds in connected speech correctly?*

Stress
- *Did I stress the syllables in individual words or in sentences correctly?*

Rhythm
- *Did I read too slowly or too quickly?*
- *Did I pause in the right places?*

Intonation
- *Did I sound interesting or boring?*
- *Did I vary my intonation, where appropriate?*
- *Did I use the appropriate intonation for questions, statements, lists, and so on?*

Variation
- *How did I vary the speed and volume of my voice, where appropriate?*
- *Did I adapt my voice for the different characters?*

Visual/audio clues
- *How did I use visual/audio clues (facial expressions and gestures, sound effects) to support the children's understanding?*

Eye contact
- *Did I retain eye contact with the children during the storytelling, to develop a shared rapport with the class?*

Pupil participation
- *Did I pause in the correct places and use the appropriate intonation, to invite my pupils to join in?*
- *Did I ask the appropriate questions, to encourage my pupils to predict what comes next?*
- *Did I ask the appropriate questions, to encourage the children to relate the story to their own experiences?*

General impression
- *How did I sound in general? Clear? Expressive? Lively?*

What do I need to improve?
- *What shall I focus on this week?*

Storybook record

Title: ....

Author/Illustrator: ....

Publisher: ....

Class/age used with: .... Date: ....

Notes

Narrative: ....

Illustrations: ....

Children's response: ....

Other: ....

Self-assessment 1

Planning interesting and stimulating learning experiences

Assess yourself as follows:
1 = *I now feel very competent in this area.*
2 = *I now feel quite competent in this area.*
3 = *I don't feel competent yet in this area, and would like to learn more.*

	1	2	3	N/A
Planning challenging lessons.				
Using familiar routines.				
Providing authentic input to create an acquisition-rich learning environment.				
Making links to other areas in the primary curriculum.				
Giving opportunities for the children to relate things to their personal experience.				
Developing intercultural understanding.				
Giving meaningful exposure to the language.				
Using age-appropriate and varied activities and materials.				
Other:				

Comments:

Self-assessment 2

Creating a positive classroom climate

Assess yourself as follows:
1 = *I now feel very competent in this area.*
2 = *I now feel quite competent in this area.*
3 = *I don't feel competent yet in this area, and would like to learn more.*

	1	2	3	N/A
Understanding that mistakes are learning opportunities.				
Creating a climate of mutual confidence and respect in the teacher–class relationship.				
Creating an inclusive classroom, and respecting diversity.				
Recognising and praising effort, and giving constructive feedback.				
Being a positive role model, and promoting positive values.				
Establishing a learning environment where the children feel confident to take risks with the language.				
Enabling the children to voice their opinions/preferences about language learning.				
Listening to and acting on the children's perspectives.				
Building a class learning community.				
Giving the children responsibility and opportunities to work independently and make choices about activities/materials.				
Using positive behaviour and classroom management strategies.				
Providing opportunities for the children to work cooperatively.				
Making effective use of classroom space.				
Using effective questioning to create an enquiring classroom and quality dialogue.				
Other:				

Comments:

Self-assessment 3

Encouraging parental support and family involvement

Assess yourself as follows:
1 = *I now feel very competent in this area.*
2 = *I now feel quite competent in this area.*
3 = *I don't feel competent yet in this area, and would like to learn more.*

	1	2	3	N/A
Creating effective communication channels between school and home.				
Enabling the children to share learning with their parents.				
Encouraging positive parental attitudes to foreign language learning.				
Fostering cooperation between teacher and parents.				
Planning activities which take the in-the-school experience into the home.				
Planning activities which take the in-the-home experience into the school.				
Supporting the parents to help their child with their English language learning.				
Other:				

Comments:

Self-assessment 4

Enabling children to experience success in early language learning

Assess yourself as follows:
1 = *I now feel very competent in this area.*
2 = *I now feel quite competent in this area.*
3 = *I don't feel competent yet in this area, and would like to learn more.*

	1	2	3	N/A
Planning and integrating learning to learn systematically into lessons.				
Discussing and reviewing learning.				
Encouraging the children to use the target language as much as possible, but with the right to use the mother tongue or the shared classroom language to help them learn.				
Using child-directed speech.				
Scaffolding learning.				
Discussing and negotiating success criteria.				
Giving opportunities to use language in context.				
Encouraging organised learning.				
Ensuring the children know what is expected of them, and how they are to be evaluated.				
Ensuring the children understand the purpose of what they have to do and its relevance.				
Giving the children opportunities to work at their own pace and personalise their learning.				
Other:				

Comments:

Action plan

Name .... Date ....

Action point: Describe the target development. For example: the teaching strategy you wish to try out or improve.

Link your plan to one of the core elements of effective pedagogy.

Steps you need to take, plus time frame.

Support/resources required.

Measures for impact and/or success.

From the editors

Teaching children how to learn is a ground-breaking book in both form and format. It provides both teachers and children with an innovative approach to **teaching** and **learning**, suggesting a series of steps which follow a **Plan, Do, Review** learning cycle.

Gail Ellis and **Nayr Ibrahim** show how successful a 'learning to learn' approach can be:

○ Teachers **plan** what they are going to do.
○ They inform the children of the purpose of what they are going to **do**.
○ They carry out these plans together, and then **review** what has been achieved.

But the horizons of *Teaching children how to learn* were constantly and excitingly widening:

Part A – Plan – presents the theoretical and methodological concepts for young children learning to learn. It enumerates the Principles for creating the conditions for effective learning and motivated and responsible learners.

Here, too, the horizons moved outwards, as the authors incorporated the stages of **Doing more** and **Sharing**, where the children's homes and families are actively involved in the learning process.

Part B – Do – offers a bank of activities for teachers to do in their own classrooms, encouraging the children to review, systematically and explicitly, **what** they have learnt, as well as **how** they have learnt.

To this end, Activity Records were added, alongside Activity worksheets, and the book grew into a fully practical course, with downloadable materials made available on an accompanying website **Toolkit**, to be eventually included in the children's own **English Language Portfolio** – their own personal record.

Part C – Review – contains additional ideas to assist teachers in evaluating learning to learn, develop their competence still further, and relate it more closely to their individual teaching situations.

Here, too, the horizons expanded, and the Principles in Part A were mirrored in such a way that Part C became an authentic **Teacher Development** course. A **Teachers' toolkit** supplies the authors' views in the form of Keys and Commentaries, and a number of templates have been added to the website to facilitate starting an **English Teaching Portfolio**.

Teaching children how to learn is a major resource, where the authors provide carefully scaffolded activities to enable teachers to develop the skills and knowledge they need to learn, to advance independently towards being successful teachers of children who are themselves learning.

It would be remiss not to mention here the work of Christine Cox, who has designed all the books in this series. In *Teaching children how to learn* she, too, has broken new ground, as she not only created the pages for the book and the templates for the website: she has played a crucial role in improving the book's transparency and apparent simplicity – always with the teacher and the children in mind.

It is, then, a book for multiple congratulations!

Mike Burghall
Lindsay Clandfield

DELTA TEACHER DEVELOPMENT SERIES

A pioneering award-winning series of books for English Language Teachers with professional development in mind.

Teaching children how to learn
by Gail Ellis and Nayr Ibrahim
ISBN 978-1-905085-86-6

Film in Action
by Kieran Donaghy
ISBN 978-1-909783-07-2

Going Mobile
by Nicky Hockly and
Gavin Dudeney
ISBN 978-1-909783-06-5

Storytelling With Our Students
by David Heathfield
ISBN 978-1-905085-87-3

The Autonomy Approach
by Brian Morrison and
Diego Navarro
ISBN 978-1-909783-05-8

Spotlight on Learning Styles
by Marjorie Rosenberg
ISBN 978-1-905085-71-2

The Book of Pronunciation
by Jonathan Marks and
Tim Bowen
ISBN 978-1-905085-70-5

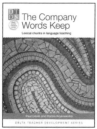

The Company Words Keep
by Paul Davis and
Hanna Kryszewska
ISBN 978-1-905085-20-0

Digital Play
by Kyle Mawer and
Graham Stanley
ISBN 978-1-905085-55-2

Teaching Online
by Nicky Hockly with
Lindsay Clandfield
ISBN 978-1-905085-35-4

Teaching Unplugged
by Luke Meddings and
Scott Thornbury
ISBN 978-1-905085-19-4

Culture in our Classrooms
by Gill Johnson and
Mario Rinvolucri
ISBN 978-1-905085-21-7

The Developing Teacher
by Duncan Foord
ISBN 978-1-905085-22-4

Being Creative
by Chaz Pugliese
ISBN 978-1-905085-33-0

The Business English Teacher
by Debbie Barton,
Jennifer Burkart and
Caireen Sever
ISBN 978-1-905085-34-7

For details of these and future titles in the series, please contact the publisher: *E-mail* info@deltapublishing.co.uk
Or visit the DTDS website at www.deltapublishing.co.uk/titles/methodology